model

Other Simon Pulse books
you might enjoy

Secrets of My Suburban Life
Lauren Baratz-Logsted

Street Pharm
Allison van Diepen

Skin
Adrienne Maria Vrettos

Indie Girl
Kavita Daswani

*The Social Climber's Guide
to High School*
Robyn Schneider

model

A MEMOIR

cheryl diamond

Simon Pulse
New York London Toronto Sydney

A NOTE TO READERS

Names and identifying details of some of the people portrayed in this book have been changed.

SIMON PULSE
An imprint of Simon & Schuster Children's Publishing Division
1230 Avenue of the Americas, New York, NY 10020

Designed by Mike Rosamilia
The text of this book was set in Adobe Garamond.
Manufactured in the United States of America
First Simon Pulse edition June 2008
1 3 5 7 9 10 8 6 4 2
Library of Congress Control Number 2007937150
ISBN-13: 978-1-4169-5904-5
ISBN-10: 1-4169-5904-1

For my parents

model

The City

There are 6.5 billion people on this planet. Sixteen of them are supermodels.

Every year hundreds of the most beautiful people travel to New York from all over the earth to become models. Most of these potential models are eighteen. I was fourteen, and this is my story.

Manhattan stretched for miles outside the floor-to-ceiling windows of IMG Models, one of the world's superpower agencies, and the first one I approached. Behind the grim-faced receptionist were ten desks where agents, also called bookers, were glaring at computer screens while talking animatedly on the phone with clients. "Yes, she can go to Paris, but only on the fifteenth." Sorry, but he's booked solid till November." The general air was one of a sophisticated boiler room.

Twenty top New York City modeling agencies hold weekly open

calls, where aspiring models are appraised by sharp-eyed agents, who decide if they want to sign contracts for representation. I was waiting to be seen, along with about thirty other potential models. A congregation of admirable bone structure if ever there was one. It was my first open call, and I was discouraged to see that all the others had portfolios, also called books, filled with professional photographs. Nervously, I clutched the backyard snapshots taken by my devoted mom. A young agent, dressed intimidatingly in black, came out and began flipping quickly through the books of the people who had arrived before me. She spent about thirty seconds on each person, then said, "Sorry, but you're not what we're looking for," as she handed portfolios back. Adrenaline buzzed through my system. The immediacy of the moment and the amount of surrounding competition made me seriously realize for the first time how much I really wanted this. Then it was my turn. The agent glanced quickly at my pictures and asked, "How old are you?"

"Fourteen."

"Hmmm," she said thoughtfully. "I like your look. Come on, I want to measure you."

I stood straight against the measuring tape on the wall, thrilled that they were paying more attention to me than they had to anyone else. "Well, that's a pity," the agent said. "You're only five-six. You have to be at least five-nine. But you are only fourteen, so you'll probably grow, and if you do, come back." She returned my snapshots, and I walked to the elevator. She smiled and called after me, "Make sure you grow, okay?"

"I'll get right on it," I said with a laugh. By the time the elevator closed, the agent had already dismissed two more people with, "You're not what we're looking for."

I walked out into the hot August sunshine and looked for a blue Taurus on the busy street. It came screeching around the corner with my dad, a Viking look-alike, at the wheel.

"Hey, pal!" he said as I jumped into the car. My dad is always smiling; he is probably the most positive person alive. "How'd it go?"

"I have to grow three inches."

"It can be arranged, my child," he said with an elaborately sinister expression, wiggling his eyebrows till I giggled.

"Hey, Dad," I said. "Why does that sign say 'wrong way'?"

"Because, pal, we're going the wrong way up a one-way street."

During the next week, I presented myself to ten more Manhattan agencies and was told to grow as soon as humanly possible. My age was also a factor, as many large agencies did not want to take the time to train and develop a teenybopper with no modeling experience.

One agency remained on my list.

I took the subway downtown, since my dad was attending his real-estate convention, the real reason we had driven from North Carolina to New York.

Platinum Models commanded the entire fourth floor of an elegant West Side building. Modeling agencies do not occupy a space, they rule it. I took in the gleaming hardwood floors, large windows, and fully equipped refreshment bar, the glass-fronted fridge stocked neatly with Snapple and little bottles of Starbucks Frappuccinos. Five other potential models were already congregated hopefully.

This was one of those defining moments that I would look back on years later, wondering if my life would be less screwed up had it not occurred. The receptionist, who looked like a boxer and contrasted sharply with the decor, squinted at me. "Here for the open call, right?" he said gruffly.

I smiled "Right."

"Okay, well you can take a seat over—"

"Ohhh my Goddddd," someone with a thick French accent screamed. I looked up and saw a man pointing at me, wide-eyed. He was wearing a hot-pink beret.

"Ooh, la la," he squealed, and ran around the corner, only to reappear a second later with a huge smile. "Don't move!" he yelled. Then, holding down his beret, he disappeared again, calling, "Rico, Rico, mon dieu! Rico!"

Everyone stared openmouthed at the boxer/receptionist, who grimaced and said, "This is what I deal with every day."

"Who was that?" I asked.

He chuckled. "That was Claude, the head booker. I think he really likes your—"

"There she is, Rico!" Claude reappeared, dragging with him a man who was shorter, less pretty, and sans beret. They both marched forward, and Claude grabbed my hand and started pumping it up and down. "I am Claude," still pumping, "and this is Rico." He looked at Rico, who was standing a few feet away, stroking his goateed chin and staring at me with narrowed eyes. He didn't say a word. Claude finally released my hand and asked, "What is your name?"

"Cheryl Diamond." I started to laugh. The whole scene was funny, but I think it was the pink beret that triggered the giggles.

Oblivious to my laughter, Claude said, "Can I see your book?"

"Well, all I have are these snapshots."

He took them, looked through a few, and said, "Ahh, good, you are *photogénique*, that is all that matters. We will get you professional pictures." He handed my pictures to Rico, who looked at them, narrowing his eyes even more. He still hadn't said anything.

"Come." Claude grabbed my hand. "You must meet the owner." I looked back and saw Rico glaring at the other potential models with deep suspicion. He shook his head at them, turned on his heel, and stalked after us, leaving the boxer/receptionist sighing in resignation.

As we rounded the corner, a redheaded man no more than five feet tall came sashaying toward us. He peered up at me and exclaimed, "Fab-u-lous! What is *this*?"

"*This* is Chérie," said Claude proudly.

"Cheryl," I corrected.

Claude smiled "Yes. Chérie. That is what I said."

Claude gestured at the redhead, saying, "This is the owner, Thom."

"Hiiii, girlfriend."

"Ummm, hi." I was starting to laugh again.

"Do you have pictures?" Thom asked.

"Rico has them," I said. Rico, who was standing stone-faced against the wall, wordlessly handed the pictures to Thom, who looked through them quickly and was instantly all business.

"Okay, you have a great look, so I would like to represent you. We have to get you professional pictures and get your hair styled. Is that cool with you?"

"Yes, definitely." I was reeling in shock at how fast this was happening, especially after all the rejections I'd had.

"Is this blond your natural hair color?" Thom asked.

I nodded.

"Amazing. Hair companies are gonna love you."

"*I* found her!" Claude chirped, raising his hand like a kid in school. Rico gave him a disgusted, if slightly jealous, look but remained mute.

Thom rolled his eyes at them. "Do you live in New York?" he asked me.

"I live in North Carolina now. My dad is in real estate, so we move a lot, but I can come to New York to work."

"Good. Right now, let's get all your measurements."

They measured my height and did not seem to mind that I was only five-six. "Just tell the clients she's five-eight," Thom said to Claude. "That'll do until she grows."

I had just learned a fundamental rule of modeling: Lie. It's all illusion.

With a tape measure they took my bust, waist, and hip measurements: 33, 24, 34. That pleased everyone, because it's important to have a ten-inch difference between your waist and hips, and it's also important that a model's hip measurement not exceed thirty-six inches. Agencies never ask how much you weigh; it's all about the correct proportions.

"Now," Thom said, clapping his hands. Rico and Claude both snapped to attention. "Get on the phone to photographers and set up a test shoot for Cheryl. If they wanna meet her they can come here tomorrow." He turned to me. "Cheryl, can you come back here tomorrow at about eleven?"

"Sure." I nodded. "This is fun." I would later learn that Thom's ability to switch instantly from silly to serious was common in the industry.

"Good," Claude said. "I will get the photographers and set up an appointment at the hair salon tomorrow for Chérie."

Suddenly I was worried. "How much will all this cost, because I don't think I can afford—"

"Ztop!" Claude said.

I ztopped.

"It is all free. Don't worry, ma Chéri, we will take care of everything. Bring high-heeled shoes and Rico will teach you how to walk," said Claude. I started toward the elevator, and all three of them came with me. As we passed the receptionist, Claude said, "This is Nick. He used to do the boxing, right, Nick?"

"Yeah," Nick rumbled, "those were the days."

As I got into the elevator, Thom and Claude said "Bye" and "See you tomorrow," while Rico just stood there, massaging his goatee. But as the elevator door began to close, the strangest thing happened. Rico waved and said, "Bye-bye, Chéri." I was too surprised to say anything, and when the door shut, all I could think was, *Rico speaks!*

"We are a boutique agency," Thom announced the next day as he opened the glass door to the booking room, which contained four computers, telephones, and a display rack with pictures of their models. Rico and Claude jumped up from their computers. "Ahhh," Rico said, "it is our little Chérie."

Thom pointed at the display rack on the wall. "We have ten female models and eight male models. Other agencies have up to three hundred, but we are very selective."

"We take only the very best," Claude said, with his nose in the air. Thom rolled his eyes and picked up one of the models' comp cards from the wall. A comp card, short for composite card, is eight by five inches of cardboard. On the front was a head shot of the model with PLATINUM MODELS printed under it. On the back were three smaller pictures, along with the model's name and measurements, all in full color with expert graphics.

"Polaroid!" Rico exclaimed.

"Yes, Polaroid," said Claude.

"Definitely Polaroid." Thom nodded.

"Yes, I think we should do the Polaroids. What do you think, Chérie?" Rico asked.

"I think we should all say Polaroid one more time." There was a short silence while I grinned at them, and then they all started laughing.

"Ooh, la la." Rico giggled. "I like this girl."

Getting Polaroided at a modeling agency is kind of like having your mug shot taken at the end of an episode of *CSI: Miami*, except models are cuter than the criminals. First you have to stand against a blank white wall, with a very serious expression, for a head shot, then one in profile, then a full body shot. It's funny, but I always look somewhat guilty in Polaroid pictures, and I blame that wholly on years of being brainwashed by TV cop shows. With a dramatic flourish, Claude placed my Polaroids in the center of all the comp cards on the wall, to show clients until my own comps were printed.

I met four photographers in the next three hours. First was Sebastian, a young guy who resembled an undernourished rock star, with shocking red hair and translucent skin. Sebastian was extremely energetic and couldn't stop bouncing around the agency. The reason for this was, of course, that he was high. But I didn't figure that out until about a year later. At the time I was so naive that I thought he was just a really happy guy. Next came two stout women, who held each other's hands a lot. The reason for this, I brilliantly concluded, was that they must be really good friends.

"She's gotta bleach her hair white," one of them said.

"Whaaaat?" everyone yelled except her friend.

"Cheryl is too cutesy, like a friggin' Barbie doll. We gotta make her look edgier."

I stared at her in horror. "I can't bleach my hair white. I'll look weird."

"That's the whole point!" she snapped, obviously exasperated with my stupidity.

Her pal spoke up. "Cheryl has potential, but if she doesn't have the guts to bleach her hair, she's never gonna be able to book a job with a company like Versace. All their girls bleach their hair white."

They were really annoying me, so I said, "Well, when Versace calls, I'll bleach my hair white." They turned bright red, and everyone else tried not to laugh.

My instinct was right. In modeling it is best not to drastically change anything about your appearance unless a client, like Versace, pays you a lot of money to do so. These women had made a mistake in their reasoning. If I bleached my hair white and then Versace didn't hire me—which was likely, since they had thousands of girls to choose from—I'd be stuck with white hair and no other company to book me.

The third photographer, Emmanuel, was shockingly normal. Claude set up shoots the next day with Sebastian the Energizer Bunny in the morning, and Emmanuel at three p.m. Rico scribbled down the address of Sebastian's studio.

"Nine a.m., Chérie," he said. "Don't be late, okay? It is very important that you are always on time."

They decided not to do a shoot with the two women, due to the strong possibility that we might all lose control and punch them.

Until that day, I had foolishly thought that I'd already learned to walk when I was nine months old, but it turns out that thing your parents taught you is all wrong. Rico informed me that I had no idea at all of how to walk. Teetering on high heels, I sashayed down the long hallway as Rico watched. I was thinking what every model thinks when she walks down a runway or in front of a client or agent: Don't trip!

I reached the end of the hallway. "You walk like the horse," Rico said cheerfully.

"What? That's not true. I do not."

"Ohh no, no, Chérie, that is not a bad thing, but you stomp your feet like the horse, clop, clop, clop." He stomped his feet up and down for emphasis. "Apart from that, you have a very nice walk. You are the ballet dancer, right?"

"Yes, how did you know?"

"You walk, how you say . . . *élégante*. Yes, is good, but I will show you how to do the walk correct. Watch me." He jogged to the end of the hall, turned around to face me, struck a pose, and came waltzing toward me, executing a perfectly feminine model's walk. Almost all models have been taught how to walk by gay men. These fashion-industry men are far better at acting and moving like women than most women are. Rico turned on some rap music with a steady *boom-boom* beat to walk in sync with, and I walked and walked for what seemed like hours. With manic enthusiasm, Rico yelled instructions over the noise of the rapper, who was chanting something about killing cops and getting more respect.

Suddenly the music stopped. Rico stood by the stereo with a serene expression. He bowed his head humbly and said, "Yes, I am the genius." Apparently, at age fourteen I had finally learned how to walk.

Every New York modeling agency has a deal with an upmarket hair salon. Models get their hair cut at the best salons for free. What better advertisement than having dozens of models walking around New York telling everyone where they got their hair done, or sitting in the salon while people walk past the window? Rico and I took the subway to Cutler on East 57th Street, a beautiful place constructed entirely out of white marble and mirrors, where a shaggy-haired man expertly cut long bangs and trimmed two inches off my hair, while being very polite to me so I would say nice things about the salon, which I will say now. It rocks.

I was having the time of my life. This is why some models just starting in the business begin to think that they are pretty special, but as I would soon learn, this period of people fawning over you is very short. The degree of pain that the jolt back to reality causes grows worse in direct proportion to how big an ego you have developed. Luckily, I didn't take the whole experience seriously, and it happened so fast that I lacked the time to develop an attitude. I remember having a deep suspicion that all the people being so nice to me probably had mistaken me for someone else. I was used to being the tall girl with a funny accent—I always seemed to have one left over from the last country I'd lived in. A classmate once asked if I was a CIA agent sent to spy on them!

On our way back to the subway, my new bangs tickled my eyelids, making me blink a lot. I asked Rico why he had not talked at all when I first met him. I still consider his answer to be some of the best advice I have ever heard.

"Chérie," he said, "sometimes it is best to watch the other people, and then decide if you want to talk to them at all."

My dad is in real estate; my first of many plane flights was at the tender age of two weeks. I grew up in Australia, Germany, and Tokyo, and I'd lived in Bombay, Cairo, and Tangier. New York is a country of its own. It's a jungle, filled with some of the world's most intelligent people, all competing for the same limited resources. Allegiances and loyalties are temporary. I could tell Rico liked me, and that he would do his best to help me succeed, but I also knew that he did not feel a similar obligation to others. As we passed a street vendor who was selling CDs, I watched Rico, the rascal, deftly slip a Cher CD into a pocket of his oversize jeans. He looked straight ahead with a satisfied smile on his face. Although he knew I saw him do it, we never mentioned it. Of course, the CDs being sold were probably stolen to begin with.

At 8:59 the next morning, I raced full speed down Greenwich Street and arrived, panting, at the door to Sebastian's studio. I pressed the buzzer and entered. Sebastian appeared on the landing of the fourth floor, dressed all in black, just as wild-eyed as before. "Hey, Cheryl," he shouted, "great to see ya. You're right on time. C'mon up." I looked up the steep flights of stairs and smiled weakly.

The studio was bright, with morning sunshine flooding in through large windows and skylights. Every photographer I have met is in love with natural light, as are makeup artists, who always work with the model sitting next to a window. Natural light is the most unforgiving, revealing all streaks or smudges and allowing the makeup artist to correct them before shooting begins.

Sebastian bounded around his huge studio, introducing me to the makeup artist, purple-haired, freckle-faced Erica, and hairstylist, a beach boy named Alexander. When they learned I was fourteen, both cooed, "Aww, she's a baby." In the modeling industry anyone under eighteen is branded a "baby." Sebastian informed me that we were going to do only "beauty shots," model-speak for head shots, because the clothing stylist was missing in action. That happens all the time; creative people are hard to pin down.

A test shoot like mine can be accomplished free of charge because models are not the only ones who need pictures for their books. Makeup artists, hairstylists, clothing stylists, and photographers all have portfolios that they need to fill with pictures of their work. It's a remarkable display of teamwork. The agency needs professional pictures in order to market its new model. The photographer and stylists need pictures to show to magazines and companies to get hired, and the model shows up because pictures are also *her* most effective marketing tool.

I stood in the middle of the studio with a stupid grin on my face, amazed that three people—adults, no less—had shown up to take my picture. Then, thinking I should at least try to act cool, I wiped the smile off my face and watched Erica, who was unzipping a large black suitcase. It was filled with every imaginable variety of makeup. "Okay," she said, "sit by the window and we'll get started." A light layer of foundation and powder took ten minutes to apply. Then she produced a black eye pencil and poked me in the eye.

"Owwwww!" I screamed.

She looked surprised. "What?"

"You poked my eye!"

"I have to line the inside of your eyelid."

"The inside?"

"It might hurt a bit. But don't blink. That would mess up the line."

I gritted my teeth. She started poking my eye again, and I had to blink.

"Don't!" she snapped angrily. "If you have to blink, tell me first."

She began again.

"I gotta blink," I said timidly.

She withdrew the pencil, I blinked, and she started again. I pouted as a pencil-induced tear trickled down my cheek. Photo shoots were supposed to be fun; they weren't supposed to hurt. Forty minutes passed, and Erica was still working on my eyes, applying shadow. I was bored, both my legs had fallen asleep from sitting still so long, and I had an incredible urge to yell, "Enough already!"

Inevitably at shoots, the makeup artist and the hairstylist will get annoyed at each other, either because one of them is taking too long, or because of the way one is making the model look. They will bicker until the photographer—the undisputed boss of all shoots—decides who's right, ending the controversy. Then they're always embarrassed by the argument and will spend the rest of the shoot air kissing and passing the argument off as a joke.

With a final flourish of her mascara wand, Erica announced I was "*fini.*" Alexander, the hairstylist, made an elaborately pained face. "Ohhh my God. Finally."

"Have you got a problem with my makeup job?" Erica shot back.

Meanwhile, I was staring at the mirror in amazement. With smoky eyes, pale lips, and blush highlighting my cheekbones, I looked three years older. Sebastian bounced over and scrutinized my face. "Love it," he declared. This remark triggered a nervous glance from Alexander, who, while pulling my hair into a neat ponytail, began praising the makeup job as a "work of art."

Stylists approach my hair in three distinctly entertaining stages.

First they gush over it, saying it is the healthiest, longest, best-looking hair they have ever seen. But as they begin trying to style it, the frustration and complaints begin. It's very difficult to keep soft, healthy hair in place. All hairstylists will tell you that, ironically, they prefer working with dry, chemically damaged, "strawlike" hair because, although not much fun to look at, it stays in place easily.

The third stage is the funniest. The stylist starts sweating and muttering swear words, then sets his or her jaw in firm determination and shakes a huge can of heavy-duty, industrial-strength hairspray. He will douse my hair for about a minute, until it actually feels like straw. Then, high on fumes, the stylist will step back with a triumphant grin because he has shown my hair who's really boss.

The show began. I perched on a wooden stool, against a black backdrop, in jeans with a towel tied around my naked chest so my shoulders would be bare for the picture. Sebastian circled me with a light meter. Although only the size of cell phones, light meters make startlingly loud *pop* sounds. Sebastian took a light reading from every angle of my face, including right next to my ear. It's a joke among models that all photographers are "pop happy," since they adore using light readers. But they are very important. If the reading is too low, the photographer knows to make the lights brighter. After all, in pictures, it's always best if you can actually see the model.

Sebastian lifted his camera. "I want you to look very serious, Cheryl, even a little angry, okay?" I glared at the camera. Sebastian grinned at Alexander and Erica, who were standing by for touch-ups, hairspray and makeup brushes in hand. "Do you see the look on her face?" Sebastian hollered. "She's a natural!"

Deeply pleased, I smiled.

"Aarrgghh!!!" Sebastian shrieked. "Don't smile, for Chrissake! You have to look edgy."

I went back to looking solemn, and Sebastian took rapid-fire photos at about one picture a second, contorting his body in every direction to get an interesting angle. Photographers get tremendously involved in their work. They will do anything, absolutely anything, to get the perfect shot. Lie on dirty sidewalks, wade into polluted rivers, balance on ladders, and other life-threatening activities all accomplished with a dreamy smile because they are, well, artists. After thirty minutes of nonstop shooting, Sebastian wiped the sweat off his brow. "Okay, let's change her hair and makeup."

There are usually three or four complete hair and makeup changes in one shoot. Sebastian disappeared into the bathroom, no doubt to pop an upper, and emerged refreshed and ready for action. The shoot finally ended at two in the afternoon. It's amazing that it takes five hours to shoot three looks, but I have never seen it done professionally in less time. Sebastian knew I had another shoot at three and told me to wash all my makeup off before leaving. Makeup artists will literally throw a fit if you show up at a shoot with makeup on; they take it as a personal insult to their skill. Once I had shoots booked so close together that instead of risking being late, I showed up with my makeup from the previous shoot still on. The makeup guy, a Frenchman, looked at me and screamed, "*Merde!* Who has done this to your face, eh?" I was too shocked to answer, so he went on. "This is a criminal to do this to such a beautiful girl . . . yes, I can see you're beautiful somewhere under all that goop. Come wash it off." He followed me to the bathroom, muttering "merde" all the way. The makeup job was really quite good, and I don't think the Frenchman actually thought it was terrible. People in the modeling industry, like dentists, love criticizing one another's work just for kicks.

There is a lot of hugging at the end of shoots, and everybody tells each other how talented they are. Before I left, Sebastian assured me he would drop off negatives of my pictures at the agency the next day.

When I left the studio, it amazed me how tired I felt. Ask any model, many of whom have played sports; they all will tell you that shoots are the most completely exhausting thing they've ever done. It's the changing of moods and poses. Contrary to popular belief, photographers hate it when you just stand there and look blank. On the other hand, they think nothing of leaving a model holding an awkward position, under hot lights, while leisurely adjusting the camera and saying, "Keep that pose or I'll become violent."

I walked uptown to Platinum Models, where my next shoot would take place in one of the agency's spacious spare rooms. There was just enough time to stop for an icy caramel Frappuccino at the Varick Street Starbucks.

A pretty sight greeted me as I entered the agency. Rico was wheeling a rack full of beautiful dresses into the room we were using for the shoot. He explained that the dresses had been loaned to us for the day by a new designer, Avante, who wanted the pictures from this shoot to show prospective buyers. I sifted eagerly through the dresses, picking my favorites, and noticed from the price tags that none of them was under eight hundred dollars. They weren't the kind of garb that I'd been exposed to at the local mall. Jon, the good-natured makeup artist with a choppy haircut, began working his magic. I had an alarming feeling of déjà vu as he stuck a pencil in my eye.

Emmanuel was the polar opposite of Sebastian. Calm, his hair neatly cut, dressed in a polo shirt and slacks, he turned out to be a nice guy and a very talented photographer. When my makeup and hair were done, I changed into one of the floor-length dresses, stepped into a pair of very tight stiletto boots, and wobbled across the room while everyone nodded their approval. In the full-length mirror I looked at myself in amazement. Without thinking, I pointed at the mirror and blurted, "I look like a model!"

That sent everyone into gales of laughter. Emmanuel, still laughing, said, "That's why we're taking your picture."

It's an extraordinary tribute to the skills of the trio—stylist, makeup artist, and photographer—that a fourteen-year-old girl, in Manhattan for the first time, can convey the illusion of wealth, worldly experience, and sex appeal. But she can. Some people would call this exploiting children. I call it one hell of a good time.

The denizens of the modeling industry enjoy acting silly, but in reality they are incredibly clever at getting their jobs done. For example, when a stylist needs high-fashion clothes for a shoot and can't find a good designer to loan them for a day, he or she simply heads to Saks and spends four thousand dollars on designer outfits. She will position the model at an angle that hides the price tags (still attached to the clothes) during the shoot. The next day all the clothes will be returned for a full refund. If a garment is too large, big wooden clothespins are used to fasten the excess cloth behind the model's back and out of sight of the camera. Ever wonder why clothes fit models so perfectly in pictures?

Fortifying ourselves with ice-cold Frappuccinos, Claude, Rico, Emmanuel, Jon, and I charged out of the agency, across the gridlocked street, to take my "location" picture, in a black dress against an ivy-covered wooden fence. Claude and Rico held giant circular light reflectors near my face and caused a near riot as everyone stomped on brakes and leaned out of their cars to see what was going on.

"Look calm!" Emmanuel shouted above the din. I gazed casually into the chaos while what is arguably the best picture ever taken of me was snapped. Four hours later, back in the studio, when I'd officially lost all feeling in my limbs, we called it a wrap.

Claude and Rico were so proud of my endurance they tugged me down the street for a smoothie.

The restaurant is worth mentioning because it was completely dark inside except for blue lights along the black painted walls—a very cool effect. As if to match the walls, the mostly male clientele was dressed all in black. New York is actually very provincial that way. As I sipped my mango smoothie, I kept thinking someone might get mad since I was dressed in jean shorts and a white T-shirt, which to my embarrassment made me glow in the dark. Rico and Claude savored purple margaritas. They got into a passionate argument later, as we walked back toward the subway, over whether I should take the number six or the R train uptown. Rico maintained that the six was more dangerous and he didn't want me being attacked by "some crazy person."

If you have never seen two slightly tipsy bookers having an argument in muggy eighty-five-degree twilight, let me assure you that it is definitely worth the price of admission.

It was agreed that I would appear at the agency the following day to review my pictures from both shoots, and I ended up taking the 6 train, much to Rico's dismay.

I was not attacked by some crazy person. Manhattan's subways are amazingly safe. Back at the hotel, I related my adventures to my dad, who listened intently, until I got to the part about the restaurant Claude and Rico had taken me to. As I described it in detail, he began laughing. "Sweetie, do you realize that was a gay bar?"

I stared at him. "Really?"

Rico was all aglow in the booking room the next day, as he inserted the CD of Emmanuel's pictures into his computer. "Look at them. They are *magnifique*!"

He was so delighted he even ran to get the receptionist, Nick, who lumbered in and squinted at the screen. "Yeah, they're purty," he said, and walked out again. Rico made a sour face. "That man has no . . . how you say . . . zest for life, eh?"

I nodded solemnly and asked where Sebastian's pictures were. Instead of answering, Rico looked elaborately cheerful and chirped, "Emmanuel's pictures are so good!"

I regarded his false smile and cautiously said, "Of course, I'm just as excited to see Sebastian's, too."

He laughed nervously. "Chérie, you don't want to see Sebastian's. Emmanuel's are so much better." By now he had broken into a sweat, eyes darting nervously. He looked so worried that I giggled. "Rico, don't lie, you're not good at it."

He looked very surprised, then grinned from ear to ear. "Chérie, I must tell you, I would like you better if you were stupid. Okay, you know that Emmanuel used the digital camera and Sebastian used the not digital, yes?"

I nodded apprehensively, and he gave a massive sigh. "Sebastian is . . . a very silly man . . . he forgot to put the film in the camera."

There was a long silence as we sat facing each other, and then for some reason that I will never be able to explain, we both burst out laughing—Rico more out of relief that I hadn't attacked him, but I thought it was genuinely hilarious. We were so loud that Nick came to see what was wrong. He stood in the doorway watching, then shook his head, muttered "Nuts," and stomped off.

There was good news when Rico e-mailed Emmanuel's pictures to the designer who'd loaned us the clothes. He liked my look and immediately booked me to appear in his upcoming runway show. That sent Claude into a state of excitement, so he e-mailed my pictures to a number of top Paris modeling agencies. Ford and Elite called to say they were interested in borrowing me.

There are four primary modeling markets: New York, Paris, Milan, and London. Everywhere else is considered a "secondary market" and therefore uncool. It is common for a "mother agency," the designation given to the first agency a model signs with, to loan its models for a few months to another agency in a primary market. The mother agency will still receive a 20 percent cut of the model's earnings, even if she escapes overseas. Chicago—where Cindy Crawford got her start—Los Angeles, and Florida are all examples of secondary markets. Models can earn big paychecks in those places, but they have little chance of booking a lucrative high-profile ad campaign. Top companies prefer to use primary market models, where only the most cosmetically blessed can even get an agency to represent them. A model could be very successful in Florida, come to New York, and be turned down by every agency in town. It's true: If you can make it here, you really can make it anywhere.

My dad had to return to North Carolina, but I arranged with Claude and Rico to come back to Manhattan in three weeks for the runway show I was booked in. They expected me to generate a lot more jobs by appearing, since other designers would be there, scouting models. Up-and-coming models get only about two hundred dollars for a runway show, but because of the exposure, most would gladly do it for free. Supermodels like Claudia Schiffer, however, receive fifteen thousand dollars per show.

We left New York, driving through the Lincoln Tunnel into New Jersey. All of Manhattan was silhouetted against the night sky, twinkling enticingly. I plastered my face to the window, keeping the city where anything can happen in my sights as long as possible.

Ten days later, back in our North Carolina apartment, nestled blissfully halfway between sleep and waking, I was dreaming of runway shows and magazine covers when my door burst open.

"Come look at the TV!" My mother's voice was so tense I didn't argue, just followed her to the living room where my dad stood, arms crossed, looking sorrowful for the first time I could ever remember.

It was the morning of September 11, 2001.

New York shut down. It was two days before I could reach Rico's cell phone to make sure he was all right. He sounded completely different. Even some of his giddy French accent had disappeared. Everything had been canceled; there was no point in me coming back to New York for at least a few months. Rico mailed me eight-by-ten-inch prints of Emmanuel's best pictures.

The total paralysis of business in Manhattan was too much of a strain for Platinum Models, located so near the World Trade Center, to handle. Four months later it, along with many other companies, was out of business. And I was back to square one.

The Launch

Square one was a pretty comfortable place to be. I spent the next couple of years after my New York adventure Rollerblading and watching, spellbound, every episode of *The Real World*, a fascinating study into the mating habits of the Youngus Americanus Screwupious.

I had completely given up on modeling, knowing I was too short to get signed by another agency. Until one day when I was sixteen, while wandering through the mall, I was stopped by a scout for a local modeling agency. Although local modeling didn't interest me, I began to wonder just how much I'd grown over the last year. I charged home and recruited my mother. Using a measuring tape and pencil to mark the wall, she balanced a copy of *Understanding Teenagers* on my head.

"How tall?" I asked eagerly.

She looked at me, smiling uneasily. "Five foot nine."

The magic number.

"Yesssssssssssssssss!" I shouted. "I'm going back, Mom!"

She leaned weakly against the wall. "Oh, dear."

Three inches can make a big difference in New York. At the open call for Prima Models, I surveyed the elegant office that took up the spacious second floor of a midtown office building. While I was waiting for an agent to materialize—they make you cool your heels just to feel superior—a pale, amazingly skinny model with dark hair and perfect features made her entrance. She sat down and, identifying me as her competition, gave me a withering head-to-toe inspection. That accomplished, she opened her portfolio so I couldn't help but see the endless pages of her beautiful pictures as she casually flicked through them. With a smirk she asked, "Here for the open call?"

"Yup." I gave her my friendliest smile.

She wrinkled her nose at my jeans and said matter-of-factly, "I'm just in from Paris. I haven't eaten in two days."

That struck me as the strangest thing I had ever heard. "Oh, I see," I said, which is what I always say when I have no idea what someone is talking about. She kept regarding me with a mocking half smile bordering on contempt, so that by the time an agent did come out I was biting my lip nervously and wondering if it was protocol to starve yourself for two days before calls. The agent had designer sunglasses perched on top of his slicked-back black hair, and the delicate scent of roses surrounded him. The smirking girl stood up in front of me and confidently thrust her book at the agent, who moodily introduced himself as Nassar. I stood glumly in her wake, contemplating why it's a rule that everyone in the modeling industry has to have an exotic name.

"You're not what we're looking for," Nassar said, handing her weighty book back.

I could hardly restrain a grin. I have always been compulsively competitive. Nassar flipped through the meager five pictures, from Emmanuel's shoot, ensconced in my recently purchased black portfolio. I waited patiently to be dismissed.

"I like your look," Nassar said. "I'm gonna show your pictures to the other bookers. Wait here." He turned and walked into the glass-enclosed booking room, where three other agents were hunched over desks, mesmerized by computer screens and talking on multiple phones, their arms flailing like octopuses. I stared after him in amazement. I had already been to three agencies and was turned down by all of them. They actually said that I was "too pretty." Meaning I wasn't "edgy" or unusual-looking enough. You may have noticed that some successful models aren't conventionally good-looking, but they have very striking features that would make you look twice at an ad with their picture on it. Models with more symmetrical, conventionally attractive features, like Tyra Banks or Heidi Klum, often have a hard time getting started in the industry. They have been known to flee to Paris, where classic beauty is still favored. London is the edgiest market on earth; the joke among models is that you can't get an agency in London without appearing to have a serious heroin habit.

While I anxiously watched Nassar behind the glass door showing my book to the other agents, I noticed that the formerly sneering girl was still standing near me, portfolio in hand, looking stunned. The glass door popped open and Nassar stuck his solemn head out. "Cheryl, we're interested in you. Come in and meet the bookers."

I felt like jumping in the air to shout "Geronimo!" On my way to the hallowed booking room, I glanced over my shoulder to see my overly confident nemesis pick up her purse and storm out of the agency, slamming the door. Victory is sweet.

The moment I entered the booking room, I felt the difference in atmosphere from cheerful Platinum Models. Here the faces of the three women bookers were grim, talking tensely into phones and looking ready to bite. The sunflower yellow walls were filled from floor to ceiling with racks of comp cards, displaying about seventy-five models. This was no boutique agency. I stood awkwardly in the center of the room, waiting for the bookers to acknowledge my existence. When they did, all three women looked me over critically as Nassar said simply, "Cheryl."

"Yeah, she has a cool look," one booker said. "Maybe her hair is too long?"

"The hair's gotta be styled, but she has a good body for runway," another declared, while staring at me unnervingly.

"Good bone structure, but do you think she still has baby fat on her face?" the third booker asked, wrinkling her nose.

Nassar spoke up. "Nah, she doesn't really have baby fat on her face, and her body is so slim it doesn't matter."

They went on casually talking about me as if I wasn't standing right there in the midst of the debate. This happens all the time to models. Clients or agents simply begin to talk to one another about you as if they are discussing a stone statue at a museum. If the model tries to join the conversation, she will be coldly ignored and not answered. At times like these I pinch myself to make sure I am still among the living.

Five minutes of intense deliberation later, they decided that I did indeed have a "cool look" and that I should meet the manager. Nassar led me to another glass-partitioned room, sat me down at a long oval glass table, and placed my book in front of me. "Wait here. I'll tell the manager to come out and meet you." He walked into a large, glass-walled office, shut the door, spoke briefly to the man seated behind the desk, and returned. "He'll be out soon." I looked intently into the manager's office, wondering how many square feet of glass it had taken to construct this agency.

The manager sat behind a huge mahogany desk with two-foot-high snarling wooden lions on either side. The furniture was far too big for him, making him resemble a chubby little boy behind Daddy's desk.

Through the glass wall behind me I saw Nassar dismiss four other girls who had come to the open call.

The manager exited his oversize office and sat across from me at the table. "Hellooooo," he said. He seated himself. "I am Fabriziou."

Sure you are, I thought, but said, "I'm Cheryl."

He regarded me with watery eyes magnified by his industrial-strength glasses. "Please do your wok for me."

"My what?"

"Your wok," he said louder.

"Ohh, you mean my walk!"

I stood, glided to the end of the hall and back just like Rico had taught me, then sat back down, knowing it had looked good.

Fabriziou appeared thoughtful. "Hmmmm . . . ," he said. "Your wok needs wuk."

Despite that, Fabriziou said he wanted to sign me, at which point I restrained a smile and told him I would need to talk it over with my mother, who would have to cosign the contract, since I was only sixteen. We agreed that I would return in three hours, at five p.m. I could have simply called my mom on her cell and asked her to come to the agency. She was across the street in Starbucks, which she calls an oasis of civilization. The real reason I postponed signing the contract was that I still had two other agencies to see that day.

Open calls are dreaded by all models. As if in united conspiracy to drive models completely insane, three agencies located at opposite ends of Manhattan will all schedule their open call on the same day between ten and eleven a.m. I am positive that someone at these agencies peeks gleefully out the window to watch models come rushing out of the steaming subway and elbow their way up the street, hopping on one flip-flop-encased foot while trying desperately to slip into the stilettos that agencies are so fond of. Meanwhile, everyone on the street gawks at all these young beauties frantically trying not to miss the open calls, because most of them can't afford to be in Manhattan for more than a week.

Once inside, the models encounter another obstacle. Many agencies don't send a booker out to look at the models, relying instead on the impeccable judgment of a slightly daffy receptionist, who, in her haste to get back to giggling on the phone with her boyfriend, routinely dismisses each one. At other agencies the receptionist collects all the models' books and takes them into another room to "show them to the bookers."

No one believes that a booker actually looks at our books, because we haven't heard of anyone being signed from open calls like that.

The best open calls are when a grumpy, overworked booker comes out and looks at the models as if we are the sole cause of all the misery in his life. Which, in a sense, we are. It makes calls worthwhile if an agency decides to sign you; but for those who don't get signed, a good 99 percent, it can be an exhausting and demoralizing experience. In smaller cities it's possible for models to freelance; but in New York, it's essential to get an agency.

My next open call was at APM Models. Their office was more informal. The agent introduced herself as Penny, and she was surprisingly friendly as she flipped through my book. I mentioned that I was a dancer; she pursed her lips thoughtfully. "Well, I like your look, but you're a little young for us. We like to sign girls with more experience." Then her face brightened. "I know a photographer who's looking for models who can dance for a shoot in *Dance Magazine*."

Butterflies tickled my stomach. For a model, being in a magazine is like finding the holy grail.

"I'll give the photographer a call now," Penny continued. "Her name is Sarah Silver." Penny sat behind her desk and reached over stacks of papers to dial. She held the photocopy I had made of one of Emmanuel's pictures, on the back of which I had written my name, cell number, and statistics. Agencies often require you to leave a picture with them if they are interested in you.

I could hear the phone ring on the other end a few times, then a recorded voice and a beep. "Hi, Sarah. This is Penny at APM," she said cheerfully. "I found a girl who is a dancer." She flipped my picture over and read from the back. "Her name's Cheryl. Height, five-nine; bust, thirty-four; waist, twenty-five; hips, thirty-five; blond hair, blue eyes. Her phone number is . . ."

That was the first time I had heard myself described only by statistics, the way someone would describe a car. It was both worrisome and amusing. It's important to remember that modeling is a business, and as a model you are a commodity. This is one of the most brutally realistic industries; no one will lie to make you feel good about yourself, and unlike your relatives, they won't like you for who you are on the inside.

Penny cradled the phone, thanked me for coming, and said that

Sarah would call me back if she was interested. Penny remains one of the nicest people I have met in the industry. Things were looking up. The next agency I went to, Classique Models, was interested in signing me. But after discussing it with my mom, in another oasis of civilization, we decided on Prima. It was larger and better known, and had a good reputation. As we sipped iced lattes, my phone rang. It was Sarah Silver. She gave me the address of her studio and asked me to come by as soon as possible to show her my book.

I could tell my mom was impressed, although she was making a valiant effort to hide it. She worries about me being a model and once told my dad that it might be a "dirty business." To which my father replied with a grin, "What business isn't?"

The studio was only a few blocks away, on Broadway near 20th Street. I restrained myself from breaking into a run to get to my first casting. It was a large stone building, and after getting buzzed in, I climbed the white marble stairs to the sixth floor. The number of out-of-order elevators in Manhattan is unacceptable. I resolved to form a protest group.

The sixth floor was freshly painted a blinding white, and paint fumes still hung heavily in the air. I knocked on number 605. "Come in," someone called.

This was the biggest studio I had seen yet, painted all white with ultramodern black furniture, the kind that looks great but you can't sit on. There was a second story, and a young woman with dark hair, dressed all in black, came down the stairs. She wore a typical intelligent, no-nonsense New York expression. She flipped quickly through my book, extracted one of the photocopies with my information on it from the back flap, and waved it. "I'll pass this on to *Dance Magazine*. Thanks for coming."

Confused, I thought, *Is that all?* Apparently it was; she shook my hand firmly and politely ushered me out. The whole encounter lasted about forty seconds.

At five p.m. I presented myself and my mother at Prima. We were ushered respectfully by Nassar to the big glass table. Fabriziou appeared. "Cherilll," he exclaimed. "So good to see you. This must be your mama."

My mother regarded him with wonder.

Fabriziou leaned back in his chair and yodeled, "Nassar, bring me the contract!" Nassar brought in three pages of paper stapled together. "Ta-dah," he said dramatically, and winked at me before leaving. Fabriziou explained that the contract was for three years, meaning I would work exclusively with them for that time and they would receive 20 percent of my earnings. Three years sounded extreme to me, so I tried negotiating for a one-year contract. Fabriziou wouldn't budge. He declared that he didn't want to work for a year at getting new pictures in my book and giving me experience, only to have me leave for another agency.

From the jilted expression on his face, I guessed that had happened to him before. Which raised the question, why did the models want to leave after one year? But I left it unasked.

Fabriziou squinted behind his oversize glasses and told us that he saw a big future for me in the industry, *Vogue* magazine as well as high-profile runway shows. I took this with my natural city-kid skepticism, because for all the high-powered reputation of Prima Models, Fabriziou just didn't seem like the kind of personality the editor of *Vogue* would beg to have lunch with.

He said he would arrange a test shoot, since the pictures I had were more than a year and a half old, and then print comp cards.

"Who pays for the cards?" I asked.

Fabriziou pushed his glasses up and began speaking extraordinarily fast. "Well, of course the model pays for the cards. It's like that at all agencies." The amazing speed at which he talked reminded me of the end of commercials for a new drug, when someone says very quickly that this wonderful new drug you have just heard about will probably kill you.

Three hundred comp cards would cost three hundred and fifty dollars. If I was going to come live by myself in New York, for the summer at least, I couldn't afford to pay for cards. Remembering something Rico had told me, I asked Fabriziou to put the cards on account. This means that instead of charging the model up front, the agency keeps a record of how much she owes and then takes it out of her earnings from jobs. Models lovingly call this "putting it on my tab."

Fabriziou was flustered, "No, no . . . we don't do that."

"Why not?"

"Ohh, well . . ." He frowned. "We don't."

"If you had confidence that you could book me jobs, you would, because then you'd get your money back right away."

"Yesss . . . we don't, you see."

"No, I don't."

"You don't see!" He leaned forward. "You need glasses?"

"No, I don't need glasses. I was referring to what you said."

"What did I say?"

My mother was looking back and forth between me and Fabriziou, as if she was at a tennis match, watching the ball.

I hid my impatience. "You said you couldn't put my cards on account. Why not? Some other agencies do it."

"Well . . . it's our policy."

"Oh, well, that's too bad." I reached for my bag and began to stand up.

An expression of panic fell across Fabriziou's face. He reached across the table and patted my hand. "Okeydokey, we change the policy."

I grinned at him. "Okeydokey."

Models' contracts are notoriously easy to break; since it's usually a minor signing, models can cancel contracts if the agency is not performing. It's also easy for the agency to abruptly drop models who aren't booking well.

I signed; Mom apprehensively cosigned, and Fabriziou looked pleased with himself. He said, "Tell me, Cherilll, why do you want to be a model?"

"To make a lot of money," I answered bluntly, just to see what would happen.

His mouth formed a perfect O. I was informed later by other models that they all get asked this question, and there is a preferred response. Smile brilliantly and say, "I'm interested in fashion, and I think it would be a great experience to model. I know it's going to be difficult, but I'll stick with it!"

Ahhh, the soothing sound of insincerity.

A lot of people in modeling, like Fabriziou, operate largely in a fantasy and try to convince themselves that there is more to the industry than money. Being realistic and telling the truth are not usually appreciated.

Fabriziou recovered from his jolt to hug me good-bye, and we agreed that I would return soon to live in New York for the summer. He offered to have me stay in Prima's model apartment, but I declined, since I had heard model apartments are notoriously cramped and uncomfortable. During the summer months, a model later told me, Prima's apartments were four girls to a room, eight to a bathroom, and Fabriziou had the colossal nerve to put eight hundred dollars a month on each of their tabs.

As my mom and I drove back to North Carolina the next day, she kept smiling to herself. Finally she exclaimed, "My God! That Fabriziou, I mean, what a *character*!"

I was sitting at the kitchen table the next morning, sleepily contemplating my oatmeal, when Sarah Silver called me. "Hi, Cheryl. The casting for the magazine shoot is today at eleven a.m." I let my spoon drop into the bowl with a hollow *plop*. There was no way I could get to New York before two. "Is it possible for me to meet with the magazine people later than eleven?" I asked. The answer was no.

I felt like crying. "I won't be able to make it, I'm sorry."

Sarah was friendly. "Okay, that's a pity. I'll give the editors your picture anyway. Maybe they can use you in a future issue." It was a standard "feel better" line, and although I appreciated Sarah being so nice, I knew I had just missed my chance. I thanked her sweetly, hung up, and screamed, "AARRRGGGHHH" so loud my mother almost dropped her orange juice.

Jersey

My cat looks like a tiger, thinks he's a dog, and eats way too much tuna. His name is Tigger, and he was stretched out in the backseat while my dad, singing our theme song, "Margaritaville," drove me to New York. I was nervous but doing an admirable job of hiding it. Tigger was coming along because he thinks I'm his mother and has a nervous breakdown if I'm not around.

I was going to stay at a hotel in Jersey—New York hotels are amazingly expensive—until I found an apartment. I had six hundred fifty dollars in saved-up cash, earned in part from being tortured by various little tykes, also called babysitting, and other forms of legalized slavery.

We drove down busy, dusty Highway 1 in Jersey, along which are about twenty equally horrible-looking motels. Among the shanties stood a Days Inn. Compared to the surroundings, it was the Ritz.

My dad carried my suitcases through the white marble lobby, while I lugged Tigger in his cage. The receptionist, who looked about twelve and proud to be wearing a suit, checked me in. All I had to do was walk out the door and catch a bus to be in Manhattan in fifteen minutes; "convenient," just as the brochure said. The room had a huge window and blond wood furnishings, "Well," my dad said awkwardly, "I have to get back home for that meeting. I love you, pal. Be good. Oh, wait! I don't have to tell *you* that, ha-ha."

I haven't done anything seriously naughty since I was eight and drove off in Dad's car. This lack of rebelliousness is a source of some embarrassment to me.

I watched from the fifth-floor window as my dad drove away. *It's only for the summer*, I reminded myself, but I still felt like running outside and shouting, "Come back!" Instead, I unpacked.

Fabriziou called the next morning and told me to come to the agency. There was to be "a meeting for all the new girls."

The two-dollar bus into the city was crowded, ninety-five degrees of pure humidity, and everyone spoke happily to one another in Spanish. Almost the entire population of Jersey City is Latino, so I could never understand what was being said. A fashionably dressed, magnificently obese young woman entered the bus and sat down next to me.

"You a model or something?" she asked me suspiciously.

She had squished me against the window. "If I survive the bus ride," I squeaked.

When I glimpsed the Manhattan skyline before we entered the Lincoln Tunnel, I got a familiar giddy feeling. This summer I was a New York model, and anything could happen!

The air-conditioning system in Prima's luxury building had

chosen that day to sputter out and die. Inside Prima's office were a dozen damp, dazed models. Fabriziou swept into the room, all five feet two inches of him, and told everyone to sit at the glass table. I looked around and decided that at least half the girls were suffering from heat exhaustion.

"Okey, now let's go around the table and say our name and how old we are, okay?" Fabriziou pointed at me. "Will you start, please?"

I groaned inwardly. This was just like the first day of school. "I'm Cheryl, and I'm sixteen."

The result of this exercise was that we heard one girl's name and promptly forgot it as soon as we heard the next one. Most of the models were nineteen. I was the youngest, except for a terrified, stunningly beautiful blond girl who was only thirteen and in New York alone.

Next, all the bookers emerged from the booking room, rubbing their eyes to wipe away the glare of computer screens. Fabriziou introduced them:

Veronika, the head booker: thirties, attractive, extremely pale, dark-haired, Russian. Spelled her name with a *k* for unknown reasons. One of the male models later speculated that it was because she was a spy from the "K" GB. Nicknamed the "Ice Queen" for her tough personality, she consumed two liters of Diet Coke a day.

La-shawnda was a plump, elegantly dressed cocoa-skinned woman who faked a snooty English accent. Harbored a pathological hatred for all models; reasons unknown. Nicknamed "The Witch" by everyone, including the other bookers.

Nassar had a pierced ear and a perfect tan. He always wore designer sunglasses perched on his dark hair and dressed only in black. Occasionally subject to massive mood swings but basically a nice guy.

Amy was a pretty African-American woman, six-one, always polite and friendly. Her nickname was "The Only Sane One in the Place."

"Okey," Fabriziou said as the bookers sat on comfy chairs near the wall. "My assistant is going to talk to you about what we expect from you as our brand-new Prima models." The bookers concealed pitying looks. An angry-looking blonde stormed out of Fabriziou's office and glared contemptuously at the models.

"This," Fabriziou said, "is my assistant, Jennifer."

Jennifer hurled a pack of cigarettes and her key chain onto the glass table with such a clatter that some of the models snapped out of their heat-induced comas. "I bet you're pretty pleased with yourselves that you're models, right?" she sneered at us. No one answered. "Well, I'm here to tell you that you're not that friggin' cool. I'm gonna make this simple for you. We don't really give a shit about you."

Fabriziou looked shocked and yelped, "No, no, Jennifer, we do give a shit about them!"

But Jennifer was on a roll. "These are the rules: You have to show up to your castings on time. I repeat, on time! You have to look perfect, don't gain any weight, don't be hungover, and remember to take baths." This shocked everyone, since we were probably the best-groomed girls in town. I felt a strong urge to giggle.

"Now, about men." Jennifer said the word "men" the way other people would say "murderers." "They are all after you, they all want to corrupt you. Don't ever, I mean *ever*, believe what one of *them* tells you. They are liars."

Jennifer forged on to tell us that New York men are basically vultures, hulking in litter-strewn alleys, waiting for the Poor Innocent Model to walk by, so they can leap out and ravish her. This didn't interest me, since I'd decided long ago not to sleep with anyone until I got married, just to confuse the hell out of people. "These men don't give a damn about you. They will use you and then change their phone numbers. Trust me. I know."

I'll bet she did.

I looked around at the other models' petrified faces and wondered how many hours of therapy would be required to erase this meeting from their memories.

"Okay now, about the bookers." Jennifer pointed at them. "The bookers are the people who are gonna book you jobs and send you on go-sees to clients, and they can choose *who* to send. So you better suck up to them, I mean really suck up, otherwise they'll send someone else; so you better be really friggin' nice to everyone here . . . where the hell are you going?" she snapped at Nassar, who had stood up.

"I have to send comp cards out," he answered wearily.

"What for?"

"The runway show."

"Can't it wait?"

"No."

"Well, who the hell's runway show is it?" Jennifer snapped.

"Calvin Klein's."

"Oh . . . umm . . . okay, then."

Nassar left, lucky guy. Jennifer turned her wild-eyed stare back to us. "I bet you think this is all gonna be fun and glamorous, don'tcha? But it's work, hard work, so don't come crying to us about how lonely or scared or sad you are. I don't care if you are thirteen, I still don't give a shit."

You-must-not-laugh, I repeated to myself.

"We aren't your friends; we give you clients to go see and that's it.

Don't talk to the bookers about your lives, because they don't give a shit either." She was getting louder and louder.

"So to recap, don't get too drunk, watch out for men, remember to take baths, and don't ever talk to us about your lives."

You-must-not-laugh.

She leaned on the table so her manic, flushed face was only inches from mine.

Do-not-laugh.

"BOTTOM LINE," she shrieked, "I AM NOT YOUR FUCKING NANNY!"

My head flew back and I burst out laughing. Almost sobbing, I had never laughed so hard in my life. Everyone stared at me. The girls, already scared, were now terrified that one of their own had lost her mind so early in the game. The bookers regarded me with confused frowns. Then I heard a solitary giggle. It was Amy, "the only sane one in the place." She covered her mouth and ran to hide in the booking room.

When I could finally stop laughing, I lifted my teary face from the table and declared, "It's just the heat." Amazingly, they bought it. The thirteen-year-old even gave me a tissue.

The meeting ended a few minutes later. Fabriziou motioned me into his office and closed the glass door. I thought I might have been in hot water for having a laughing fit, but Fabriziou scribbled an address down and handed it to me. "This is a photographer. He can do a test shoot with you at two p.m. today, okey?"

I was relieved. "That's great."

Fabriziou looked serious. "Now, I don't want you telling the other girls that you are doing a shoot so soon, because they will be jealous." He pointed through the glass at the models milling around. "They are just 'summer girls.'"

That puzzled me, but I nodded. "All right."

He was pleased, "Good girl. Ahh, you have such pretty hair, I'm going to talk to Clairol about you. Okey, okey, bye-bye." His damp little hand massaged my arm in farewell.

On my way out I waved to the other models, most of whom were in the booking room taking Jennifer's advice and sucking up. The funny thing is, I never saw Jennifer after that day. Perhaps she was fired, or perhaps they locked her in a closet so she wouldn't disgrace the human race any further.

I had two hours before my test shoot, so as I was leaving Prima's building I asked the security guard if there was a bookstore nearby.

He was about forty, wearing a fancy navy blue uniform with lots of buttons and a captain's hat. "Biranajeje Kukubona," he replied in his native Kinyarwanda.

The best thing about Manhattan is all the *interesting* people you meet.

Walking up Sixth Avenue, I pondered the definition of a "summer girl" and wondered why Fabriziou said "okey, okey" all the time.

The photographer's studio was near Greenwich Village, on the west side of Manhattan, where the quaint streets run in all directions and you can get lost in five seconds flat. The Village is the prettiest section of the city, but I was oblivious to that as I held my massive paper map up like a sail in the muggy breeze. I hadn't bought a small laminated map yet, so I wrestled with the four-by-four-foot monster, the kind that once unfolded will never, ever refold. Finally I crumpled it into a ball, hurled it into a trash bin, and marched off feeling wronged. A cop gave me directions. Manhattan cops are the best. First of all, they don't mind being called "cops," and they actually enjoy helping people get unlost.

Most photographers' studios are located inside imposing buildings that resemble warehouses; the hallways are bright white, the studios massive, and the decoration minimal. The door to James's studio was open. A cheerful young guy who somewhat resembled Will Smith, but without the protruding ears, peeked out from behind a rack of elegant dresses.

"Hey, Cheryl, come in."

He jogged the length of his sunny studio and took a good look at me. That made me nervous, because I'd heard that photographers will only shoot a model they really like the look of. I've heard horror stories of models being abruptly turned away if photographers think they look different from the pictures that the agency has shown them.

"You have a great look," James said.

"Oh, good." I sighed in relief.

The rest of the studio was empty. "Do you have a makeup person coming?" I asked.

"Yeah. She's gonna be a little late, but you can play on the computer till she gets here." James pointed at two computers against the wall. I sat down at one. James shook his head. "Makeup people are always late, or they just don't show up."

An hour and a half later, Nina, the makeup artist, finally stormed into the studio tugging a suitcase filled with hair appliances, gels, and every color of makeup on earth. "James," she announced in thickly accented English, "now, I would have been on time, but you forgot to confirm."

"I did confirm!" James said through clenched teeth.

"Nyet, you didn't, otherwise I would have been on time. I'm very prrrrofessional, James."

They glared at each other for thirty seconds while I prayed she wouldn't leave. Then they both chuckled, hugged, told each other they were talented, and promptly forgot all about it.

Nina was worth the wait, and although she used very little makeup, the effect was stunning. James positioned the lights, rolled down blue background paper, and placed a wooden stool in front of the camera. "Okay, Cheryl, put this on." He held up a black dress with an eight-hundred-dollar Saks price tag still attached, "Don't take the tag off, I'm gonna return it tomorrow," he said with a wink. I ducked behind the paper backdrop and pulled on the dress, hiding the price tag up the right sleeve.

I sat on the stool as James took light readings and Nina coached me on my pose. She arranged my legs crossed, with my hand tucked limply under my chin, and commanded me to look "ethereal." When James inspected it on his two-inch digital camera screen, he screamed, "Oh my God, this is hotttt!"

Three hours and three dress changes later, we all bear-hugged good-bye. With the dreamy smile photographers get when they have gotten "the shot," James promised to drop the disk off at Prima the next day.

Out on the street, I phoned Fabriziou to let him know the shoot went well; he had told me to always call in after shoots. That sounds like he cared about me, but in reality, he wanted to make sure I hadn't disappointed James, who was a very important photographer to Prima.

I took a walk down Canal Street toward the subway, passing through Chinatown; the sidewalks were so crowded that the sea of people flowed over onto the road. Yet miraculously, no one bumped into each other. It's a finely choreographed dance of sidestepping, edging along sideways, and managing to walk very quickly with a cell phone glued to your ear. The open-air stalls where merchants sell raw fish, fake Vuitton handbags, and knockoff Rolex watches are packed so close together that there isn't an inch of wasted space. The merchants hold up watches and shout, "Weal Wolex watch, twenny dollar!" The noise is terrific. I felt alive; in other cities I had been bored without even realizing it, but it's impossible to be bored in Manhattan.

In summer, the tunnels of Manhattan's subways are like ovens, but the trains are so efficient that everyone uses them. Business executives stand next to homeless men, Goths next to yuppies, and in the grand tradition of New York they all get along and mind their own business.

You have to take a few steps into the subway tunnel from the stairs before a wave of heat hits you. I dodged businessmen hurrying off the train with their briefcases held in front of them as path-clearing battering rams, and studied the multicolored subway map on the wall. Unable to decipher it, I approached an angry-looking woman in the little glass information booth and asked which subway I should take to the bus terminal. She scowled, shoved a folded paper replica of the map on the wall at me, and turned her swivel chair away from me.

"Ummm . . . okay," I said, and went back to the wall.

There are a startling number of subway lines in Manhattan, one for almost every letter of the alphabet, and if that doesn't get you, there are others numbered one through nine. You hear people saying, "So I was at Forty-second Street and I take the W downtown, but whaddya know, it doesn't stop at Twenty-third, so I get off at Canal to take the N or R uptown, but it turns out I get on the downtown and the next thing you know I'm across the river in friggin' Brooklyn."

When I stumbled, exhausted, into my hotel room, the sight of Tigger stretched out on the bed in air-conditioned bliss made me so jealous that I stood under a cold shower for half an hour.

In the morning I marched out of the hotel into the blinding sun and went exploring the hood in search of breakfast. All of Jersey City is crammed with aluminum-sided, box-shaped, two-story houses in various colors, making every street look depressingly similar to the last one. On a corner I found a tiny deli advertising breakfast, the kind of corner store going out of business because of chain restaurants.

Capitalist pigs.

The inside of the deli was cramped and smelled deliciously like the sausages being fried by the middle-aged chef with slicked-back hair and a grease-spotted T-shirt. He looked up with a toothy grin. "Yo, what can I getchoo?" he said.

The "getchoo" sounded like a sneeze. I contemplated whether or not my mother would let me eat here, decided she wouldn't, and sat cheerfully at the counter.

A young, hungover couple eyed me while I ordered toast and sausages. The woman's overly made-up face wore a contemptuous sneer, and the man leered sleepily. I smiled at them, trying to maintain peace in the Northeast.

"You ain't from around here, are ya?" asked the chef.

"How did you know?"

Instead of replying, he started to chuckle, and so did the comatose couple. When the chef recovered, he asked amiably, "So whutchoo doin' in Joysey?" Again the "whutchoo" sounded like a sneeze, and I watched my frying sausages protectively.

"I'm going to college in New York," I lied. Saying I was a model would provoke too many questions.

"Yo, that's cool, NYU?"

"Umm, yes."

He handed me my breakfast plate. "You know"—he squinted his eyes—"you should be one of them fashion models like in the magazines."

The hungover guy piped up, "Yo, I wuz thinkin' the same thing."

His girlfriend fixed him with a murderous gaze, then grimaced at me. "Not in those sneakers you ain't."

I looked down at my favorite sneakers, white when I bought them for thirty-five dollars, now a light gray, scuffed, torn, muddy, and to me, completely beautiful. I lifted my chin. "I like them."

The woman rolled her eyes and snorted.

The chef was leaning around the counter, trying to get a look at my famous shoes. I finished the yummy sausages and asked him, "What's the best way to find an apartment in Jersey?"

"Around here in Joysey?"

I nodded.

"You look for the 'For Rent' signs in windows of the houses."

"Great, thanks." I paid my bill, only $2.50, and stood outside in the rapidly increasing heat. A group of teenage boys approached with a boom box turned up to full volume, shouting at one another. They were wearing baggy jeans and ridiculous "tough guy" expressions. As they walked along, the guy with the boom box began swearing at his friend, who angrily raised his hand and smacked Mr. Boom Box on the side of his head. At that exact instant, Boom Box's pants fell down, exposing red boxer shorts with adorable little pink hearts on them. I bit my lip hard, trying not to laugh. This could be why I never found most teenage boys attractive, something my father is positively delighted about.

I decided to go apartment huntin'. It doesn't take long to get the hang of it:

1. Pick a street you like; failing that, pick one you aren't afraid to live on.

2. Avoid vicious, snarling miniature dogs with delusions of grandeur.

3. Look for FOR RENT signs in windows and write down phone numbers on sweaty palm, or knock on doors.

The first door was opened by a short, squat woman in her eighties wearing curlers and a flowered muumuu. She looked up at me and asked, *"Qué? Qué?"*

I gave her my most charming smile. "I don't spe—"

"Qué quiere?"

"I can't understa—"

"Qué pasa? Qué es?"

In a flash of inspiration, I yelped, "Apartmentito!"

Her eyes crossed.

I tried again. "Apartmento?"

"You want apartment, come in." She opened the door.

I followed her flowered derrière up creaking stairs. "How many bedrooms does it have?" I asked.

"One."

"How much per month?"

"Seven hundred."

She unlocked the door and swung it open. It was a great place with lots of windows. I puzzled over why it was so cheap until I looked out the window and saw a charming view of a small graveyard, full of old, chipped headstones with moss and overgrown weeds partially obscuring the names.

"You want apartment?" she growled from the doorway, fists firmly planted on her hips. I had the thought that maybe the cemetery was populated by former tenants who had displeased her. I tried one of my jokes on her. Pointing out the window at the graveyard, I said with a grin, "I hear people are just *dying* to get in there."

She wasn't willing to get the joke. "You want apartment?"

"Nah." I shrugged. "I didn't know there was a cemetery in the backyard."

"You afraid of the ghosts?"

"I'm not afraid!" I said indignantly.

"Then why don't you want apartment?"

"Because it would be depressing to look out the window every morning at dead people."

We started down the stairs. All of a sudden, she announced, "Six seventy-five."

It took me a moment to get it. "Oh, no thanks."

She bared her teeth. "Six fifty."

"Really, no thanks." I slipped by her, out the door, and beat it down the steps to the street.

My cell phone rang, and I actually jumped.

"Hello?"

Fabriziou started talking very fast. "Hellooo Cherilll, I have proofs of your pictures for the shoot. Come by the agency, okey?"

"Great. How do they loo—"

"Okey, bye-bye." Click.

Conversation à la Manhattan.

Baaf, the security guard, was at his post in the lobby of Prima's building. "Hello," I said, raising my hand to my brow in salute.

He beamed, showing dimples. "Muraho, amakuru yawe?"

I nodded and waited for the elevator.

The street doors opened, and into the lobby, straight out of a magazine, strolled a real live male model. This was an interesting development. He looked like a male version of me; blond, blue eyes, about eighteen, wearing the kind of bewildered innocent expression that suggested Fabriziou had driven by a potato farm in Idaho and kidnapped him.

The elevator opened. We got in, and I pushed Prima's floor.

We ignored each other.

Completely.

There is something ridiculous about pretending that a person standing two feet away from you doesn't exist. The side of my mouth was starting to twitch, when I noticed the portfolio he was carrying. It was translucent blue, with blocky printing spelling out PRIMA NEW YORK MODEL MANAGEMENT. It looked very important. I desperately wanted one.

The elevator opened, and I walked quickly to Prima's door, intent on asking Fabriziou for one of those portfolios. There was a high receptionist's desk inside the agency, so high that you couldn't tell if anyone was sitting behind it, unless you stood directly in front of it. No one had ever been there before, so I breezed past.

There was a high-pitched shout in a German accent. "WHERE ARE YOU GOING?"

I froze.

From behind the desk rose a strong-looking woman in her late forties with square features and black hair pulled tightly back into a bun, her blue eyes hardened. She reminded me of the woman in the James Bond movie who tortured people with electrodes.

"What do you want?" she barked, leaning forward menacingly.

"Ah . . . um, I'm here to see . . . ," and realized I had temporarily forgotten his name. "Far . . . Farizio?" God, this was embarrassing.

"You mean Fabriziou," she said.

I let out a relieved sigh. "Yes, I'm Cheryl. He asked me to come."

"Siddown!" she said. "I'll tell him you here."

I dropped into one of the elegant chairs and started breathing again. She turned to the blond male model, who was standing near the door with an oddly dignified expression.

"What you want, Eric?" she yelled.

"Hello, Hilda," he said very calmly. "I'm here to see Nassar about new comp cards."

"Siddown, I tell him!" she commanded, then lifted her phone and savagely punched a button. Inside the glass booking room I saw Nassar innocently lift his phone and wince as Hilda screeched in his ear, "Eric here!"

Nassar got up from his desk and opened the door. The sounds of clicking keyboards, multiple phone conversations, and a shouted "Fuck!" spilled into the reception area before he shut the door. Taped to the inside of the glass was a sign reading, NO MODELS IN BOOKING AREA!!!

Nassar was dressed all in black, earring aglitter, silver sunglasses perched on his hair, very cool. He gazed adoringly at Eric, then noticed me. "Hi, sweetheart," he said.

I was shocked that someone was actually being nice and grinned from ear to ear. "This kid never stops smiling." Nassar chuckled. Not knowing what else to do, I kept smiling. He was still giggling as he led Eric to the oval table and scanned his book for pictures to use on the comp cards. I was now alone with Hilda, who was still standing, sorting through papers and looking dangerous. A fountain was built into the wall, with water trickling down a beautiful stone slab to splash onto pebbles at the bottom. At first the sound was pleasant, but after ten minutes, it began to remind me of a faucet dripping maddeningly. Fabriziou, or Fab, as I had begun to call him mentally, glided in from his office, clad in designer jeans and a loose white cotton shirt. "Cherilll," he said, spreading his arms and giving his signature chipmunk smile. I stood, towering over him by half a foot. He placed his hands on both my shoulders while simultaneously tugging me down a little and rising up on his toes. He mashed my left cheek with his cheek, made an air-kissing sound (Mmwhaaaa) and repeated it on the flip side. How icky. I am really, really not a touchy-feely person.

Then Fab looped a hand around my waist and headed for his office. The glass door was held open by a small, fierce-looking wooden lion, matching the two on either side of his desk; a large window flooded the room with sunshine. He sat behind his desk, nestling comfortably into a reclining, cushioned black leather chair, while I squirmed on a solid carved wooden monstrosity. The back of my chair had bumpy animals chiseled into it so that the only way to sit without stabbing yourself was on the very edge of the seat with your back ramrod straight. Fab searched through the stacks of papers on his desk and handed me five sheets of photographic paper with ten small pictures on each.

"Wow, these are great."

"Yes, I checked the best ones."

There were red check marks next to one on each page.

"I will get those five pictures printed, okey?"

"Sure. I can take them to a printing place myself if you want."

"No, no, I send them out for yoi."

"How much does the printing cost?"

He waved his hand dismissively. "Not much, don't worry."

"I'm not worried." I smiled. "I'm just wondering because it goes on my account, right?"

"Yes, we get it printed by the best, they give us a discount, it's twenty dollars."

"Twenty dollars each?" I said, surprised.

Fab leaned forward, eyes narrowing. "Cherilll, this is New Yok," he informed me. "That is the standard price. We are professionals; we know what it costs." He gave me a hard look for doubting him.

I shrank against the chair back, momentarily forgetting that it was a torture device, and shot bolt upright again. "Right, send them where you think is best."

His face softened. No longer impatient, he said gently, "Cherilll, we want to help you, okey, so you have to trust us." He gave a chipmunk smile.

"Yes, I trust you." I nodded. That was sincere.

He looked me in the eye. "Good, that's good. Now you need comp cards and a book."

That activated me. "A book! Do I get a blue one?"

He smiled fondly, while I, realizing that I had just acted sixteen, tried to appear mature.

"Yes, here." He pulled a bubble-wrapped package out of a drawer, removed the wrapping, and handed the book to me. I accepted it solemnly, while trying to figure out a way to get my hands on the bubble wrap and pop it.

You like doing that too—just admit it.

Fab began talking happily about the pictures to use on my cards. I wasn't really listening because after ten minutes of awkward perching on the chair, my entire right leg had fallen asleep. I concentrated on wiggling my toes until Fab said, "Okey, stand up, I'll measure you for the cards."

For good reason, modeling agencies will never believe the measurements that models claim to have. So before printing comp cards, out pops the measuring tape. My leg wouldn't move. I stood up, using the desk for support. Fab didn't notice I was on one leg as I held my arms out like a scarecrow for the bust measurement.

"Thirty-four," he announced, and wrote it down.

Next I had to roll my shirt up to my ribs to get an accurate waist measurement. No matter what time of year it is, the tape is always ice-cold, causing me to flinch and the measurer to snap, "Don't suck in."

"Twenty five . . . and hips thirty five." He wrote the numbers down and looked surprised that they matched what I had already told him. Feeling returned to my right leg in the form of a colony of ants marching up and down. "Are we putting Cheryl Diamond on the cards, or just Cheryl?" I asked. Often models go by their first name only, since so many are foreign, and who can pronounce Zvaldechmirova anyway?

Fab grinned enthusiastically. "We will put both your names on the cards, it sounds good. Cherilll Diamond, yes, it's a groovy name." He was being serious.

"Do you get along with your mummy and daddy?" he asked out of the blue.

It was annoying and amusing, the way he always spoke to me as if I were a four-year-old.

"Yes, we get along."

He looked happy. "Are you good friends with them?"

"Oh yes, they're very nice." I was getting bored.

"What does your daddy do?"

"My *father*"—I paused, letting "father" sink in—"is in real estate."

"And are you friends with him?"

Yes! Goddamit, yes! "Yup."

He seemed satisfied. "Good, good, I want to make sure you're happy. I'll give you a call when your cards and pictures are ready, okey?"

We both stood, and Fab scooted around his desk to repeat the air-kissing ritual. He looked up at me adoringly. "Cherilll, you are such a sweet girl, such a happy personality."

"Thanks." I was discreetly trying to back out of his grasp.

"Okey, okey, bye-bye."

Gratefully, I left his office and was passing the booking room when Veronika, whom I could see hunched behind her computer, looked up and motioned for me to come in. The NO MODELS IN BOOKING AREA!!! sign froze me, but Veronika kept impatiently waving her hand, so I opened the door like the hard-core rebel that I am and stood just inside the room.

"Don't just fucking stand there. Come over here," Veronika commanded.

I thought that was funny and grinned at her while squeezing by the other bookers' desks. As head booker, Veronika had the biggest desk, nearest to the window.

"Hi, Veronika."

She leaned back in her leather chair and looked at me. "What's your name?"

"Cheryl Diamond."

"Okay, bye." She went back to typing.

I just stood there. She looked up at me impatiently. "What?"

"Is that all you wanted?" I asked awkwardly.

Veronika sighed in annoyance. "Yes, I have to know your name if I'm going to be your booker. Thank you. Good-bye." She began typing.

I said, "Bye" to her bent head and, feeling like an idiot, made my way back toward the door. From her desk, La-shawnda shot me a look that could freeze the Sahara at noon. With a fixed smile, I hurried by Hilda's command post and into the hallway. I leaned against the wall and, for no good reason, started laughing.

Outside, the sun beat down on the yellow cabs caught in a traffic jam on Sixth Avenue. They all leaned on their horns as if it would make a difference. One of the cabbies leaned out of his open window. Sweat streaming down his face, he shook his fist at the cab in front and screamed, "You bastard! Go! Go forward. I'm going to kill you."

A head emerged from the taxi in front of him and shouted hysterically, "Shut up! Shut up! I'll kill *you*!"

The pedestrians smiled appreciatively.

I walked up Eighth Avenue past the shops with fluorescent lights flashing XXX DVDS, ADULT ENTERTAINMENT, GIRLS LIVE NUDE. Even though it was one in the afternoon, a few heat-exhausted men were straggling in, probably seeking the air conditioning more than girls. On the corner of 37th Street, huge, pulsing orange lights read GRAY'S PAPAYA: HOT DOG 75¢. A line extended out of the partially enclosed snack bar. I studied the long queue of people and noted optimistically that there wasn't a tourist among them. So it had to be good. You can tell a Manhattanite from the tourists because New Yorkers dress in black, talk constantly on cell phones, and wouldn't be caught dead in an "I ♥ NY" T-shirt. I joined the line on the sidewalk as my cell rang. It was my mom, making sure I hadn't been sold into slavery. I was overjoyed that she called, because it gave me an opportunity to talk on my phone and look cool.

"How's it going with finding an apartment?" she asked cheerfully.

A vision of the cemetery apartment flashed before me. "I . . . ah . . . I'm working on it."

"Good, honey. When you find one, leave a deposit so they hold it, and we'll wire the money to the bank on Friday."

"Sure." I was distracted by everyone pressing into Gray's Papaya. Fifty-gallon stainless-steel vats stood in a row against the wall, labeled PAPAYA, COCONUT CHAMPAGNE, and PINEAPPLE. Empty Dasani water bottles hung from the ceiling, and the white walls were covered with colorful signs: NO GIMMICKS, NO BULL, THEY REALLY DO TASTE GOOD.—NY TIMES. And PAPAYA IS GOD'S GREATEST GIFT TO MAN. Gallon-size dispensers of mustard and ketchup were getting mobbed by construction workers, businessmen, druggies, and one elegantly groomed man in a white suit and red silk shirt who was definitely a pimp.

He stared at me.

"What's all that noise, Cheryl?"

"Mom, I'm in the coolest hot dog place. I'll call you tonight, okay?"

"All right. Your dad and I are going white-water rafting this weekend!"

"Are you kidding me?"

"No, really."

I tried to picture my petite, sophisticated mother crashing down a river. "Wear a life jacket."

"I will, pumpkin. Talk to you tonight."

She has always called me pumpkin. I have no idea why.

The staff rushing back and forth behind the counter managed to look like cheerful Hawaiians, each wearing a button on his or her shirt reading POLITE NEW YORKER. A promise they actually live up to. The businessman in front of me shouted his order while simultaneously talking on his cell phone. "Cover the short on my swissies . . . two dogs, everything on 'em, medium papaya for here . . . and I want to go long on the euro."

I stared at him, amazed by the multitasking.

The Hawaiian smiled at me. "Whaddyowantmiss?"

I wasn't prepared, and people began glaring at me impatiently. "Ummm . . ." Then inspiration hit. "One dog, everything on it, medium papaya, for here." I was smiling proudly while he rung it up, when a shadow descended over the cash register. "Let me get that for you, darlin'."

The pimp flashed a celebrity smile and pulled out a wad of cash fastened with a gold $-shaped clip. In a perfectly choreographed movement, he placed his thumb on one end of the hundred-dollar bills and fanned through them. The druggies eyed the money with comic longing.

"I'm paying for it," I said, and handed five dollars to the amused guy behind the register.

Still beaming, the pimp began, "Now now, honey."

Despite myself, I smiled at him. "Man, this is a total waste of your time."

He looked at me and let out a thoroughly pleasant laugh. "All right, gorgeous." Even in the crowded surroundings he managed a sweeping bow, winked at me, and walked out. I waved. What a city. Collecting my change, hot dog, and drink, I squeezed into a space at the end of the counter facing the street. Never having tasted papaya juice before, I took a cautious sip, and discovered that it was cold, sweet, and frothy. The dog was equally good. Always eat where New Yorkers eat. The businessman was still talking about his "swissies," which I figured were Swiss francs. He was the most unbelievably tense person I had ever seen. Brown eyes darting constantly, taking nervous little bites out of his hot dog, he said through clenched teeth, "No, just five contracts. But now. Before it hits one point two zero. And there's a *deadline* on those swissies. You know what that deadline means, huh?" Shoulders hunched to his ears, he yelped, "It means if we don't make it, I'm dead." Abruptly he hung up and placed the phone in his breast pocket. His hand re-emerged clutching an orange prescription pill bottle. Squinting his eyes, he tried to align the childproof cap so it would open. I watched in fascination as he clawed at the top, which wouldn't budge. Then the cap popped open and his face lit up in delight. He rolled two white pills onto his palm, tossed them into his mouth, and took a last swig of papaya juice. He wiped the sweat out of his eyes, took three loud, panting breaths, and stormed out to conquer the city.

It took me thirty minutes to zoom back to Jersey, where I dedicated myself to finding an apartmentito. Divine intervention struck a couple of sweaty hours later, when I surveyed a sunny one-bedroom place going for seven hundred fifty a month. There were feminine furnishings and frilly curtains, as well as lots of pictures of Jesus. One of them had holograms for eyes that followed you watchfully all over the room. The landlady, who appeared sane, informed me that the present occupant would be moving out in five days, on Monday morning. Taking some of her furniture, all of her pictures, and leaving the fridge. Praise the Lord. I gave her a three-hundred-dollar deposit to hold the apartment until Monday. We agreed that she could keep the money as a security deposit once the rent was paid. I wore my serious, dependable face, and she seemed impressed that I was carrying three hundred dollars in cash. Everyone adores the sight and smell of cash. Even Jesus had his eye on it.

I made my way back to the hotel to find Tigger lying on his back, pink paws folded over his white tummy, making a deep dent in the pillow. No one has a right to be that content.

When I counted what was left of my money, I noticed there was a slight deficiency in my fungible assets. At least that's what Alan Greenspan would say. The hotel was draining me, and I wanted to have extra money to get basic furniture for the apartment. Instead of bothering my parents, I decided to move to one of the cheaper motels in the morning. My reluctance to ask for money originated when I was ten and my mother informed me that money did not grow on trees. I told her that I already knew that, otherwise why would I stand there blabbing when I could be out picking.

At about nine p.m., my mind having turned comfortably to tapioca after some serious TV watching, I decided that I really needed some Doritos.

My name is Cheryl, and I'm a Doritos addict.

I pulled on a sweatshirt and headed to the hotel's gift shop for my fix. Inside the elevator, Muzak played. I pushed the button for the lobby and watched the doors close. The elevator stopped on the third floor and a naked man walked in.

He had strategically positioned pages of the *New York Times* wrapped around his waist like a towel. He smiled at me in apologetic embarrassment. I was in complete shock. The doors closed. My brain started functioning again. I realized that he looked more embarrassed than I felt; in fact, he looked kinda funny. Thin, pale, average-looking, with a mop of brown hair falling onto his forehead. He seemed so miserable that I began to feel protective toward him. Then I got curious. *How did this happen?* The doors opened onto the lobby, and the man, still clutching his newspaper around himself, said with immense gallantry, "After you, miss." He bowed slightly.

Never in my life have I wanted so much to laugh, but I bit my cheek and said graciously, "Thank you." I stepped out into the lobby and, restraining myself from breaking into a run, walked calmly to the gift shop.

A buzz, made up of confidential whispers, began in the lobby as Newspaper Guy walked to the front desk. The tired-looking man who was guardian of the gift shop was staring open-mouthed, straining to hear the conversation. I could hear bits of what Newspaper Guy was saying, ". . . girlfriend went nuts . . . don't know . . . threw me out . . . crazy . . . unbelievable! . . . very embarrassing." The hotel receptionists were restraining smiles and promising to get his clothes, while trying to herd him back into the elevator, and out of sight. I paid the no-longer-sleepy cashier, got quickly into the elevator and retreated to the relative safety of my room. You gotta wonder what he did to make his girlfriend so mad.

Morning dawned bright, hot, and sticky. I packed my bags and chased Tigger around the room, trying to get him into the cat cage. In a heroic tackle across the bed, I caught him by one paw and packed him in. With all the trouble he gives me, it must have slipped his mind that it was none other than *moi* who had rescued him from a rainy alley when he was six weeks old. Kids!

In the lobby I called a cab. The guy at reception seemed sorry to see me go. A taxi screeched to a halt outside. As we sped down the highway, radio blasting salsa music, hot air rushing in from the open windows, I surveyed a storage place offering one month for a dollar and a string of dilapidated motels. When I saw one that might withstand the elements for another week, I yelled over the music, "Turn in here."

He swiveled around in his seat, no longer watching the highway, and shouted, "WHAT?" The taxi veered ominously toward the next lane.

"Look at the road!" I yelped.

"WHAT?" He frowned.

Sensing that my young life was in danger, I pointed forcefully at the fast-approaching driveway. He nodded wisely and made an expert turn, the back tires burning rubber like a car chase in a movie. He came to an abrupt halt in the courtyardlike parking lot and gave me a toothy smile. I sighed, handed him a five-dollar bill, and said, "Wait here please."

He nodded.

I glanced into the cat cage on the backseat to make sure Tigger had survived. He looked roughed up but alive. I got out, hauling the cage with me, and deposited it safely on the raised sidewalk that surrounded the parking lot. I didn't want to leave Tigger on the backseat; I was 97 percent sure that by the time I got back, the cab driver would be cooing, sticking his fingers though the grid of the cage, and traumatizing my sensitive cat. While walking toward the motel's office, I cast a quick glance over my shoulder and read the license number on the cab. When I was seven, I watched a cab drive off with a trunk full of a tourist's luggage. I can still see the tourist bounding down the dusty road, shouting, "Come back!"

I repeated the license number in my head, then opened the office door. Air-conditioning hit me like a cool wave. A peroxide blonde sitting in a glass cubicle eyed me through her mascara. "Help ya?" She had a low, gravelly voice. With the tip of a fake red nail, she flipped open the top of a Marlboro pack, extracted a cigarette, placed it where red lipstick outlined a mouth, and lit up.

"Yes, I'd like a room." The sound of my voice seemed to annoy her. She sucked on her cigarette and scowled.

"How much is it per night?" I asked.

"Fifty bucks." She seemed to swallow the smoke, never blowing it out.

"Do you allow a cat?"

"Yeah, but if it wrecks the room, you pay." She pointed a red talon at my face.

"He's very well trained. May I have a key to look at a room?" I kept a paranoid eye on the parking lot.

She stared at me. "May."

I frowned. "What?"

Shaking her head, she rasped, "You said 'may I.'"

"Yeah, I did." I leaned forward to see if she was all right. She made a sound like a chainsaw starting.

"May I," the chainsaw wheezed again, followed by a coughing fit. I realized she was laughing. A key clattered into the metal tray. I picked it up, still staring at her in wonder, and walked out.

I inspected the room quickly. The walls were paneled with imitation dark wood; everything else was an inoffensive green. It was clean. As I walked toward the cab, I noticed the driver had gotten out. He was squatting in front of Tigger's cage and poking his finger through the grid, cooing, "Kitty, kitty."

Sometimes you just can't win.

After not helping me unload my bags, the driver informed me, "Five dollars for waiting."

He was cheating me, but I was too tired to argue. I handed him three dollars.

"That's only three," he said.

"Yes," I agreed.

Back in the office, the blonde had recovered and was smoking another cigarette, appearing bored. I paid her fifty dollars, hauled everything into the room, locked the door, and let a traumatized Tigger out onto the carpet worn thin by the thousands who had preceded us.

As I looked out the window at yellow tufts of grass straining through cracks of bleak, sunbaked asphalt, I thought, *What's the worst that could happen?*

Down and Out

Someone was screaming. It sounded far away and unimportant, as everything does when you're sleeping. It became louder and more hysterical. Annoyed, I cautiously opened one eye and surveyed the room. The drapes were drawn, and it was dark except for the digital clock glowing 9:32 a.m.

"You bastard!" the voice screeched.

I got out of bed and tripped over Tigger, falling flat on my face.

He has a habit of stepping in front of my feet in an attention-getting strategy. It works. Massaging my cheek, I peeked out the drapes and gawked.

It simply wasn't possible for this to happen twice in twenty-four hours. A completely naked woman was standing in the center of the parking lot. It was not a pretty sight. Painfully skinny, with leathery creased skin and bleach-fried hair that had two inches of black roots showing, she stood unashamed, energetically screaming a string of swear words at a huge, fully clothed man framed in the doorway of a room.

Was it a hot new trend to throw nude people out of their rooms? A few maids and guests milled around outside, seemingly bored by the spectacle. The man roared, "Shaddup!" and hurled a pair of sneakers toward the raging woman, closely followed by underwear, jeans, and a T-shirt. They fell in a rumpled heap at her feet; she made no move to pick them up. There was something absurdly brave about the woman continuing to scream at the guy instead of putting her clothes on.

There was still fight in her. I admired that. Finally the guy slammed the door. The woman pulled her clothes on unhurriedly, swore a few more times, and stormed off.

Never a dull moment here in the Garden State.

Fabriziou called my cell to give me an itemized list of how much money I owed Prima:

Comp cards (300): $350
Prints of pictures (5): $100
Portfolio (1): $40
Total debt: $490

Wonderful! He went over the list again, and I felt a slow throbbing begin between my eyes.

"Thanks, Fabriziou, that's good to know."

"Okey, Cherilll, but don't forget what you owe."

The throbbing was getting faster. "I won't forget."

"That's good, bye-bye." He hung up.

I looked at the phone in the silent room and frowned.

The next morning, Friday, the outside world seemed to be behaving itself.

My mom called in a state of extreme excitement due to her imminent plunge down a raging river. She told me to confirm with the bank that the money she'd wired to me had arrived. I enjoyed a meaningful discussion with an automated voice at 411 and another at the bank, finally reaching a person in the wire transfer department who confirmed that the money was there. When I called my mother back she said enthusiastically, "Right, pumpkin! We'll be back Monday!"

I said good-bye and the line went dead.

As I left the room in shorts and a T-shirt, on my way to get breakfast, a throaty voice barked, "Hey!" I turned to see the blond, chain-smoking gatekeeper.

"Are ya stayin' another night?"

"Yeah." I gave her a pleasant smile to see if she would thaw.

"Well, ya gotta pay now." Apparently not.

I reached deep for my inner Buddha. "Okay," I said, and followed her into the office. After feeding the dragon fifty dollars, I wandered back out into the humidity and almost collided with a small, bouncy man. A few long wisps of white hair were plastered over his shiny head. Watery, slightly bloodshot blue eyes looked up at me; his nose was a road map of red veins. Definitely an alcoholic.

He smiled charmingly. "My wife and I saw you from our window." He gestured to one of the rooms. "And I had to come ask you, are you a model?"

Uh-oh.

"Umm, no."

"Well, you should be! I used to be an acting agent before . . ." He let the sentence hang. He bobbed up and down on his toes and asked, "How long are you staying at this fine establishment?"

I smiled, looking at the crumbling motel. "Just a few days, and you?"

"Well, actually . . . we've been living here for three years."

"Wow!" My eyebrows shot up.

"You get used to it."

I ate pancakes at a nearby diner. After a few ominous sneezes and a tickling in the back of my throat, it occurred to me that I might have caught a cold from a sneezy woman on the bus. I vowed to hunt her down and take away her cell phone.

You have to hit where it hurts most.

I quarantined myself at the back of the bus to New York. The bank was one of those cavernous, intimidating places; it looked like it had been hacked out of a single giant hunk of white marble. These banks make you feel small, insignificant, and shabbily dressed.

I shuffled up to a teller's window. She told me to speak with an assistant manager and pointed commandingly at a row of desks. "Go there."

I went. I picked the least threatening person, a middle-aged lady, and told her about my transfer. She began typing fluidly. I have always envied people who can type that fast. It just looks so cool.

"Yes, I see it here," she said.

"Great."

"But it won't be posted until noon Monday."

I frowned. "What do you mean by posted?"

"The money has arrived, but you can't withdraw it until Monday."

"Why not, if it's there?"

"It's our policy."

I was beginning to hate all policies. "Well, I actually need it now."

"The only person who might authorize that is the manager."

"Can I speak with the manager?"

"She's not here." That seemed to satisfy her.

"When will she be?"

"Maybe tomorrow between eleven and one."

"All right, but why does the bank have to keep my money over the weekend?"

"Policy," she replied flatly.

Bankers love the word "policy." They probably name their kids Policy Beckwyth III.

I didn't know at the time that banks routinely hold money for twenty-four to forty-eight hours to earn overnight interest on the millions transferred every day. Banks have to make a living too.

From behind her desk, the woman was fixing me with a glassy stare that meant further discussion was useless. I got up and went outside to call for help.

When I dialed my parents' cell phone, it skipped directly to voice mail without ringing. I left a message, feeling increasingly uneasy. Like a lot of people over forty-five, my parents are allergic to technology. If the phone was out of range or not working, they might not even notice. Pondering the situation, I decided it would be best to wait for a call back from my parents and return to the bank tomorrow.

Back at the motel, I went through my pockets, spread all the money out on the bed, and counted what was left: forty dollars. Yikes!

Saturday morning dawned ominously, without a call back from

Mom or Dad. My cold had definitely taken hold, and I felt the beginnings of a fever.

I arrived at the bank by eleven a.m. and asked the same deskbound woman if I could speak with the manager.

"Not here," she replied flatly.

"Will she be in later?"

"No, come back on Monday," she stated with smug finality.

On my way back to the bus, I tried my parents again and got voice mail. As the shuttle sped under the Hudson River, I scripted my negotiation for credit at the motel until Monday, thinking I could always leave my passport with them for security.

Confidently approaching the motel's office, I glanced casually toward my room and froze. The door was wide open. I ran across the parking lot. Stumbling into the room, my eyes still adjusting to the suddenly cool dimness, a warm body smelling of Marlboro smoke and sweat brushed by, carrying *my* suitcase. I dropped to my stomach and checked under the bed, then the bathroom, confirming the worst. Tigger was gone.

"Damn," I said through clenched teeth, pursuing the suitcase out the door.

Setting the suitcase down, dragging deeply on a cigarette, the receptionist stared vacantly into the distance.

In a restrained voice, I asked, "Where is my cat?"

"Dunno." She shrugged, her gaze shifting suggestively to the speeding cars on the highway. In the ninety-degree heat, I shivered. Then it occurred to me that Tigger would be more likely to run away from the highway; in the opposite direction was a densely wooded hillside. The receptionist was trying to scare me and now regarded my frightened expression with a slight smirk.

"Why are you taking my bags out?"

"It's past noon and you didn't pay, so I need fifty bucks or you gotta leave."

She was really enjoying this. Dropping all emotion from my face and voice, I offered her thirty dollars and my passport until Monday.

"No." She knew I would pay her, but she *wanted* to kick me out and would, no matter what I said. Her close-set blue eyes watched me carefully, searching for a reaction. Never had I been so panicked in all my life. But to my amazement, I was able to appear calm. I walked to the pay phone near the office, feeling her eyes on the back of my neck, and called a taxi without knowing where to go.

While waiting, I scoured the hillside's impenetrable wall of blackberry thorns and brambles, calling Tigger's name. After a couple of minutes, holding back tears, I returned to the room and carried my small bag and empty cat cage to the driveway. Just then, the resident alcoholic bounded around the corner. "Leaving us so soon?"

I shrugged. "She won't let me stay because my money arrives on Monday."

"That can't be! They've let me stay for three nights until my check arrives." He raised his hand. "Worry not, I'll go talk to her." He scurried to the office. I felt a twinge of hope, probably because I had no one else to call. After a minute, he returned, shaking his head in disbelief. "I've never seen her this angry for no reason."

"Thanks for trying." My voice was raw from the sore throat.

"Are you sick?"

"A little." Understatement of the millennium.

My taxi pulled off the highway, a cloud of dry dust behind it. The trunk popped open and I lugged my bags toward it, the drunk skipping along beside me.

"You know," he said, "there was this woman who used to live here, and once she couldn't make the rent." I barely listened, loading my bags in. "So she stood on the corner till a car stopped. Well, she came back with the money."

I looked up at him, at his eyes twinkling with cruel amusement.

As the full meaning of what he had said struck home, I felt my jaw clench and very quietly said, "Leave me alone."

His eyebrows went up and he walked away, still with a faint smile.

I slammed down the trunk. The driver's window was open; there was no meter inside.

"How much to the storage place up ahead?" I asked.

"Eight dollars." It was no more than a couple of minutes away.

"I'll give you four."

He looked at my eyes. "Okay."

In the small, neat office of the storage company, a fan lazily stirred the hot, sticky air. An old, nearly emaciated man regarded me sleepily from behind a desk and explained in a monotone the terms of "First Month for One Dollar." Apparently there was a registration fee, a service fee, and a lock purchase fee, amounting to twenty dollars. Since my first priority was to unload the bags, I paid him.

Pushing a trolley with my luggage, I punched in the five-digit code at the heavy security gate, and it rolled open. Moving through the complex of two-story, freshly painted concrete buildings, I opened the door to the last one and felt the welcome rush of cool, stale air from the interior. A vast padded elevator lifted me to the second floor; windows along the concrete corridor dimly lit the individually locked five-by-five-foot compartments. I put my bags inside and caught sight of the Prima portfolio in my open shoulder bag. The model apartments the agency kept in Manhattan were looking pretty good right then. I dialed Prima's number on my cell. It was Saturday, and there was only a taped message saying they were open weekdays, nine to six. Standing there in the soundless building, I realized that for the first time in my life I was completely alone.

I slipped the key into the pocket of my jeans and walked back toward the motel on the residential street above the highway. I looked through the thick foliage at the vague outline of the motel below and began calling Tigger again. A man walking by with his wiener dog asked sympathetically, "Lost your cat?"

"Yes, how did you know?"

He pointed at the trees and said, "In there is a whole colony of wild cats. Pets get lost in there a lot."

"Do they come back?" I watched his expression carefully.

He gave an overly confident smile. "I'm sure yours will! Don't worry about it."

I sighed, wondering if Tigger had a chance against an army of feral cats. I felt my fever rising in the sun and walked off in search of food and air-conditioning, so I could plan for survival until Monday.

The Journal Square PATH station, where you can catch a train from the center of Jersey City to Manhattan, is busy 24/7 and resembles the bar scene in *Star Wars*. The square is an odd blend of a few newer buildings surrounded by complete, crumbling poverty. People in suits rush for trains while drug dealers and homeless people lounge in disarray under the sparse trees. A row of fast-food restaurants disperses cheap eats to rowdy teenagers and exhausted-looking mothers with screaming babies.

People rushed by, a mixture of Indian, black, and Hispanic, with a couple of young white Jehovah's Witnesses in suits, intent on saving souls. Made uncomfortable by their stares, I bolted for the air-conditioned refuge of McDonald's. Inside, sugar-high kids ran back and forth squealing. The scent of french fries hung heavily in the air while I checked the dollar menu and ordered a double cheeseburger. A quick mental calculation revealed that I now had nine dollars left and 48 hours to go. Surprisingly, this didn't alarm me. I had somewhat shut down since Tigger disappeared, and I viewed the money situation as just a fact.

As I bit into the burger, an annoyed and frustrated-looking man with a Red Sox cap entered and surveyed the restaurant impatiently. His gaze fell on a skinny, wild-haired guy, who immediately tried to disappear behind a large woman, who was unaware that she was being used for cover. The Red Sox fan walked menacingly toward the young man, who began to sweat, while a weak, guilty smile played on his lips.

A sense of danger pervaded the place. Everyone, including children, fixed their eyes on their burgers with great concentration. I slumped down in my seat and watched the action from the corner of my eye.

The Sox fan threw a powerful right hook, which was skillfully ducked as the little guy bolted for the door, giggling hysterically.

Just as he pushed open the first of two glass doors, Red Sox landed a hard kick on his bum that catapulted him through the second door and sent him stumbling onto the street. The wild-haired fellow immediately sprinted off, both hands clutching his behind, while his pursuer closed the distance. Animation returned to McDonald's, everyone eating happily as if nothing had happened. The counter girl shrugged and said tiredly, "Next, please."

I made a feverish decision. Despite Tigger being a nuisance

sometimes, he had always been a good-hearted, loyal pal, and I loved him for it. So I would find him if it was the last thing I ever did, and that horrible bitch at the motel wouldn't have won. With a rush of head-cold-induced motivation, I marched out, head held high, to avenge all the wrongs perpetrated on my friend.

I lasted about two minutes before I got dizzy and leaned against the peeling wall of a building to catch my breath. What struck me, looking at the streets, was the complete hopelessness of it all. Buildings that had long ago been given up on, too far gone for repair. People trudging by, faces dulled by the knowledge that they would never get out of here; this was their life, their prison.

I came to a second decision, never to settle for less than I was capable of just because it was easier.

The smell of damp earth and rotting leaves was strong as I called Tigger's name into the gloomy forest, wondering if he could even hear me. The sun was starting to set, the sky turning soft pink. As often happens with fevers, I got chills. I walked back to the storage place to get a sweatshirt.

A tough-looking woman was hurling bags into a storage locker, while yelling threats at a cute three-year-old boy, who had plastered his back to the wall in terror. His mother's frizzed red hair made it seem like a brush fire had erupted on her head from frustration. I pulled on a baggy sweatshirt and tied my hair back in a bun; from now on, I was keeping a low profile. My dad had given me a copy of *Catch-22*; I fished it out of my bag and set off.

There was a twenty-four-hour coffee shop one level belowground at the PATH station, and I figured it was the safest place. In contrast to the chaos aboveground, the lower level of the station was comfortingly bright, clean, and new-looking. I ordered a coffee at the counter and reluctantly parted with another dollar. I took a seat and surveyed the terrain. It was actually an okay coffee shop, with individual tables and a clientele of broken-looking pensioners, office workers, and train operators.

I cracked open the book and tried to fool myself into forgetting what was happening by glaring at the pages. Somewhere in the third chapter I had a vision of Tigger hiding in my new sneakers when he was a kitten and focused harder on the words, which were starting to swim. I looked up and saw a woman walk in with jerky steps and lay a shaky hand on the counter. "Coffee," she rasped. She reminded me a lot of the buildings outside, once new, now so quickly aged, and of the neighborhood, coarse and desperate. She couldn't have been more than thirty-five, but she looked at least fifty, face scarred from punches, yellow-gray hair, her wiry body constantly in motion, searching for a fix. Looking closely at her features, I saw that she had once been pretty.

She scanned the café with a hunted expression, moving in little spastic jerks, unable to keep still. As a stoop-shouldered, graying man shuffled past, the woman stopped him. Showing rotting teeth, she croaked, "Wanna have some fun?" The man shook his head tiredly and began to walk out. A look of desperation came over the woman's face. "Just give me a few bucks"—she was breathing heavily—"I . . . I . . . need something . . . okay?" But the man had left. This was the first time I had seen someone in drug withdrawal, and she looked ready to die. One of the sleepy-eyed men working behind the counter went over to the woman and said gruffly, "You can't do that here. You gotta leave."

"Just listen, man—"

"Get lost."

"Fuck you." She stumbled out.

That whole scene scared me—the fact that wanting a drug would make someone do anything, absolutely anything, to get it. The night wore on. I began seeing double—the whole world had become twins; so I rubbed my eyes and saw everything in triplicate. That amused my delirious brain, and I considered having a good laugh before logic kicked in and I realized this was probably not a good sign. I ran cold water in the massive restroom of the station and looked in the mirror. Apart from my cheeks being flushed and my eyes glassy, I didn't look sick. The water tap was one of those annoying things you push on to get a gush of water for two seconds before it shuts off when you need it most. The temperature choice is Lava Flow or Siberian Winter.

Splashing freezing water on my feverish face and hitting the handle every few seconds, I became briefly angry with my parents. What was the point of raising them for sixteen years to be abandoned like this? After drying my face with those brown paper towels that smell funny, I got another cup of coffee and stared at my book.

Business in the café started to pick up, with harassed people placing orders. The clock said six a.m. I had survived!

This amazed me.

Cautiously standing, my bones cracking back into place, I felt like going for a walk. I rode the escalator up to ground level. The milky morning light made everything hazy. There is something unreal, almost dreamlike, about not having slept when everyone else has. As if by staying awake I had gained some secret knowledge that everyone else was lacking, maybe a head start on the day—or maybe the fever was affecting my brain. The air was warm and humid, a clear sign that it would be a scorcher. I took some deep breaths and refrained from having any more deep thoughts.

After my ritual, unsuccessful Tigger search, I found a park; yellowish grass and benches perched at the top of a hill. Sitting on a bench, I looked down at the massive abandoned factories in the distance, the soot-stained walls and broken windows seeming on fire in the orange-red sunrise. Dawn can make almost any place beautiful, but then it just got hot. Church bells chimed in the distance; Sunday morning had arrived. Children paraded by in stiff church clothes, eyeing the playground longingly. I finished *Catch-22* and concluded that it was a damn good book, even if I had been delirious from chapters four through six.

The flu had really kicked in. It felt as if I had been recently run over by an eighteen-wheeler. Remembering the library I'd passed on the way to the park, I decided that if it was necessary to die, it should at least be somewhere literate. Of course, when I got there, it was closed. Which made it abundantly clear that this was going to be One of Those Days. I feigned positivity and went to a nearby Internet café, in case my parents had e-mailed me. There wasn't any coffee at the so-called café, which ruined my positive mood. I opened my e-mail and scanned the new messages, junk mail and nothing from my parents. I leaned back in the chair, staring at the screen, and sighed. Then one e-mail caught my eye, from laura@dancemagazine.com. I opened it.

Hi, Cheryl,
A few months ago, your picture was given to me
by photographer Sarah Silver. We are planning a
five-page spread for the anniversary issue of our
magazine. Please give me a call so you can come by
and try some outfits on; we are casting this weekend.
All the best,
Laura

Her contact info was below. I wrote it down, cautioning myself that this was only a casting and she would be seeing many other models. The hawklike counter girl eyed me as if she had just eaten a lemon. I paid a dollar for the computer time and winked at her, just for kicks.

Outside the door, squinting from the sun, I dialed Laura's number. The e-mail had been sent yesterday, Saturday. Would she be in the office?

"Laura, *Dance Magazine*," said a friendly voice.

"Hi, this is Cheryl Diamond. You e-mailed me about the magazine shoot."

"Oh yes, great, we're casting today. Can you come by our office?"

I spun around and inspected my face inches from the Internet café's reflective window.

"Ahh . . . ," I said while assessing the condition of my reflection. It would do. "Yes. What time is best?"

"Two p.m. You have our address from the e-mail, right?"

"Yes, I'll see you then."

We hung up. I checked the time on my watch: twelve forty-five. The magazine's office was at 50th Street and Fifth Avenue, which meant I really had to get a move on.

I hurried across the street to catch the bus and hauled myself, wheezing and exhausted, aboard. Having a cold is every young person's preview of what old age will feel like.

I needed my portfolio, high heels, and a change of clothes, so when the bus neared the storage place, I gave the driver *another* dollar and hopped off. Quickly unlocking the storage compartment, I walked in and began randomly pulling clothes out of my bag, guaranteeing that they would never fit back in. I chose a nice pair of jeans and an elegant black sleeveless top. I stubbed my toe on the suitcase and checked that no one was in the hallway. I changed; stuffed stilettos, portfolio, and my remaining four dollars into my black shoulder bag; brushed my hair; put on mascara, flip-flops, and a light khaki jacket; and went.

I barely avoided falling asleep on the pleasantly sweltering bus to Manhattan by playing Space Dude on my cell phone. Giving the driver two dollars was an emotionally debilitating experience, and I walked quickly uptown, checking the time: 1:47.

A few minutes before two o'clock, I was still four blocks away. Have you ever tried running with the flu?

Don't.

I limped, sweating, into the white marble lobby of the magazine. Behind a security console, the big guard looked at me suspiciously while I panted and took the high heels out of my bag. Stepping out of my flip-flops into the stilettos, I took my jacket off and folded it and the sandals into my bag—a routine models repeat millions of times over their careers. As I stood up too quickly from my bag, a wave of vertigo made me lean my forehead against the cool marble wall. I had the urge to collapse giggling; the guard was now watching me with a mixture of awe and curiosity. I presented myself at his desk and said, "I'm here to see Laura at *Dance Magazine*."

He narrowed his eyes at me. "Okay, I need to see some ID, and you have to sign in."

Ever since 9/11, they practically want to test your DNA before letting you into any building. I passed him my ID and started to sign in.

He studied my laminated card and said, "Nice picture."

I looked up sharply to see if he was kidding—since I look extremely guilty in all passport-type photos—but he seemed serious. He phoned Laura upstairs to confirm that I had an appointment, and

I rode the elevator up; it's harder to get into that building than to get into Harvard.

Entering the magazine office, I saw rows of desks and a large conference room on the left. A tall, pretty blond woman with a sprinkling of freckles seemed to be the only person in the office. She stood up from her desk and smiled. Laura looked through my black book and said I looked like Uma Thurman in the picture where I hold a real-looking butterfly near my chin. I smiled happily at the compliment.

"I'd like you to try on some leotards that we'll be using in the shoot." She motioned for me to follow her into the conference room. A long, polished wood table dominated the room, and framed covers of the magazine's past issues hung on the walls. Laura lifted a light purple leotard with spaghetti straps from a padded leather chair and said, "It's from Danskin." Handing it to me, she added, "This is the best place to change. I'll close the door." She smiled and went out. It puzzled me that she was so genuinely nice. I had begun to expect everyone to be furious with me for no reason.

I undressed, pulled the leotard on, and padded barefoot out of the conference room. Laura was waiting outside. She carefully inspected me, and I felt oddly at ease. "Turn slowly, please," she said. I rotated in a slow circle. "Good," she said, one finger on her chin in concentration. "You have very long legs, that's good."

I nodded.

"Okay," she chirped. "You can change back now, thanks."

I said sure, and went back into the conference room. I had absolutely no idea what was going on, or if I was doing it right. I neatly folded the leotard on a chair—Mom would be so proud—and returned to the office.

"Have you been in New York long?" asked Laura, who was looking through my book again.

"Not long, but I really like it."

"Great city, great people. Have you been around to agencies yet?"

"Yes, I signed with Prima recently."

"Oh . . . were you signed to them when you met with Sarah Silver?"

"No, not yet."

"Since your agency didn't get you this casting, I would rather deal directly with you. Is that okay?"

"Sure." If I ended up getting this job, I decided to simply give Fab 20 percent of whatever I earned.

At the time, I didn't know that the reason many clients try to circumvent the agency and deal directly with the model is to avoid paying an "agency fee." This is separate from the 20 percent cut of a model's earnings that an agency receives. It is an additional 20 percent of a model's fee that the client must pay directly to the agency.

Agencies hate to admit that although they take 20 percent from the model, they are actually getting 40 percent. Because whining, "Look how much work we do for you, and all we get is 20 percent" wouldn't be as guilt inducing if the model knew they were getting double that.

"I'm going to show your pictures to the editor, and we'll decide which models to cast later today." Laura handed my book back to me. "Thanks for coming."

She seemed less enthusiastic than before.

"Nice to meet you." I smiled and walked back toward the elevators, absolutely sure that I had blown it. The adrenaline had faded, I felt hungry and sick, and I wanted to go home—wherever that was.

Fifth Avenue between 40th and 60th streets is home to some of the most expensive brand-name boutiques. Couture-clad women step elegantly from limousines and into shops, while people in business suits on their way to or from work avoid colliding with tourists, who stop walking, without any warning, to snap pictures. I strolled down Fifth, distracting myself by looking at window displays. Some women looked me up and down, then scowled. It will never cease to surprise me that women who have oodles of money could be jealous of a sixteen-year-old kid with two dollars in her pocket.

Life is weird.

A homeless man sat cross-legged in front of an elegant store; a cardboard sign spelled out something about him being in 'Nam. In the window of the boutique, an elegantly calligraphied sign read, CUSTOM-MADE MEN'S TIES. I was frowning at the sign, trying to figure out why anyone would need a custom-designed tie, when a couple stopped near me and the man boomed approvingly, "Look, honey, custom-made ties!"

The man sitting on the sidewalk patted the ground next to him and smiled. "Custom-made concrete."

Despite my condition, or maybe because of it, I started to laugh.

The homeless man chuckled, obviously proud of his joke as he said, "You've got a good sense of humor."

The couple had walked off. "It was a good joke." I grinned at him.

He squinted from the sunlight as he looked up at me. "It's amazing how few people appreciate subtle humor now; you have to be vulgar to make an impact." He shook his head sadly, while I stared at him in awe. "You're . . . ah . . . very well spoken."

"I used to be a professor."

"Really! Of what?"

"English literature. You couldn't feed a hamster on what they pay."

I smiled. "But won't your friends help?"

"They think I'm going to ask them for a loan. And nothing, trust me, nothing, scares people more." He winked. "Except maybe having to give it."

"You should *not* be homeless," I said.

"Ahh, but life is unjust."

For the next three hours I browsed through Barnes & Noble on Forty-eighth Street, picking out interesting books and magazines, then leaning back in one of the chairs Mr. Barnes and Sir Noble so generously provide. Hardly ever have I seen people actually *buying* books there. Mostly everyone lounges around, happily reading books from cover to cover.

At six p.m. my cell rang. It was Laura. I held my breath.

"Well, Cheryl, you see . . ." This was not a good start. "We've seen a lot of girls and haven't come to a decision yet on who to feature. It's a very important issue for our magazine, so we want to take our time to decide."

I could live with this. "Definitely, that's a good idea."

"I'm sorry that I told you we'd know tonight. . . ."

"Oh, that's okay." The suspense was killing me.

"Good. We will absolutely know for sure tomorrow morning, and I'll give you a call either way."

The "either way" sounded ominous.

After hanging up, I went back to reading. It seemed like a few minutes later when a sharp sound made me open my eyes and realize that I had dozed off. The sound was a woman dropping a heavy book near me, which she now sheepishly picked up. I rubbed my eyes and checked the time: eight forty-five p.m. I drank two gallons of water from the fountain and stepped out into the humid night. Manhattan is beautiful after dark and surprisingly safe, but if you're unfamiliar with the city, it can be confusing and scary. By then I was completely exhausted, and thinking about anything was much too hard an activity to even consider. I was operating on automatic. Like a deranged homing pigeon, I parted with the last of my money on the bus. I was now entirely, and literally, penniless. It was an interesting feeling, almost peaceful, to know that this moment is what human beings probably fear most and spend lifetimes in windowless cubicles to avoid. Yet there I was, sixteen years old and somehow not afraid. I leaned back in the seat with an air of nonchalance that comes only when you truly have nothing to lose, and watched the hypnotizing row of lights through the Lincoln Tunnel.

We all make decisions that, in retrospect, are mildly insane but at the time seem perfectly logical. So when the bus neared the place where Tigger had disappeared, I yanked the stop cord instead of going all the way to Journal Square. I was going to find him, goddamn it! I stepped off the bus, confident in the knowledge that things could not possibly get any worse, and tottered toward the forest. The air was almost liquid with humidity. I wheezed Tigger's name a few times. Then, in a moment of delirious heroism, I extended a flip-flop and stomped into the woods, ignoring mosquitoes and thorns cutting into my feet. Some yellow light from the streetlamp managed to filter through the dense branches. "Tigger, come here," I commanded.

No result.

I tried a few more times before realizing that my feet were bleeding and that a thousand bugs had fallen deeply in love with me. My chin started to wobble up and down, but this was no time for sentiment, I was on a mission! "Tigger!"

I realized, for the first time, that he was truly gone. In the forest, or maybe on the streets, he couldn't hear me and I wasn't going to find him. All the energy left me. I pushed branches out of the way and made it back to the deserted sidewalk. Streetlights cast pale circles of light onto the black asphalt. A bird gave a high-pitched tweet and landed on a branch, making the leaves rustle in the bordering forest. Everything else was quiet. I sleepwalked down the street without an idea of where I was going but appreciating how silent it was except for the bird. I reached the end of the block and frowned, then listened carefully; the *tweet* had morphed into a distinct, faraway *meow*. There was a crashing in the forest. I turned to stare. Tigger catapulted through a bush onto the sidewalk and, still meowing, limped toward me. There was blood on his front paw and a vivid red scratch across his nose. The fur on top of his head was wet and stood up like a Mohawk. He looked happy.

It was all too much for my nervous system. I sat down on the curb and put my head in my hands. Tigger appeared at my side, purring ecstatically; without using his front paw, he managed to climb onto my lap. I gave Tigger a tearful hug that might have broken a few ribs. He put his head on my knee and gave a long, relieved, human-sounding sigh. I smiled. Life wasn't so bad after all. Technically, of course, it was midnight, and I was sitting on a curb, starving, broke, sick, bleeding, with a battle-scarred cat. On the bright side, I was alive, with a 50 percent chance of surviving the night—and I was still cute.

Yes, things were definitely looking up. That's when it started to rain.

I found this immensely amusing; who cared anymore? Leaning my head back, I closed my eyes and caught raindrops on my tongue. Tigger, who hates getting wet, was slumped across my lap like a melting watch in a Salvador Dali painting, too exhausted to move. I considered just passing out on the sidewalk, leaving a kindly old lady walking her pet poodle, Frou Frou, to find us in the morning. The drama of that situation appealed to me, and the papers would love it. Real human interest stuff. Instead I picked Tigger up and, knowing that he had not eaten in almost two days, headed for the storage place where a box of kibble awaited. The rain poured as I cut down a residential street to the highway. Car headlights shone on the falling raindrops, making them look like nails hammering the concrete. The soggy cat in my arms started to whimper, so I unzipped my shoulder bag, put him in, and partially rezipped it. I ran up to the gate, fumbled through the side pocket of my bag for the paper I had written the entry code on, and punched it in.

Nothing happened.

Just Book Me

I checked the digits and tried again; the sliding gate didn't budge. Glaring menacingly at the numbered panel, I said, "Don't do this to me!" The gate wasn't intimidated and stood its ground.

This called for desperate measures. Looking guiltily over my shoulder, I pushed my bag through the metal bars, then grabbed the top of the seven-foot gate—a technique learned from vast childhood experience of climbing into places I wasn't supposed to be. I summoned all my remaining energy and jumped up, managing to get my stomach and one leg draped over the top. Then I realized I couldn't move. The metal bar across the top of the gate was pressing into my belly so I couldn't breathe well, my head and torso hung upside down inside the complex, while my leg pointed at the highway. At these moments in life, you gotta retain a sense of humor, and this was really, really funny. The blood rushing to my feverish head, I giggled helplessly.

The rain streamed on. I tried heaving my leg over, but it just made me laugh. Getting rained on upside down is annoying when the novelty wears off, so I squirmed forward, swung my leg, slipped off the wet metal, and landed on my bum inside the complex. God, I'm good.

I stood up gingerly and grabbed my bag, hobbling toward the last building. I unlocked the door and stepped into the cold, vast, pitch-black hallway. I groped along the deserted concrete hallway for a light switch, while my eyes adjusted to the dark. I saw a white knob like a microwave timer on the wall. I eyed it skeptically. I have learned from past disasters that when I push buttons or flip switches just to see what happens, alarms go off. I pressed on the knob and nothing happened, so I twisted it, and instantly bright fluorescent lights came on, while the timer ominously went *tick, tick, tick*. The maximum it could be set for was forty-five minutes, but it sounded like a bomb about to go off. The elevator doors opened on the second floor, which was unlit except for some pale moonlight filtering past the raindrops on the windows. I turned the fluorescent glare on, my flip-flops making squishing sounds down the hallway. In front of my compartment I picked a limp Tigger out of the bag. He stood, head drooping, while I unlocked the latch and went inside the shadowy compartment. We were a mess—soaking wet, cut, and hardly able to move (although Tigger's Mohawk hairdo was really cool).

After a lifetime of avoiding cat cages, the little rascal limped into the open cage and plopped down inside. I smirked triumphantly. There was a sharp *tok* and all the lights went out. Aware of a whispery sound, I peeked out at the moonlit hallway. A shadow moved on the wall, looking exactly like a human arm reaching toward me. While I stood watching the arm in horror, a loud crack sounded behind me. Jumping two feet in the air, I saw a tree branch being hurled forcefully against the window by the storm. In a moment of mental clarity, I knew why the gate hadn't opened: At night, storage places have sensors turned on that can detect if a car is in front of the gate. If it is not there, even the right combination doesn't work. They probably do this to keep people like me out. The clarity lasted a few seconds, and then I was terrified. I started to notice sounds from the other darkened hallways, menacing creaks downstairs, and more shadows playing across the walls.

So far in my life, I have never been more petrified than at that moment. But hey, there's always tomorrow. I tried not to shiver and organized a mental to-do list: Walk down hallway, turn corner, turn lights on. If I walked down the hall, someone could come up behind me, and yet it was turning the mysterious corner that scared me most. The tree branch kept banging on the window along with torrents of rain. Now I was sure there was someone moving stealthily around the corner. The best thing to do, I concluded, was to stay absolutely still and postpone death by a few seconds. Frozen against the wall, wondering if the murderer could hear my heart thumping, I thought of something that turned my knees to jelly. If I screamed here, or even outside, no one would hear.

Then everything changed. I'm not sure how, but suddenly I just didn't give a damn anymore. After all I had been through, this was not the time to have a nervous breakdown, and I wasn't going to tremble against the wall all night. To hell with the evil murderer around the corner, the hell with the world in general, I wasn't going to take this! Confidently turning my back on the shadows, I marched angrily down the hall toward the dreaded corner ahead. To make sure I wouldn't change my mind, I ran the last few yards and skidded around the bend to confront a dark, empty hallway. Breathing hard, I twisted the light switch and, squinting at the sudden brightness, jogged along the other corridors to find every one deserted. I walked slowly back toward my compartment, thinking this over. It would, I thought, be possible to live an entire life in fear of an unknown obstacle lurking around the corner. When confronted, there might be nothing there, or there might be an actual enemy, but it's better to face it than to hide. Tigger was sleeping peacefully, sprawled on the blanket inside his cage; I lifted his bloody paw and saw only a superficial cut. He would live; maybe we both would.

I left the door to the compartment open and sat on the long windowsill, leaning back and stretching my legs out. I rested my burning forehead against the cool glass and watched the storm rage outside. A very bright white light appeared in front of me. It was annoying, so I opened my eyes and saw the sun. Startled, I tried moving, only to discover I had caught arthritis overnight. I brought a creaky wrist to eye level and squinted at my watch: eight a.m. It's amazing how you can have seven hours of sleep and feel worse when you wake up. Then it hit me; I had made it! It was Monday morning, and I was still in one piece and reasonably sane. My face in the compact mirror looked pale, with no focus in my glassy eyes. I plugged my cell phone in to recharge and pulled on a blue tank top and my khaki jacket to cover the scratches on my arms from the previous night's wilderness trek. Tigger lazily opened one eye as I locked him in his cage, picked it up, and set off for the bank. The clean morning air felt good as I tapped the code into the goddamn gate, which opened obligingly and let me out.

I got on a bus to Manhattan, slid Tigger under the seat, and sat back to contemplate my escape. Halfway through the tunnel, I was still figuring out the best way to get off a bus without paying the driver.

When the doors opened at the corner of 40th and Eighth Avenue, I let a few people congregate in front paying the driver. Using my skinniness, I held Tigger's cage in front of me and slipped between people off the bus. The driver spotted me and yelled, "Come back!"

Yeah, right. I ignored him and walked calmly around the corner into the crowds of Eighth Avenue. I didn't feel the least bit guilty; the world had been pretty rough on me lately, and it was time for a little payback. At the bank, I hid Tigger behind a potted fern near the entrance and went to take care of business. The transaction is blurred by exhaustion, but I remember two things: I got the money, and the bank didn't intimidate me anymore.

Like a finely tuned eating machine, I disposed of two hot dogs and a coconut juice at Gray's Papaya. I felt a little better on the bus back to Jersey, as I secretly counted out the correct amount of money for my apartment and tucked it into the bank's envelope. Self-righteously, I paid the driver and hauled an increasingly heavy Tigger along the sweltering sidewalk. Still a block from the apartment, I put the cage down and panted. My phone rang. "Hi, Cheryl, it's Laura from *Dance Magazine*."

"Good morning!" I said cheerfully.

"Oh, yes, I've shown your pictures to the editor, and the thing is, she likes your look, but . . ." Uh-oh. "Since this is such an important issue, we're having the models we really liked come to a callback today so the editor can see you personally."

To tired to think, I said, "I see."

"So can you come in at eleven today?"

Today I was scratched all over and doubted that I could make it to the end of the block, much less Manhattan. If they saw what I looked like today, the job was gone.

In panic, my brain kick-started. "Well, today I'm booked solid until evening," I said breezily.

"Hmm . . . I'm really sorry about this decision taking so long. Can you get away for about fifteen minutes? She really wants to see the models before booking them."

Sweating under the ninety-five-degree sun, my legs starting to buckle, I became extremely frustrated. I'd already been to their damn offices, and she had promised to make a final decision this morning. At this rate, I'd be ninety before they figured out who to use.

Without thinking, I sighed in annoyance and said, "Just book me."

There was a shocked silence on the other end.

I cringed. *And in the competition for dumbest things ever said . . . Cheryl Diamond wins!*

Laura still hadn't said anything. It was one of those moments when the first person to speak loses.

I kept my mouth shut.

In her usual friendly way, Laura said, "Oh . . . ah . . . okay, I'll have to talk to the editor. I'll call you back, all right?"

"Yes." She hung up, and I slapped a palm hard against my forehead.

I picked the cage up and trudged on. The apartment was in sight—another block and I could collapse in peace.

I pushed the landlady's buzzer. She appeared and saw me and Tigger on her porch like shipwreck survivors. "Ohh look, kitty cat." She smiled and squatted down to poke a finger into the cage and coo at him. With a clever marketing campaign, Tigger could become an international sex symbol.

She looked up at me happily. "How was your weekend?"

"Educational."

"Oh, good," she said absently.

I handed her the bank envelope, and predictably, her face lit up. So would mine if someone gave me seven hundred and fifty dollars in cash. She opened the flap, saw the green bills, and warmly said, "Come in, come in."

"Ah, how kind." I smiled to hide the sarcasm and carried Tigger up the stairs behind her. She opened the apartment door and asked, "Where are your bags?"

"Coming later."

Inside the apartment I looked around with blurry vision, satisfied to see that the couch, fridge, and coffee table were still in residence. Jesus, of the watchful eyes, had left the building. Ceremoniously, the landlady gave me the keys. "Thanks," I said as she departed, clutching the bank envelope to her breast. When the door shut, the imitation wood molding along the side of it came loose and arced down, bonking me on the top of my head. Stars exploding in front of my eyes, I held up the piece of molding and waited for my ears to stop ringing, only to discover that it was my cell phone.

"Hullo," I croaked.

"It's Mom! We're back!"

I sat down on the floor, laughing weakly, while the plastic wood hung off the wall like a giant question mark.

"Why are you laughing?"

"The apartment I just moved into is falling apart."

"You found an apartment! How was your weekend?"

"I have a cold. I survived."

My phone stared to buzz. "Hold on, Mom, I've got another call." I pressed the send button and said hello.

"Hi, it's Laura."

I frowned. "Oh, hi."

"So I've talked to the editor, and we've decided to just go ahead and book you!"

I almost fainted. Unable to speak, I sat on the floor with my mouth open.

"Cheryl?"

"Right, yes, that's good."

"Are you free for shooting on Thursday?"

I paused a moment, as if I had to think about fitting it into my busy schedule. "Yes."

"Great. It's a five-page spread, two other models will be in it, and the pay is eleven hundred and fifty dollars."

"Ah, okay."

"I'll send all the info to your e-mail, and I'll see you at the shoot."

We said good-bye, and I stared straight ahead. "Mom, you're not going to believe this."

"What?"

"I'm going to be in a five-page spread in *Dance Magazine*."

"NO!"

"Yes."

"NO!"

"For God's sake, Mom. Yes."

She shouted to my father in the background, "Pumpkin's going to be in a magazine!"

A few minutes later I walked to the corner store, after giving my mom an extremely sugarcoated version of my delightful weekend. A "little problem" had occurred at the bank, followed by a "talk" with the hotel, and the final assurance, "Everything's fine, I just have to sleep this cold off." I would tell the whole truth some other time; things are less scary to parents when told in retrospect. At the store I bought a big, yummy-looking bottle of aspirin and a jug of water. For my loyal companion there was kibble and a litter box. I'm a good mother. Back at the apartment, I popped five aspirin, splashed my face, put everything out for Tigger, and hugged the couch adoringly. I slept eighteen hours straight, waking up sprawled half off the couch at seven a.m. My fever had broken; the universe was unfolding as it should.

There is a positive side to going through a rough experience; you really appreciate life's simple pleasures afterward. Floating in a hot, soapy, scented bath for an hour, I noticed a deep scratch on my right arm near the shoulder. It would leave a narrow white scar. I began mentally sifting through possible tall tales that I could tell about how I got it. A thorn in the forest just wasn't cool enough. *A shark bite while deep-sea fishing? A collision with an eagle while paragliding over the Everglades?*

I like the scar, a reminder of the thin line that separates safety and chaos. I got it wrestling a croc. Really.

I was feeling fondly toward my apartment's previous denizen because she had left so much furniture, including the bed frame. All I would have to get was a mattress. All the Jesus posters were gone except for a small religious scroll in Spanish, which hung above the door that tried to kill me. It got me thinking: Did I believe in God? Staring philosophically at the showerhead, I decided I did. But not the kind of God most people visualize—the benevolent fatherly figure nestled among the clouds, like Santa Claus in a toga. I have taken a good look at this world and come to the conclusion that God exists, but he sure has one hell of a sense of humor.

I used the morning to transfer all my bags from the storage place to my apartment by cab. At noon my cell rang. "Cheryl, this is Veronika at Prima." Her voice was cold with the almost unnoticeable Russian accent. "I need you to go to"—at machine-gun speed—"Peak Performance Gym, Fifty-fourwesttwenty-firststreet, eighth floor, gottit?"

Scribbling frantically, I replied, "Yes, got it."

"Fabriziou said that your walk needed work. There's a runway expert, a friend of his, in town. The new girls are at the gym with him, so go there now."

I was annoyed; my walk did *not* need work. But I said, "Thanks. Is Fabriziou in the office?" Now would be a good time to tell him about *Dance Magazine*.

"No, he's at the gym, go there. Take stilettos." Click.

I was getting used to being hung up on; in fact, I was starting to expect it. Dressed in a jean skirt and white short-sleeved top, with high heels in my bag, I set off. After the physical exertion required to run up and down stairs in the subway, I was feeling a bit of postfever limpness. As I walked into the building's marble lobby, the security guard looked up; maybe he wanted a blood sample.

"I'm sorry, miss, the elevator's broken. You'll have to take the stairs."

The gym was on the eighth floor. I leaned my head back and groaned. The security guard chuckled. "That's what everyone's been doing."

I smiled at him and opened the stairwell door; it was dimly lit, with long flights of narrow stairs. Without air-conditioning in there, each breath was heavy with humidity and dust. By the third floor I was seriously rethinking my modeling career. At the eighth landing I hauled the heavy door open and entered the air-conditioned gym. It was huge, spanning the entire floor, windows looking out at the blue sky and tiny people below. Ultramodern machines that could pass for torture devices stood in rows.

I spotted Fab, dressed in flowing white, at the far end of the gym, surrounded by the "new Prima girls." A tiny man dressed all in black, who looked like a square-jawed, tough, annoyed ninja, was barking orders. The runway expert.

I walked past some hunks pumping iron, intent on proving once and for all that I had a good walk. Fab stood on tiptoe to kiss the air near my cheeks and tell me I was late. The runway expert was leaving to catch his plane to Milan.

I felt sick. Eight goddamn flights of stairs!

Fabriziou was watching my face intently, no doubt seeing that I was pale.

"Have you been sick?" he asked.

"A little. I'm better now."

He told me to go ask the runway guy to stay an extra few minutes and watch me walk. The black-clad ninja listened to me coldly and snapped, "Put high heels on, I watch you walk, quick quick." As directed, I retreated to the other end of the gym, stepped into stilettos, and with a hard, haughty, runway look, stalked leggily toward Ninja Man. Fab and the models watched, pretending not to. I maintained eye contact with the expert.

Stop. Pose, one hand elegantly on bony hip. Turn. Walk away, remembering to lift knees high on each step and place one foot directly in front of the other. *Like a drunk deer*, I thought, and grinned, which was okay, since my back was turned.

I stopped and walked to the ninja for his opinion. Stone-faced, he said, "Keep shoulders farther back and lift your chin higher. You have good walk."

"Thanks, I'll take your advice," I said, because I liked the guy.

He looked at his watch. "Must go." He bowed slightly to me, then waved to Fabriziou, who was talking to the girls and didn't hear the runway expert compliment my walk. Damn.

In a *whoosh* of black cloth, the ninja exited. I looked out the window and saw a black Lincoln limo with a chauffeur waiting for him curbside. Cool.

I turned from the window. The girls were giving me the once-over, and some looked mildly hostile. I gave a small I-come-in-peace smile. They lost interest, or pretended to do so.

My cell rang. It was Veronika again. "Cheryl!" she said commandingly. "There's a runway show tomorrow night that we are putting on to promote the agency."

Can-I-be-in-it? Can I? Can I?

"It's going to be very big. All the top industry people are coming and we want the new girls to come help out. Also you're going to be seen when you mingle with the party."

I thought it over. Was this going to require me to expend energy?

"That sounds interesting. How would I be helping?" I asked cautiously.

She sounded friendlier. "You won't be doing any work, we've hired people for that. The models who've been with us for a few years are going to walk the runway, and you would hand them their outfit changes during the show."

Hmmmmmm.

Veronika went on, "You're going to be in shows soon, so you have to learn how it works backstage. . . ." A hint of menace invaded her voice. "I would consider it a *personal favor.*"

I broke into a big grin. She was counting on me remembering the "suck up to your bookers, they are the ones who get you calls" speech. There was a smile in my voice, "I would love to come help out, especially as a favor to you."

She laughed. "Good . . . I appreciate this. Get a pen to write down the info."

Wednesday. Rehearsal: Noon to three p.m. Show: Nine p.m. to midnight. At Vue (an exclusive club)*, 151 E. 50th.*

When Veronika said good-bye, I could still hear the amusement in her voice.

"Yoo-hoo, Cherilll," Fabriziou sang from where he was seated on a cushioned bench-press machine. Next to him, tossing her dyed blond hair, sat a girl I remembered from the scare tactic meeting. She was twenty-four, the oldest of the new girls. Emily? Emma?

I walked over, still in my stilettos and hauling my bag, wanting to see his surprise when I told him about booking *Dance Magazine*. As I neared them, he asked me, "Are you coming to the show tomorrow?"

"Yes, it sounds fun."

Fabriziou and Emily/Emma's heads were at my stomach level, but there was no more space for me on the bench. I started to say, "There's this magazi—"

It happened so abruptly that I was completely disoriented. One moment Fab was smiling up at me, the next, a sharp pain was traveling up my left arm and I was being pulled down and sideways. My high heels wobbled, but I remained standing, hunched over. I looked down. Fab's little hand was wrapped around my left upper arm, his thumb digging into a nerve that made the rest of my arm limp. Fabriziou's face was inches from mine. He was still sitting down, maintaining good pressure on my arm. Emily/Emma's surprised face moved to the other side of the bench, and she pretended not to watch.

Fab's voice was cold, with much less of a goofy accent. "Cheryl, I don't like you lying to me; you still owe the agency money for your comp cards and prints. You were supposed to ask your parents for it."

I was completely confused by my life. My head started to throb again, my arm hurt, my chin started to wobble. No one except Emily/Emma was aware of what was happening, and she was pretending to study her shoes. Fab managed to look mean and smug simultaneously.

I snapped.

I rotated my arm in a circle, so that he had to break his grip, and straightened up. Involuntarily my fists clenched. I really, really felt like punching his surprised face.

A tiny, delicate gasp came from Emily/Emma, who was watching me in alarm.

An unfamiliarly confident voice said, "No." I realized it was me.

Fabriziou seemed confused, sitting with his hands clasped together, trying to get his innocent look in place.

"We had an agreement, Fabriziou. That money comes from my first job. So get me bookings and you'll get your money, understood?"

He cleared his throat, appearing casual. "Okey." He broke eye contact and gazed out the window. "Okey, so I see you at the show?"

His accent was baaaaack.

I considered his question. He still had the pictures from my book, I didn't have negatives, and I actually wanted to go to the show. I nodded.

He forced a friendly expression. "You were going to tell me something?"

Dance Magazine.

"Nope," I said, slinging my bag over my shoulder and walking toward the door. Shoulders back, chin up, as advised by Ninja Man. None of the other models had even noticed the incident, it was that quiet—although one of the gym hunks was frowning at Fabriziou while trying to get a better look at my upper arm. I opened the staircase door and heard it shut firmly behind me. Safe. I stomped down the staircase in my high heels, hurrying so I could get far away.

This kind of intimidation is quite common in the industry, although it is usually only verbal, a way of making sure a model will do as the agents say in the future before investing a lot of marketing in her. It had nothing to do with the money I owed. If a model offered to pay off her tab, Fabriziou would almost always tell her to keep the money, he would continue to bravely shoulder the financial burden. Guilt. He knew how to use it. What had happened back there was simply a test that backfired.

My experience was quite tame compared to what some other models have had to go through. Supermodel Carmen Kass, at fourteen, left her hometown in Estonia and went to Milan alone. Milan is one of the tougher markets, with more predators than others. After a while, it was so unpleasant that she decided to go home. Her agent refused to let her leave and confiscated her passport. She had to threaten him with a knife before he gave it back. It's a very glamorous industry.

At the seventh floor, I realized that Fab had picked that exact moment to intimidate me because he knew I was tired and off guard. At the sixth floor, sweating from the lack of air-conditioning, I sat down on the steps and pouted. Dust motes swirled in a shaft of soft light. Watching as one grain danced helplessly in the light and then got lost among all the rest, I visualized myself as one speck of dust among billions.

I was having a midlife crisis. At sixteen.

I started crying. The weekend, losing Tigger, it all added up. Fab was only the trigger.

The miserable bastard.

I sobbed energetically for a few minutes; then it hit me. The way I handled him back there was . . . cool. I sniffled, feeling immediately better. It had become clear that if you turn the other cheek, in this town at least, people consider you their permanent doormat. Now that the rules were established, I was more relaxed. I put my flip-flops on and jogged down the rest of the steps. I smiled at the security guard as I barreled through the lobby and out the door.

No more Mr. Nice Guy.

Nice Girl.

Whatever.

The next morning found me, red-faced, tugging a mattress upstairs, while the teenage delivery guy wheezed and pretended to help by pushing. I debated letting the mattress go just to see the look on his face as it plowed into him.

"Hey, man, are you going to push or just stand there?" I asked, sweat beading on my forehead.

"I *am* pushing," he said.

"Let me put it this way. Do you want a tip?"

He seemed to ponder it briefly and then started pushing. The great thing about being young is that you can bounce back from traumatic experiences at lightning speed. Two days after limping into my apartment, I was feeling pretty darned good as I skipped downstairs to go food shopping.

I had discovered the first thing that happens when you move into an apartment. Everything falls apart. It's because the landlady simply neglected to say that all the drains are blocked, the shower only dribbles, and the door is homicidal. But the rent was cheap, so I considered this fair. I opened the front door and came face-to-face with my landlady. "H-h-how is the apartment?" she asked apprehensively, edging toward her door.

"Ahh." I smiled. "Marvelous."

She seemed confused. "Really?"

"Yes, the funniest thing happened, you know the molding around the door"—her eyes were wide while listening—"came loose and bonked me on the head."

She fumbled, unlocking her door.

I continued happily, "I took a closer look, and it was actually being held there by Scotch tape. . . ."

"Really, bye-bye." She smiled guiltily and escaped into her apartment.

TV teaches you that when you get your own place, you're supposed to throw a wild party, get drunk, and break things. It doesn't matter what, just break stuff.

This proves that you are grown-up.

I have a different theory: Unpacking groceries and doing my special interpretation of the moonwalk to Billy Joel's "Movin' Out" blasting from the CD player, I took a swig of milk directly from the container. Laugh all you want, but drinking milk from the carton is the true expression of total independence. I slid in my socks toward the fridge, milk jug raised in one hand, then I skidded to a stop without spilling a drop. Yup, I've got skills.

Veronika had told me to dress casually when I reported at noon for duty at Vue, but to bring a dress to change into for the show later.

I got off the bus at 40th and Eighth Avenue, descended into the maze of underground subway tunnels, and promptly got lost in my search for the E train. I walked in circles like a confused country bumpkin, dressed in jean shorts, T-shirt, and flip-flops. Wandering down the massive main tunnel, I spotted a foot-high plastic black-and-white sign screwed onto a concrete girder above my head.

OVERSLEPT, it read, in block letters. I walked on; three girders ahead was another one.

SO TIRED. I jogged forward.

IF LATE.

GET FIRED.

WHY BOTHER?

WHY THE PAIN?

JUST GO HOME.

I had to smile. Leave it to New York to put "inspirational" messages in the subway.

Eventually I found the E train and watched three of my peers, with their hats on sideways, do a great break-dance as we sped uptown. Teenagers are the salt of the earth. I say this not just because I am one but because without us, what would everyone else have to worry about?

In the sunshine I crossed Third Avenue and continued down elegant 50th Street. Past a uniformed doorman in his fifties standing at attention outside the five-star Kimberly Hotel, I searched for number 151. I wandered back and forth a few times in confusion before the hotel's doorman took pity on me.

"Are you looking for something?"

"Yes, Vue."

"Oh, it's right there." He pointed to a medieval-shaped black door without a number or visible sign.

"Why don't they mark it?" I asked, exasperated.

"If they had to, it wouldn't be cool," he said with a smile.

The massive door was locked. I pushed a buzzer.

"Whozzit?" asked the intercom.

"Cheryl."

"Are you one of the models?"

"Yup."

"'Kay."

With a forbidding *creeeak*, the door was hauled open by a chubby man holding a washcloth.

"Hi. I'm cleaning up, the other models are already here."

From behind him came the sound of girls talking. One said loudly, "Shit!" Yes, those were definitely models. The inside was beautiful, hardwood floors and a long, sweeping bar. Mr. Intercom directed me through an archway, and my jaw dropped. I was in a huge oval room whose ceiling was two stories high; there were velvety couches on raised platforms near the walls, where the models were sitting. A four-foot-high, T-shaped runway was being assembled by workmen in the center. I walked toward most of the same girls from yesterday's runway class at the gym and was happy to see that they were all dressed in shorts and flip-flops. That went down as the only time I have ever been dressed correctly at an event. I smiled and said hi; they nodded sleepily at me as I plopped down on a couch. "Shit," said a dark-haired, green-eyed girl, glaring at her cell phone. "It always dies on me!"

No one had any reaction.

This was going to be fun.

I leaned forward. "Where are the bookers?"

"They're on their way, it's all very hectic, and their limo was delayed," said the green-eyed girl.

"My name's Cheryl. What's yours?" I asked her.

"Kahla." She turned away from me, frowning at her cell, abruptly tuning me out.

Well, la-di-da.

I slumped back on the couch and closed my eyes to wait. Twenty minutes passed. The sound of the front door smashing shut reverberated through the club, followed by stomping footsteps. Bookers exploded through the archway, shoulders tensed, chins jutting, snapping at one another. Nassar led, a vision in black, delicately dabbing sweat from his face with a black silk hankie.

"It's too fucking hot out there," Veronika declared, looking pale next to Nassar's flawless tan. With great squeaking and stress, racks of clothes were wheeled in. "Over there, over there"—Nassar said, pointing as Amy pushed the clothes—"and don't tip that limo driver, he was late, teach him a lesson . . . Jesus! The incompetence, am I right?"

The bookers nodded grimly.

Four shining chrome racks were eventually lined up, bursting with designer outfits. Nassar finally spotted the ten of us, sitting in plain view. "Oh, look!" he said. "The models are here!"

Nassar sat next to me. "Omigosh, busy, busy, the girls who're walking the runway are going to be arriving in a sec to rehearse. We'll pick their outfits and organize, organize this show! Okay, ladies?"

We all bobbed our heads. He rushed off toward the clothes racks. I looked around the couches. None of us had any idea why we were there.

One by one the runway models arrived, clones of us, except they were a few years older and possessed a thing called "style." Designer sunglasses, expertly worn jeans, high-heeled boots, studded belts, and understated jewelry. All the new models immediately looked down at their own outfits with newfound distaste. The runway had been assembled, but the workmen were reluctant to leave. They gawked disbelievingly at us and at the arriving models. Veronika shooed them out of the way.

"Ming!" Nassar squealed. "Get up there and walk, girl!"

A very slim girl with long black hair, the bangs nearly covering her eyes, smiled and headed for the steps to the runway. Nassar turned to us. "Look at her. Ming has one of the best walks in the business." I watched intently. Nassar stood a few yards away from the end of the runway. Ming posed four feet aboveground, enjoying the moment. She locked stares with Nassar and lifted her knees absurdly high, proceeding down the runway with her hips pushed forward.

"Oohhhhhh, yesssss." Nassar sighed. "That's the walk." He was glowing, arms raised, like those people on religious TV when they find the Lord. He was still congratulating Ming when I went to take a look at the clothes. Casual wear by Jennifer Lopez's new line, JLO; tight little athletic shorts and matching jackets. There were elaborate dresses from other designers that looked confusing to get into.

"Nice, huh?" said Amy at my side.

"Great." Looking up at her, I noticed a row of windows on the second-floor level that looked down on the entire club. "Is that the office?" I asked.

"No, it's the VIP room. It's awesome. People can see everything from there."

"But only Very Important People, right?"

She giggled, the only booker not on the precipice of a nervous meltdown.

At runway shows, there is a lot of waiting involved. First the organizers go crazy arranging everything. Then the models sprint in all directions trying on clothes, while the organizers stand by. Basically a runway show is everyone going nuts in cycles.

Nassar talked tensely on his cell. "Annabella, you have to come for fittings now. . . . Don't pretend you don't understand English! I know you speak it! . . . You're not sick!"

An accented voice protested loudly on the other end.

"Annabella, if you're gonna be in the show, you *must* get here now." He hung up and yelled to Veronika, "She'll come."

A ten-foot-square white projection screen was being hoisted at the back of the runway. A technician fiddled with the projector. The bookers chose which outfits would look best on which model. Wearing the outfits, the models emerged from the large marble bathroom to be solemnly inspected.

When an ensemble "worked" on a certain model, she stood against the wall and Nassar snapped a Polaroid. The developed Polaroid was taped to the wall with the model's name written on it. The model's name was also written on a label—like elastic luggage tags at the airport—that was tied around the hanger carrying the outfit. Each girl would have three or four wardrobe changes during the show. Polaroids helped the bookers decide in which order the models should walk.

Nassar ran out of Polaroid film. "Does anyone feel like going out to CVS for film?" he called.

Most of the girls nodded, but I walked over to him, wanting to get out of there for a while.

"You're Cheryl, right? The one who always smiles."

I grinned obligingly.

"Okay, we need six hundred instant film, Polaroid, thirty photos in a three-pack."

I repeated it back to him. Impressed, he handed me a fifty-dollar bill.

The bright sunshine was a jolt after the club's dim lights. I sauntered over to my pal the doorman. "Hi."

"Hello. How was the club?"

"You were right, it's cool. Is there a CVS around here?"

He gave me directions. I repeated, "Six hundred instant film, Polaroid, thirty photos, three-pack" all the way there. CVS was comforting because it looked exactly like all the ones I had ever been in. A severe-looking woman got the film from behind the checkout counter. I was immensely proud of remembering what to ask for. She rang it up: fifty-five dollars. I made up the difference with my own money.

Nassar ran to greet me inside the club. "Ooooooh, thank you, thank you, was it fifty dollars?"

"Fifty-five."

He handed me a twenty-dollar bill out of his wallet and, waving the film, announced, "The eagle has landed!"

"Which one is mine?" demanded a highlighted blond model in her midtwenties, as she scanned the club. Nassar rubbed his chin and, spotting me as the nearest warm body, said, "Ummmm . . . Cheryl!"

I eyed them cautiously. Nassar continued, "Cheryl, this is Hillary. She's walking in the show. You can help her." He smiled a bit too widely and disappeared.

Hillary locked gazes with me and sniffed. Then she sighed in resignation and looked me up and down.

"Well?" she asked, hands on hips.

"Well, what?" I said very calmly; she seemed volatile.

"Well, which are my outfits? What order are they in? Which accessories are mine? You know!"

"Actually, I have no idea."

"You . . . don't . . . know!"

"Nope."

Hillary didn't know what to do. She looked in all directions for help in dealing with this imbecile. "Kid, you need to know. It's your job to know. So go figure it out."

I smiled a little, "Hillary, it's not my job. I'm doing this as a favor for Veronika. Besides, look around." I swept my hand at the chaos surrounding us. "No one knows what's going on yet."

Her mouth was open, thinking of something to say. I gave her a friendly smile, all her past transgressions forgotten, and walked off.

Amy jogged up to me. "Is she giving you a hard time?"

I paused. Better not to make a problem. "I think she's just wondering about what order the clothes are in."

"Oh, I'll show you."

We threaded our way though the pandemonium. The projectionist hit the projector: "Goddamn machine!" Veronika pointed at a spot on the runway while yelling at the workmen, "There's a bump here, a girl could trip!" Nassar on his cell: "Annabella, stop it! I know you speak English!"

Polaroids were falling off the wall. Amy reinforced them with more tape while pointing vaguely at shots of Hillary and explaining the order, in a way that made it clear she hadn't decided yet. All the while, clothes slipped off the slick wooden hangers, forming colorful puddles on the floor.

"Thanks, Amy, I'll be back for the show tonight."

"If you could come back at nine, it would be great. Thanks so much for helping."

"It's fun," I said truthfully, watching the projector fall.

On my way out, Hillary blocked my path and barked, "Did you figure it out?"

Without breaking my stride, I said, "Yup" and got out of there. It was two o'clock. Most of the new girls were leaving gratefully along with me.

I had to have caffeine; it was vital to maintaining my sanity. A Starbucks loomed ahead. Ahhhh. I sat by a window. With an iced caramel Frappuccino sweating on the table in front of me, life seemed livable. One of the new models was standing timidly near my table, even though others were empty. "Can I sit here?" she asked.

I was shocked. Someone being nice: Inform the media! "Sure."

She dropped tiredly into the chair and put her iced coffee next to mine. Brushing light brown hair off her face, she asked, "How many of the bookers, do you think, are gonna survive the night?"

I laughed. Her name was Allison—"call me Allie"—and she was eighteen years old and living in Fab's Upper East Side model apartment.

"How is it there?" I asked.

"God! You wouldn't believe it. There are way too many models there; some of the girls are sleeping on the floor. The whole bathroom is moldy, I saw a huge roach, and the air-conditioning's broken."

"But other than that, pretty good?"

Allie choked on her drink, then giggled into a napkin.

A few minutes later, a shadow descended over our table. I looked up to see Hillary.

"What are you guys talking about?" she demanded.

I was officially sick of her. Would she give me no peace?

"Well?" Hillary snapped.

"We were talking"—I grinned—"about how annoying you are."

Hillary gawked at me. "Well, you know . . . ummm . . . I'm sorry about that, but I'm under a lot of stress."

"Don't worry about it."

Hillary and I smiled at each other, old pals. She took her drink and set off down the street.

Allie leaned forward across the table. "Wow! She's so scary, I can't believe you said that to her!"

I shook my head. "I'm more surprised than you are."

We split outside Starbucks, agreeing to meet outside Vue at nine p.m. I went exploring. Manhattan is one of the few cities where you can wander around observing the interesting/weird citizens and be completely entertained. When my legs gave out, I lounged around Barnes & Noble.

At 8:55 p.m., I ducked into the Kimberly Hotel next to the club to change into my dress. Some of the other models were there with an identical mission. In the bathroom I put on my All-Purpose Little Black Dress and heels. Night had fallen, but the air was still hot and humid. I stared at the scene outside Vue. Red velvet ropes stretched far down the block to accommodate a massive line. Women dressed in designer cocktail dresses, men in suits—and gigantic, square-jawed bouncers to block them all from entering before being checked out. The bouncers held clipboards with entry lists attached. I saw a group of seven models standing away from the velvet ropes, aloof from the crowd, and went over. Allie waved at me. "Hey, Cheryl, check out the line. They're running out of block space."

I smiled appreciatively. "Are we going in now?"

"The bookers say some people are still getting the club ready, the doors are gonna open at around nine fifteen."

The average age of people in line was forty; they stared at our little group of overly tall girls.

"I jus' sooooo tired of this heat," said probably the most beautiful girl I had ever seen. Five-eleven, long black hair, brown eyes, and a fierce, pouty expression. "Every day, heat, heat, heat." She fanned her perfectly tanned face.

"That's an interesting accent. Where are you from?" I asked.

"Brazil. What's your name?"

"Cheryl."

"I am Annabella."

I laughed.

"Why you laughin'?"

"You were pretending you couldn't speak English on the phone with Nassar, right?"

She smiled proudly. "It work, I no go to rehearsal, only show. Hee-hee."

Nassar—all in black, of course—came bounding down the street. "Hey, girls, you don't have to wait out here, we have a suite at the hotel."

We followed him into the small, luxurious lobby. Models were lounging on sofa chairs, some of our group dropped off to chat. Nassar had me and Annabella by the hand. Wisely, he was not letting her out of his sight.

Allie hopped into the elevator ahead of us. As we rose, Nassar told us excitedly about how totally stressed he was. The doors opened and we padded down a thickly carpeted hallway. I lagged behind, apprehensive about going into the hotel suite. Allie did a goofy twirl. "I like this hall."

Nassar rolled his eyes.

He threw open the huge double rosewood doors of our prep suite. Sound poured out, and Allie marched confidently through the door, while I peered in cautiously from the hallway, gazing at a large, brightly lit living room that used to be very elegant before Prima Models invaded. Clothes were piled on the couches; makeup bottles, tubes, and sponges were scattered on tables; while models and bookers dashed in circles. Cans of Diet Coke—the official drink of models—were grouped in six-packs at regular intervals around the suite. I watched from just inside the open doorway so as not to get run over. A red satin dress was traveling across the room, hiding everything but the gray alligator shoes of the carrier. Shimmering, the gown was placed reverently over others. The diminutive Fabriziou was revealed. This should be interesting.

He spotted me, and a dreamy smile spread across his glowing face. "Cherilll, hellooo. Oooooh, you look sooo beautiful." He danced toward me. His moist little hands very gently connected with my elbows; adoringly, he smooched the air at a safe distance from my right cheek. "Mmmwhaa." Repeat performance on left: "Mmmwhaa." He gazed up at me with deep love. I looked down at him with a small, genuinely amused smile.

"Oooh, Cherilll, you will have so much fun in the runway show." Looking at a six-pack, he asked, "You want a Cokey-Coley?"

I really started to smile. Fab was torn away from his new favorite model by Veronika, who dragged him into a corner to discuss a dress. This was only one day after the "incident" at the gym. Very nicely done. The little guy had guts.

"What's so funny?" Allie was studying my face, waiting to be let in on the joke.

"Life in general. Do you want to go back downstairs?"

"Yeah, it's way too busy up here."

We sipped Diet Cokes as the elevator descended. Allie said happily, "I just think Fabriziou is so silly."

Subconsciously I touched my left upper arm, knowing *that's exactly what he wants you to think.*

The situation outside Vue had escalated. More people had joined the line, and bouncers were carefully selecting names from a VIP list and then letting them in.

A few shining black limos pulled up outside the club. Expensive people got out, argued with the bouncer about being let in, then joined the queue, which now stretched around the block. Women's diamonds glittered in the moonlight; people were trying to sneak by the bouncers, who weren't taking it and growled, "Are you on the list?" Allie and I approached the ropes, confused. Everyone was yelling at the bouncers; neither of us had been to a club before. The meanest-looking bouncer—think Arnold in *The Terminator*—sensed us wavering outside the velvet cord and barked automatically, "Areyouonthelist?"

Then he scrutinized us carefully. "Never mind." Another bouncer said, "Let them in." Allie was annoyingly holding onto my wrist for support in this sea of loud noises.

"Get the fuck to the back of the line!" a woman in the queue screamed at us. There was a clicking sound as Arnold, the bouncer, unclipped the velvet rope.

"You didn't check the list! I'm on the list!" the woman yelled, blood red nails reaching for my free arm.

Allison whimpered as Arnold My Hero stepped between me and

the nails, allowing us to zip into the club. People yelped protests in our wake. I heard the woman scream, "DO YOU KNOW WHO I AM?"

This was a different entrance from the one we had used during the day—a pitch-black hallway, music pulsing from ahead, an even bigger bouncer guarding a stairway. "Ladies," he said, motioning grandly toward the stairs. Automatically we started climbing. Halfway up Allie giggled delightedly, "Oooooooh, we're vee-eye-pees."

The VIP room stretched importantly before us: long, glittering bar, cushioned booths softly lit with candles. And I thought downstairs was cool. We oohed and aahed appropriately. The only women up there were half a dozen young models and a few black-clad ladies in their forties who looked extremely intelligent. The rest were well-tailored men who stood in groups sipping drinks, talking about what we had no doubt were very important things. They looked at us appreciatively.

"Allie . . ."

"Yes?'

"You're cutting off my circulation."

She looked down at her white-knuckled hand, still gripping my wrist, and released it, laughing. We walked to the row of windows and inspected the rapidly filling club below. Music pounded and lights swirled along the runway. Apparently the projectionist had beat some sense into his machine, because the ten-foot projection screen was flashing "JLO Fashions by Jennifer Lopez" and "In association with Prima New York Model Management." Annabella's insolent face materialized on the screen, looking straight out of *Vogue*. Amazing graphics blended a succession of fashion shots displaying Prima's models. Funmi smiling on the cover of *Elle* magazine, Tamiyo and Danielle heading campaigns for Aveda and United Colors of Benetton. It's understandable why the crowd outside was so frantic to be let in. People will wait for hours, in all kinds of weather, to be let into one of Manhattan's trendiest clubs. Often they are still turned away.

But there I was, sixteen and in the VIP room, my God! In order to get in quickly, you have to be a female model or very rich and influential. Looks and Money, the two go hand in hand.

Literally.

Allie summed it up: "Wow!"

A booth was free, so we sat down to regroup and were joined by two blond models. One sat very straight, afraid to move lest she damage her hair, which she constantly smoothed. The other snapped her fingers to emphasize every statement. I didn't mind Hair, she was nervous. It was Fingers who annoyed me, because she was pompous.

"I tell Fabriziou that I want a contract with Prima, like, now!" Fingers snapped her fingers and continued, "But he wants to see what some clients think before he commits to signing me"—I listened carefully—"and maybe in a month he'll sign me to a one-year contract. I said I wanted a three-year, but he says the max he does is one year."

I was smiling. Good ol' Fab, he was stringing this girl along. Why? An interesting question, because I was asked to sign immediately and told a three-year contract was the minimum. I looked carefully at Fingers. She was beautiful but a little under the crucial five-nine height requirement.

I turned to Allie. "How long is your contract for?"

"One year."

I asked Hair, "How about you?"

"Oh, me?" Stroke platinum blond tresses, "I don't have one . . . um . . . yet."

I said conversationally, "Has Fabriziou gotten any of you a test shoot so far?"

"No."

"No."

Fingers: "No, but I'm gonna. It's six hundred dollars plus prints—my parents are paying. Then maybe he'll sign me."

I leaned back out of the conversation and thought. It all fell into place. Summer Girls. Fab saying, "Don't worry about them, they are just summer girls. Don't tell them about your shoot." Girls with no signed contract and therefore no obligation on Prima. He was clever; how much of a kickback was he getting from the photographer? I wondered. Probably 30 percent, a referral fee.

He would then see if there was any response from clients regarding the model. If there was, she would be signed; if not, she would be effortlessly dropped at no expense to Prima. It amazed me that they didn't see this.

This thing Fab had going didn't concern me or Allie. We had signed contracts and all expenses on account. The rest of Prima's business was legitimate—ad campaigns, the cover of *Elle*, and a decade as a respected New York agency proved that. I wondered if Prima's owner, a former female model, knew what Fab had going.

I also realized that these two girls didn't want to see the truth. They wanted to be New York models for the summer, something very few people can do; so let them.

Fingers declared, "I'm going to tell Fabriziou that I could go to Tokyo and get a hundred-thousand-dollar contract right away." She snapped her fingers. A contract like this is signed by the agency that will represent the model, guaranteeing a hundred thousand dollars in profits in the first year or the agency makes up the difference. It is usually done only with established models.

Fingers lied on. "I've been offered, I can go there like that!" She snapped again.

"Why don't you?" I asked.

"What?"

"Why don't you just," I snapped my fingers, "go to Tokyo." Pleeeease.

Not getting the sarcasm: "Oh, cuz New York is a primary market, less money, more you know, prestige."

"I'm thirsty," I announced.

Hair, "The drinks up here are free, for models anyway."

I got up, pondering how much this event, the club, drinks, runway, was costing Prima. Probably around two hundred thousand dollars—and worth it for the publicity. I sipped Perrier, trying not to sneeze and to appear sophisticated at the same time.

"Hello there," said a slender, silver-haired man balancing a martini.

"Hi," I said.

"Now tell me, how are you enjoying the event so far?" Politician smile.

"I like it."

"Ahh, excellent, will you be in the runway show later?"

"No, I just signed recently."

"That's an outrage!" Insincere indignation. "If they want to promote an agency, you should be in the show."

"Can I quote you?"

Delighted laughter. "How clever! Aha ha ha."

He recovered. "I'm taking a guess, you must be, hmmm . . . nineteen?"

I hesitated. Was I supposed to tell my real age?

"She's sixteen," chirped Allie at my elbow, solving the dilemma.

"Sixteen! My, how mature. Now tell me, how do you like New York?"

"It's . . . informative."

"Ahh, and what have you discovered so far?"

"Everything is corrupt."

Silence, then, "I was forty before I figured that out. I'm sixty-five now, would you believe it?"

"No, you look younger," I said dutifully.

"Ohh, you charmer, you!"

"Ha-ha."

"Ha-ha."

He asked me out to dinner. I hid my surprise, invented a jealous boyfriend, and escaped with Allie.

We saw the thirteen-year-old model standing in confusion at the center of VIPdom and struck up a conversation. In timid spurts, she revealed that she was the oldest of twelve children from a farm in Nowheresville. No wonder she looked traumatized; her parents had packed her onto a bus to New York to stay in Fab's model apartment. When I asked questions, she answered, "yes" or "no," while her glazed eyes looked beyond me into space. After the summer, she would go back to the farm, but *who* would go back? Probably a very different girl. Thirteen is far too young to enter one of the hardest businesses, in the toughest city, without a parent for backup. Then again, maybe so is sixteen.

Amy, the sane booker, looking more like a model, spotted us and hurried over. "Cheryl, Allison, can you go down to the club? Behind the runway they're going over the order of the outfits."

We pounded downstairs, leaving the rarefied atmosphere. The club was packed. A wave of people swept Allie away. I squinted into the whirling lights and saw her surprised face at the other end of the room. Undertow.

A quick tap on my shoulder. I turned to see Emily/Emma. She chirped, "Hi," over the music, with the fake cheerfulness that girls use to disguise their real purpose. The last time I saw her she was watching Fab squish my arm at the gym.

"Hey," I said pleasantly, and started to turn away.

"Wait!" She looked back and forth furtively, adjusted her skimpy top, and hooked a finger into the belt loop of her jeans, "So what's up?" she asked.

I thought this over. Where to begin?

She gave a fake smile that didn't reach her eyes. "So, are ya having fun?"

I smiled and leaned forward. "What is it that you really want to ask me?"

Her smile vanished, eyes shifting, she turned partially away from me, and I noticed her jeans had strategically placed holes all over the bum and thighs. Elegantly dressed men and women were hiding smirks as if wondering, *Who let her in?*

She took a cautious step away from me, crossing her arms protectively, and snapped, "Well, if you want to be so direct."

"Yeah, I'd like that."

In an angry burst: "I need to be signed to Prima, so basically, I didn't see anything happen at the gym. Whatever you're planning to do about it, I'll side with Fabriziou. I don't give a shit about you."

How quickly they learn. She ended with a nervously triumphant smirk, backing away a little more.

I opened my eyes innocently. "What happened at the gym?"

She blinked rapidly. "Are you kidding?"

In an imperious British accent, "Dahling, I nevah, evah kid."

"You're really fucked up."

I allowed myself to be carried off by the crowd, then edged along one side of the runway to the back of the club. Another huge bouncer—obviously there was an endless supply—guarded the hallway leading to the restroom. He let me pass, asking, "Prima?" I nodded. In the hall the temperature instantly rose fifteen degrees, from too many panicked bodies. I was bumped against the wall by a stray clothes rack as the bookers waved various outfits and said:

"This one goes second on Lindsay."

"It's better third."

"More continuity."

"We have to decide!"

"Actually, I think that's Carolyn's outfit."

Glad to see things progressing so smoothly, I saw my former nemesis Hillary and smiled. "Hey, Cheryl," she said neutrally, and pointed at a chrome rack. "These are mine. See the labels? This one first, this second, this third, and this one fourth, okay?"

"Okay." I was relieved she wasn't calling me kid again.

Hillary moved off; I pressed out of the saunalike hallway. Faceless silhouettes moved sedately to the now louder, pounding music. I leaned against the runway near Allie and shouted in her ear that Hillary was actually being civil. She looked doubtful.

"The girls say some of the Knicks are coming tonight."

"The what?" I yelled back.

"Knicks . . . it's a basketball team."

"Oh," I said, embarrassed that I didn't know.

Hillary appeared at my side, gave me a small smile, and talked to Annabella, while monitoring me from the corner of her eye.

I felt a firm tap on my shoulder. It was one of the intelligent, black-clad ladies from the VIP room. She assessed me through designer glasses. "Hello," she hollered up at me. "You're beautiful, great hair. I saw you from"—she motioned at the bank of VIP room windows that looked down on the entire club. "I'd like to talk to you." She pointed toward a couch along the wall. Standing around me listening were Allie, who looked interested; Annabella, who seemed typically indifferent; and Hillary, whose eyes narrowed and jaw set as she looked between the woman and me.

On the couch, she introduced herself, a name garbled by the music. "You're newly signed to Prima?" she asked, while studying my waist-length hair intently.

"Yes."

"I know Fabriziou"—did I imagine amusement in her eyes?—"worked with Prima before. Is that your natural color?"

"Yes."

"Do you have a card with you?"

"They're still being printed."

"Hellooo!" Fab hovered, chipmunk smile in place.

His arrival had an interesting effect: A slight smile appeared on the woman's face. Apparently, I wasn't the only one.

"You've met Cherilll. Isn't she so beautiful?"

"Yes. I want to use her as a hair model."

"Okey, good." He saw the bookers waving frantically at him. "I must go now. So good to see you, Marlena, bye-bye."

She grinned, watching him move away. "What do you think of him?"

I froze. Then I remembered what my mother had said. "I think he has a lot of character."

"Oh, he's a character all right." She laughed. She typed my cell number into her phone—another technique for bypassing the agency fee—and headed back for the stairs to the VIP room.

"What'd she say? What'd she want?" Allie squealed, charging up to me.

"She might use me as a hair model."

"Kewl, very kewl, lets go back upstairs."

The VIP room was slightly more crowded. Fab sat on an ultra-modern white couch surrounded by four serious middle-aged men. A knee-level table with ice buckets holding Cristal champagne, sparkling glasses, and bottles of white wine was in front of them. Fab stopped us as we passed and hissed in our ears, "These people, very connected." Then he addressed his companions: "These are two of our lovely new models. Cherilll is only sixteen, and Allison is eighteen."

The men smiled and complimented us. Fab gushed, "Cherilll, Allison, sit, sit, have some wine or champagne."

"I'm fine, thanks." I smiled. Allison shook her head.

"Is that for religious reasons?" one of the men, good-looking in a slippery way, said with a grin.

"No." I laughed. "I just don't like the taste much."

"Why not?"

"Yes, why not?" asked another.

"I'm not sure," I said cautiously.

"Well, you're gorgeous, so you don't have to be sure," said the slick guy. "Other than modeling, what have you done?" he asked us.

I kept silent, having the feeling that they were playing a game, but not sure what. Allie, standing nervously next to me, blurted an answer. "Nothing."

"Oh, really." He hadn't taken his eyes off me. "So basically"—a wink—"your looks are all you have going for you."

They all laughed in a supposedly friendly way.

Fab was engrossed in a conversation with a passing woman in black.

Humiliated, I felt queasy as blood rushed to my cheeks.

He looked regretful. "Just kidding, now. Tell you what, you're forgiven. Have a seat, I'll get you a drink."

Forgiven for what?

Allie moved to go sit with them. This time I grabbed her wrist and forced a smile at the bastards. "Nice meeting you, but we still have to get ready for the show."

I tugged the dead weight of Allie through the crowd. Our silver-haired friend was hitting on the thirteen-year-old model. "Tell me, do you have cows on your farm?"

"Yup, we've got all kinds of animals."

"Ah, and what color are the cows?"

"Um, black and white, you know."

"Ahh, naturally . . ."

We charged into the VIP restroom, which looked like an elegant lounge. Allie plopped onto a sofa, her head in her hands. I leaned against a marble counter. Complimentary hairspray, creams, perfume, and stockings were neatly laid out.

"What the hell was that?" Allie blinked a tear away.

"They're just playing mind games."

"I looked like an idiot. You were really cool, though."

"Believe me, Allison, I looked like an idiot too."

She smiled weakly. "Why'd they do that?"

"Cuz if they make us feel like idiots, we might sit with morons like them."

"Ha ha ha." She lay down on the couch, slapping a cushion.

The nicely chubby uniformed attendant smiled at us while stacking towels. Allison bounded up, eyeing the counter with free goodies. "Ohh, what's all this stuff?" She started sniffing various perfumes like a connoisseur. I could tell she had made a complete recovery, but the encounter had hit me deeper. I hate being used as an amusing toy. Allie began a heartfelt conversation with the attendant, who proved to be more interesting than a lot of the vee-eye-pees. Her boat from Cuba had crashed and she, Manuelo, Juan, and Someone Else had to swim though an electrical storm before dragging their seaweed-adorned selves ashore in Florida. I believed 10 percent of it and begged for more.

"These are desperate men, they have the guns, eyes like the coyotes—" The restroom door banged open, interrupting the attendant's speech. Annabella charged in. "Showtime!" she yelled, and marched out.

We scuttled downstairs and squished our way to the back of the club. Organized chaos reigned as half-naked models tried to find space to dress. The bouncers were on high alert, letting only models and bookers into the hall. Looking around, I was sure that this would never pull itself together in time.

"Hey, kid! Come over here." Hillary pointed to the ground near her bare feet.

I didn't budge.

She stormed over, obviously still angry about the hair-modeling thing. "Are you deaf or what, kid?"

"My name's Cheryl," I said tiredly, wanting to go back to my apartment.

"Whatever!" The hellion was back.

Deep breath. Hellllp meeeee.

"The order's been changed." Hillary smirked.

I blinked.

Her eyes glittered dangerously as she madly waved clothes hangers around like a traffic cop. "Now it's this one first. Then this, this, this. Got it?"

"Uh-huh, sure."

"You better not mess it up, kid." She stalked off.

I smiled ruefully at her retreating figure, refraining from talking back because I felt some sympathy for her. People's rudeness is usually in direct proportion to how unsatisfied they are with their own lives.

Annabella whispered confidentially in my ear, "Don't worry. Hillary's just jealous because of the hair modeling, and you're eight years younger than her." We shared an exasperated eye roll.

A second staging area was set up behind the projection screen hanging at the back of the runway, allowing models to travel unseen from the hallway to the far side of the runway where the steps were. I peeked out from behind the projection screen and saw another technician heave a video camera the size of a boom box onto his shoulder and train it on the catwalk. Funmi—the smiling girl who graced the cover of *Elle*—rushed by in only skimpy panties. I idly wondered how much a guy would pay to be in my position. In life you seem to be placed in environments according to your indifference.

Veronika, seeming in control, wielded a red Sharpie and wrote reminders—"green necklace for Lindsay"—on Post-its and stuck them to the wall. The guests sensed imminent runway action and grew quieter. A current of anticipation crackled through the dense air.

Hillary was at my side, in panties and bra, swearing, "Damn it! My first outfit! Give-it-to-me, kid."

"Oh, for Chrissake. You're the one who knows the order."

"I showed you the fucking order, you're just stupid."

The other models were watching Hillary disapprovingly.

Hillary turned red. "THIS ONE! THIS ONE, THIS ONE, THIS ONE! GOT IT?"

"Oh yeah, seared onto my memory." Small smiles all around.

She had unwittingly changed the order again—the red outfit used to be first. Solemnly she whisked her "first" dress off the hanger and stomped into it. Zzzziiiiipp.

She faced me with forced calm. "The reason I need you, Miss Whatever Your Name Is—"

"Prunella McGillicuddy." My favorite alias.

"Aarrggggh. I need you to have my next outfit ready as soon as I step off the runway. Otherwise I can't be ready in time, okay?"

"It'll be ready." Anything to make her stop speaking.

She stood in line for the runway behind Annabella and a few other models.

All the lights shut off.

A giddy murmuring ran through the club.

The catwalk was suddenly illuminated, a white fluorescent T in a sea of darkness.

Not a sound in the room.

Boom, boom, boom, heavy pulsing music to match the heartbeat.

I grabbed Hillary's next outfit and stared, mesmerized, at the catwalk from the hallway. Everyone in the audience was looking up at the shining T, mouths slightly open in anticipation. Annabella was on the runway in a short skirt and elegant top, with a proud, angry expression as she glided to the end of the catwalk. Annabella paused to pose; as she turned back, the next model immediately skipped up the steps and started walking. The cameraman had a live video feed, so that when Annabella walked, a larger-than-life image of her strutted in time on the projection screen. The purpose of a model is to act like you loathe the audience. They are scum. Look down your nose at them, and strangely, they love it. Hillary was coming off the runway, calm, aloof, until she was out of sight of the audience. Then she rushed toward me, tearing her clothes off like a maniac. "Hurry, hurry, goddamn it!" She jumped into red velvet JLO athletic shorts, already taking off running toward the line of models, while I bounded after her with the matching jacket. Instantly it was Hillary's turn again. She growled over her shoulder, "Be faster next time." I attributed that to stress.

I had the next dress, a white strapless, ready as she charged off the runway toward me. Shorts, jacket, and bra were jettisoned along the way. Other models bumped into us as I pulled the zipper up . . . it wouldn't move.

"HURRY UP, KID!"

The problem wasn't the zipper. It wouldn't go past her waist because the dress was too small for Hillary.

Should I tell her she wasn't skinny enough? "It won't budge."

"FIX IT!" Her shouts were almost drowned by the music.

Abruptly a hand grabbed the top of Hillary's dress, holding the zipper together. Annabella, her face calm from experience, snapped, "Suck in, Hillary!" And to me, "Zip."

I gritted my teeth and pulled up as hard as I could. Annabella yelled, "Suck in harder."

Zzzzziiiipppp, it's up. Hallelujah.

I was sweating. Annabella scrambled toward the runway. As her stiletto hit the first step, her face became calm, serene, just been to the backstage spa. If that's not talent, what is?

Hillary knew that the zipper wasn't faulty. She stabbed at a simple dress with her name tag on the hanger. "This one next, kid!"

I started thinking very quickly as she joined the line. I saw my bag, which I had left safely behind a clothes rack. I saw a neon EXIT sign. I saw Post-its. I grinned.

Sharpie in my fist, I scribbled on a Post-it and stuck it to Hillary's final dress. I slung my bag over one shoulder and walked out from behind the screen. Everyone was focused on the catwalk. I passed easily to the stairs for the VIP room. Over my shoulder, Hillary walked stiffly down the runway in her too-tight dress. The bouncer smiled at me. "It's you again!"

"It's meeee." I bounded upstairs.

All the VIPs were pressed against the observation window; I passed unseen into the restroom/lounge. I waved at my friend the attendant, closed the door to a cubicle, and changed out of my dress into shorts, T-shirt, and flip-flops in record time. I headed for the door, smiling manically at the attendant, probably giving her another story to tell. . . . "There was this crazy girl . . ." I stormed out the door and came directly face-to-face with Fab.

"Ooee, Cherilll, you going home already?"

"Yeah, it was a great show. Congratulations."

The VIP room was clapping in appreciation of the runway show.

"Thank you, thank you. You helped so much."

He kissed the air near me again and I headed for the stairs. The Knicks were there after all, a group of seven-foot giants who made me feel short. The head booker, Veronika, stopped me. "Cheryl, thanks so much for helping. I'll talk to you soon."

"You're welcome." We exchanged the first genuine smile of the evening.

I jogged downstairs, glad Hillary had managed to get the last dress on by herself. I learned one very important thing that evening: Perrier tastes just like seltzer, but everyone is afraid to admit it.

Midnight outside. Warm and quiet, relaxing after the pandemonium. I was walking down the street, slightly surprised that I had managed to survive my adventures of the past week, when I smiled, recalling the Post-it note that I'd stuck to Hillary's last dress.

Red marker on yellow paper: "You're on your own, kid."

Shooting

"Wheyagoin'?" asked the cabdriver.

"Thirtieth and Ninth." I panted from humidity and excitement in the taxi's backseat.

I'm gonna be in a magazine. *Eeeeeeeeee.*

Morning sunshine illuminated the swarms of New Yorkers rushing across Sixth Avenue outside the PATH train station. I felt very Manhattan because I was in a hurry, sleepy after Prima's party last night, high on caffeine and on a deadline. Must get to *Dance Magazine* shoot by eight thirty a.m.

Zooming up Fifth Avenue at six miles per hour, I lounged in jean shorts and a white button-up top, chosen because it could be removed without pulling over my head and smudging a makeup job. A massive black Hummer appeared at the passenger side of my taxi and tried to cut in front of us. Cursing, my driver didn't allow the urban assault vehicle to wedge in. The light turned red and we pulled to a stop directly alongside the Hummer. "LUNATIC!" my driver hollered.

"Uh-huh," I said sleepily.

Slowly, menacingly, the driver's window of the Hummer lowered to reveal a perfect replica of Mr. Clean. Probably with Navy SEAL training. Buzz cut, features set in stone, dead blue eyes, massive tree-trunk arms. He leaned out his window and said in a gravelly bark, "Just who the hell do you think you are?"

My cabdriver was incensed; he fully lowered the front passenger window and began yelling across the empty seat.

"Oh, you want some, huh?" Mr. Clean growled.

"I not afraid of you, asshole!"

"What! You should be afraid, very afraid!"

The light changed. We remained stationary. Mr. Clean got out of his Hummer. My driver growled in anticipation.

Sensing impending doom, I shouted, "Go!"

"I not afraid!" he hollered at me.

"Go! Drive!"

"I will punch him!"

"Ohhh no, you won't!"

"Yes!"

"I'm gonna be late!" I screamed.

Mr. Clean crossed in front of the cab. I lunged for the door to escape, trying to unlock it in time . . . too late. Cars honked madly as they accelerated all around us. I had no way out.

Mr. Clean at the window: "Get out, worm!"

I stuck my head through the foot-square opening in the bullet-proof glass separating back and front seats. "Please go!" I pleaded.

The driver looked at my disembodied head with interest. "He insulted me!"

"Yes, he's a rotten bastard, now GO!"

In a calm voice, holding eye contact, he said, "I not afraid he punch me."

"If I'm late, *I'll* punch you!"

He smiled.

"Let's go!"

He floored it, tires screeched, my shoulders jammed forward against the glass. Burning rubber, we flew forward. I fell back forcefully onto the soft backseat and stole a look through the rear window at Mr. Clean. He was stomping his foot in the middle of Fifth Avenue.

The Eduardo Patino studio entrance was a large street-level pane of glass, like a department store's display window, except with shades. I was impressed. When I pressed the buzzer on the door, Laura appeared, smiling, and opened up. "Cheryl! Hi, great to see you. How are you?"

"Great, you?"

"Awesome!"

I took in the studio, by far the coolest I had been in. Clean white lines stretched back to where colored backdrops stood. Sunlight streamed through the street window, falling on the chest-high makeup counter. Two jeans-clad models sat on tall white canvas director's chairs along the counter. Both smiled and waved. Laura introduced the models, the makeup artist, and the redheaded hairstylist, who was firing up her straight iron. Names, names, names. Too many, too quickly. I couldn't remember a single one.

"Ahh, hello," said a good-looking, dark-haired man.

"This," Laura said, "is Eduardo Patino."

I smiled and shook the photographer's hand. "You must be hungry," Eduardo said. "They need some time to finish these models." He motioned at the makeup artist and hairstylist, fanatically absorbed in their work. I was led to a fully equipped kitchen, where muffins, bagels, fresh fruit, and coffee—COFFEE—were laid out. Blueberry muffin and steaming coffee in hand, I exchanged Manhattan taxi horror stories with Laura. Eduardo was deeply absorbed in taking light readings near the brightly colored backdrops. Huge fifteen-foot-long rolls of paper were suspended ten feet off the ground from metal poles. They were unrolled like gift wrap, down to the floor and along it, and were secured to the ground by tape, creating the backdrop.

A tomboyish assistant scuttled back and forth with the *pop*-producing gadget. The blond model appeared, beautifully made up, to capture a muffin. She smiled at me and said, "Your turn."

I settled onto the makeup stool.

"Hello. Ohh, good, you don't have any makeup on. . . . And honey! Did you wear that shirt for *moi*?"

Grinning, I replied, "Yes, I did."

"I love you," he declared.

"Oh, I know!"

"Ha-ha."

How to Inspire Adoration in Makeup Artists 101:

1. Wear a button-up shirt.

2. Don't wear makeup.

3. Stay completely still. Movers will be poked with an eye pencil.

Rubbing moisturizer on my face: "You know, Cheryl, I love New York, but guess what? I have to go to L.A. soon."

"Why?"

"Ooooh, I'm the makeup artist for *Trading Spaces*."

"Really?"

"You bet, sweetie."

"Is it fun?" I asked.

"A blast, omigosh! Guess what they gave me as a present?"

"Hmmmm," I said, while he dabbed foundation on with a sponge. "A chainsaw?"

"No! Yuck! A tool belt designed to hold all my makeup."

I laughed, imagining him wielding lipsticks and powder brushes like a nail gun.

"Should we put them on?" he asked Laura.

She squinted. "They're pretty long naturally."

"Everyone else is wearing them."

And so, for the first time, fake eyelashes were applied. A slim strip of glue along the base of the fake lashes, and then they were stuck to my suspicious eyelid. When the glue dried, my eyelids felt amazingly heavy with the extra weight. I adopted a sleepy, dozing expression, which delighted everyone. After forty-five minutes the makeup was excellent, all the focus was on my now giant Bambi eyes. I batted my eyelashes at the mirror while the hairstylist straight-ironed a few waves.

Activity mounted. The clothes stylist whirled different dance ensembles while she matched them with accessories. Laura's assistant perkily offered her advice on a scarf. The clothes stylist gave her a polite, do-not-invade-my-expertise-turf-unless-you-are-higher-on-the-totem-pole look.

The mousy tomboy taking light readings was expert at fading into near invisibility. No one introduced her; she didn't expect it. *Pop, pop, pop*, the drumbeat of her existence. My, how cynical I had become. I secretly christened her Poppie as she scurried around in worn dungarees and a striped T-shirt.

"Cheryl . . . yoo-hoo . . ." The clothes stylist was smiling, crystal jewelry asparkle. "You were a million miles away. Can you try this on?"

"Sure."

Into the spacious gleaming bathroom. I locked the door and wiggled my toes on the extra-furry bath mat while changing. Ah, life's simple pleasures. I exited to be inspected, hearing a flurry of comments from everyone.

"Ohhh, that looks good, but which shoes?"

"Accessories?"

"I'll handle the accessories!" from the clothes stylist.

I remained cautiously mute.

In the next half hour, I changed stocking colors three times, settling on black. Various necklaces, scarves, and bracelets were hung on me. I daringly made a suggestion to the clothes stylist, to see where I stood in the pecking order. She listened attentively, then said, "Good idea." A polka-dot top was wrapped around my waist and fastened with a clip at the back, to make it like it was meant to be a skirt. To further confuse things, a scarf was folded and tied around my waist like a belt. Black boots that I'd brought with me finished it off. Cool. It took forty-five minutes.

It's surprising how many experts it takes to make a shoot progress smoothly. Hair, makeup, clothes stylist, Poppie, Laura's assistant, photographer, Laura. That's seven people, not including the models.

The two other models were already shooting a look together. We would be photographed in duos and maybe, just maybe . . . a solo shot—depending on who was chosen for it. I stood near the windows, trading one-liners with the makeup artist. I heard Eduardo instructing, "Good, move farther forward, strong look, yes." Laura appeared, took one look at the windows, and started laughing. The makeup artist and I turned around. Pedestrians were crowding, pressed against the glass, hands shading their eyes, peeking through the blinds at me. I waved. Laura closed the shades tightly and peeked out to make sure the coast was clear. My adoring public dispersed.

"Got it, great job," said Eduardo, and the models headed toward the clothes stylist for their next outfits. Laura waved at me. "Cheryl, you're up." I walked toward the bright backdrop. I was about to step onto the yellow background paper that extended along the floor, when a little voice yelped, "Ooh, wait a minute, please." Poppie was kneeling around my knee level. "H-h-have you ever worn these boots outside?"

"Yes."

"I'll have to tape them. Just a sec."

Looking down, I saw a black imprint of my boot where I had started to step. If I had walked on the backdrop, dirty footprints would have shown up in the photos. Poppie returned with white electrical tape. I lifted one foot up behind me, and, tearing it with her teeth, Poppie applied strips over the sole of my boot. Then, to be sure, she scrubbed at the soles with a dry towel. I was embarrassed, wanting to say, "You don't have to do this, there are openings at McDonald's," but she seemed to actually be enjoying herself.

"All done." A victorious peep.

"Thanks." I joined the dark-haired model at the center of glaring yellow.

Eduardo approached, camera in hand, and explained how he

wanted us to pose. "Jumping in opposite directions, Cheryl in front, very strong look." He demonstrated how we should move, with Laura helping.

"Okay, let's go." His camera at the ready, he counted, "One, two three, jump!"

We danced in opposite directions, captured in bright flash. There was a stab of pain in my feet when I landed on my three-inch stiletto boots, not intended for dancing in. I was surprised to see our picture appear immediately on a formerly blank television screen behind Eduardo. The image was studied. "Good. Cheryl, lift your knee higher and move the skirt." Eduardo was in the Zone, focused and excited as only photographers can be.

Poppie took more light readings.

We jumped, again . . . again . . . again.

"One, two, three, go!"

"That was very good. Knees higher, girls, one, two, three, go!"

My feet were killing me, but I was also in the Zone, as only an ultra-ambitious, determined sixteen-year-old can be.

"Excellent," Eduardo said. "I think that one was it."

Laura nodded happily.

"But just in case . . . we'll shoot a few more," he said. "One, two, three, go."

Ouch.

Twenty minutes of nonstop shooting later: "Okay, great job."

I stepped gingerly to the edge of the yellow paper, leaving my boots on the towel. The dark-haired model gave me a worried look. "In those boots your feet must really hurt."

"Oohh, yeah."

Two startling revelations:

1. 70 percent of models are actually nice.

2. Modeling is hard work. Just look at our feet.

Laura rushed over. "Cheryl, you're on right away again." The clothes stylist was holding up my next change, a green leotard and striped leg warmers. "When you've put that on, you can get your hair and makeup changed. Awesome pictures," Laura said.

My hair was pinned up like a lion's mane, and extra mascara was added; I stepped into different shoes. Showtime. I was paired with the blond model. We stood stationary, shooting fierce looks at the camera. After fifteen minutes, Eduardo chuckled. "Cheryl, would it be possible for you to open your eyes?" With all the weight on my eyelids, it was a necessary reminder to appear awake. Laura, the angel of mercy, declared, "Lunch—the girls are exhausted." What a brilliantly, superbly, magnificent idea.

We had all shot two looks, with two or three remaining, depending on who was chosen for the solo shot. Menus from a favorite local restaurant were produced; the salads were said to be "deeeeevine." Laura's assistant collected orders, which were changed multiple times. Creative people just can't make up their minds.

The food arrived via a starstruck delivery boy, and Diet Cokes were passed around. Complete silence descended. It was food time. Show some respect. My cell rang. It was Veronika, creating an awkward moment as I set my Asian chicken salad aside and went into the kitchen so she wouldn't guess I was at a shoot.

"I've got a call for you tomorrow, got a pen?"

I jotted the info down. She asked, "Got it?"

I said yes, and she hung up.

I shot two more looks with the blond model, who was a lot of fun, but the hot lights, six hours of shooting, and stiletto heels were taking their toll. Laura's assistant had been sent out on a mission to find refreshments. I was taking a break from shooting and watched her unpack the goodies, multicolored pastries all made from rice. Luckily, from growing up in Europe, I have managed to avoid the uniquely American love/hate, obsession/disgust, pathological-fear-of-calories approach to food. We are the only culture to "refine" all the vitamins out of food, and then "enrich" it. Laura was bouncing excitedly. "Did you get the bubble tea?"

Bubble tea? I was cautiously intrigued. Ice clinked gently in the glass. The tea, mixed with milk, was a creamy brown. At the very bottom were large, black, pearl-like objects. "What *are* those?" I asked Laura.

"Tapioca! The straw is extra big, so you can suck it up along with the tea!"

I stared at her. Was this voluntary?

But in a bizarre way, it looked good. I took a tentative sip, chewing on the springy tapioca that shot up through the straw, and became instantly addicted. Emboldened, I picked up a pastry that resembled a squished, congealed ball of cold rice dyed pink. I discovered that it tasted like a squished, congealed ball of cold rice dyed pink. Oh well, I still had my tea. The rest was irrelevant.

Having shot four looks, I thought I was done, until Laura handed me an all-black outfit. "We're going to do a solo shot of you in this."

Yesssss.

"Okay, sure."

The hairstylist emptied almost an entire can of hair spray onto my head in order to make it behave in an updo. High on the fumes, I watched Eduardo roll down light blue background paper. He said, "I like your nose. I want to do a profile shot of you sitting down; you can do it barefoot." Poppie took this as her cue to scrub vigorously at my bare feet with the towel. Sitting at the center of blue, I was instructed to hold my hand elegantly at eye level and gaze at it philosophically. A hand is a hand is a hand . . . or is it?

The other models had already left. Everyone else was packing up. There was a calm silence, except for the rhythmic click of the camera. "Aaaand that's it!" A big grin from Eduardo. "Cheryl, excellent job, you really know how to pose."

Smiling sleepily: "Thanks."

The makeup artist pried the fake eyelashes off.

"Wow," I said. "That didn't even hurt!"

"I, my dear, am an expert."

I dressed in my own clothes and flip-flops. Laura, who was obviously giddy about the shoot, said, "Awesome." I wondered how someone as nice as her had slipped into this industry. "We'll be sending the checks out in about three weeks, if you write down your address."

I was probably going to need the money sooner. "Would it be possible for me to pick it up at your offices?"

"Sure. I'll call you when it's cut."

I hugged everyone good-bye and saw Poppie at the other end of the room, busy gathering up electrical cord. In her own world. I walked over and said hi; she looked up from her perpetual kneeling position. "Uh . . . hi."

"Thanks for helping."

She watched me in total puzzlement, as if I must be joking and would, any second, yell, "Psych! Gotcha!"

"Bye." I smiled.

"Uh, okay." She was still shaken to the very core of her being . . . or something like that.

It was past six p.m.—eight hours of shooting later—when I stepped out into the lazy evening humidity. Really, the best thing about modeling is all the free food.

The PATH train sped underground back to Jersey. I sat across from a small, timid woman, neatly dressed and bespectacled, who let out a tiny delighted gasp and turned the page of her romance novel. On the cover was a hunk with absurdly large muscles and jaw, whose shirt was conveniently in tatters. He was hauling an unconscious, nearly naked belle out of the ocean; she seemed suitably helpless. I have only one problem with romance novels: They give people completely unrealistic expectations. Mostly it's that the male heroes are far too sensitive and perfect. These men do exist in real life, but in real life they are gay.

Dusk was falling as I entered the corner bodega near my apartment. A group of rowdy drunks, resembling badly groomed cavemen, stood on the opposite corner roaring insults at one another and collapsing in giggles. The middle-aged store owner sat despondently behind his counter. I saw the object of my desire, a Campbell's tomato soup can, part of a giant stacked pyramid near the counter. As I picked up two cans, the store's door smashed open, rebounding off the wall. Instinctively I stepped behind the soup can tower. Peeking out, I saw a hairy dirt-caked beast storm in. "ROOOAARRR." He was one of the drunks, very drunk. Wild, bloodshot eyes popped out of his head. "AHA . . . HAHA . . . HEEEEE . . . ORRRGGGG."

I palmed one of the cans, ready to bonk him on the head. The drunk wore a big, manically happy smile and hadn't spotted me. The owner looked bored. The drunk stumbled to the fridge, leaned against it, giggling, and extracted some bottles of Coke. He careened toward the counter and leaned against it. "HEYY, MY FRIENND . . . HOOW'S IT GOIN'?"

I began to see some comic value in this scene. As the owner sat with a bland, tired expression, the drunk grabbed fistfuls of chocolate bars. Gathering them and the Coke bottles in his arms, he shouted, "OKAYYY, MAN, I'LL PAY YOU TOMORROW, HEE-HEE!" and barreled out the door.

I took this as my cue to exit from behind the soup and calmly approach the counter. "Friend of yours?" I asked.

Not in the mood for jokes. "No, that is the third time this month!"

"Can't you do anything about it?"

"Nooo, if I tell police, he will wreck my store." He shrugged. "It's okay, he not take much." Lines of worry and exhaustion were etched in his face as he rung up my soup. "Two dollars."

"I'll pay you tomorrow."

We stared at each other seriously, until I grinned and handed over the money. He let out a long, relieved sigh. "Ohh, you scared me there."

I had to tell someone about my first magazine shoot, so I called my mother and told her to calm down. Whenever I'm excited or worried about something, I always command my mom to relax and take it easy, for Chrissake!

Morning sunlight slanted through the blinds; cold-nosed Tigger nudged my cheek. I rolled out of bed, all my muscles sore from the shoot, and did a John Wayne walk into the kitchen. My cell rang. Guess who?

"Hellooo, Cherilll, this is Fabriziou at Prima."

"Hi." I wondered why he felt compelled to announce himself, when no one else on earth sounded remotely like him.

"I have your pictures from Kevin's shoot and your comp cards. You can come by and pick them up."

"Great. I'll be in around noon."

"Okey, okey, bye-bye."

Hilda, the do-as-I-say-or-die receptionist, was at her post at Prima. I had changed a lot since our last encounter.

"WHAT YOU VANT?"

I gave her a big smile and walked right by, around the glass corner and into Fab's office. He was on the phone. "Yes, Abercrombie on Thursday, two p.m." He looked up and waved as I sat in the torture chair. Still on the phone, he handed me a small, already open cardboard box. I extracted one of my newly printed comp cards. A head shot on the front, two smaller full-body shots, and my statistics on the back. Fab had miraculously made one inch vanish from my waist measurement and added one to my height.

He cradled the phone. "Cherilll, you like?"

"Yes, very much."

I wondered if Hillary, the model from hell, had mentioned the little note I stuck to her last dress. Apparently not.

He presented me with a large paper envelope. "Your pictures from Kevin's shoot."

I looked through the eight-by-tens, amazed at how well the prints had turned out. "What do you think of them?" I asked Fab.

He looked nervous. "What do you think?"

"They're great!"

"Yes, yes, I think so too."

It became a running joke among the Prima models that Fab was terrified of giving a concrete opinion on anything. When models were annoyed with him—which was often—they would casually ask what he really thought of something, just to see him squirm.

Now that I had done a shoot for a magazine, I was hungry for the next step. "Will you be sending me on runway castings?"

"Cherilll, you have the look for runway, but you need to develop your book."

"You mean get more pictures?"

"Yes. You will be competing against the best models in New York, and they have full books, with tears."

"Tears" is model-speak for when you are featured in a magazine, then tear your picture out and put it in your book. Clients *love* tears. It proves someone in the industry knows you are alive.

"I'll get tears," I said with certainty.

"Ooee, Cherilll! You are so confident, that's good." *I'm confident, you dope, because I've already done the shoot, and if you hadn't tried to amputate my arm, you'd have 20 percent.* "But Cherilll, it's very difficult to get in a magazine. Very, very competitive."

"If I get tears, will I be sent on runway castings?"

The *Dance Magazine* with my pictures in it would be out in two months.

"Cherilll, Cherilll, you must be patient."

I hate people telling me that. Patience is a character trait of someone who never gets anything done. I can only be patient if there is a logical reason for it. "How about if I get more test shoots?"

"Yes, talk to Veronika, you need a lot more shoots. A very editorial look."

There are two categories in modeling:

Editorial (or high fashion): Appearing in high-fashion magazines like *Vogue*, *W*, and *Vanity Fair*. Doing runway shows for companies like Calvin Klein, Chanel, etc. This is the most prestigious category, the most competitive, and the lowest paid. A model appearing on the cover of *Vogue* is paid only four hundred dollars. You have to be at least five-nine with a unique look (edgy), no cookie cutters here, and dahling, you simply must have high cheekbones. All supermodels are editorial.

Commercial: The smiling models in catalogues and toothpaste commercials—basically, anywhere a model is smiling, that's commercial modeling. It's very well paid to compensate for the disdain high fashion has for anyone looking cheerful. Some supermodels, like Heidi Klum, are both commercial and editorial.

I was glad Fab thought I was editorial. "Okay, I'll talk to Veronika."

I added my new pictures to my book and tucked some comp cards in the back flap. Fab tried to do the hug-kiss-kiss ritual. I put my arm between us and shook hands with great sincerity. He seemed pleased.

Making my escape down the hall, I detoured into the "No models allowed" booking room, where two male models, both blond, were stocking up on their comp cards from the display racks on the wall. La-shawnda shot me a look of contempt from behind her desk. I could never understand what her problem was, but Veronika was the head booker, so who cared? I smiled at La-shawnda, just to prove that I wasn't sinking to her level. Nassar waved. "Hi, babe."

"Hiya, Nassar. How's life?"

"Busy, hon."

Veronika was in her perpetual rictus, pale hand glued to the mouse. She raised her face. "Hey, Cheryl, aren't you supposed to be at the call?"

"It's not for another hour. Fabriziou wanted me to ask you about finding some test shoots to develop my book."

"Hmmm, yeah, I'll look for photographers. But Cheryl, it takes time to find a really good one willing to shoot for free, and there's no point in shooting with just any photographer."

Was I being given the runaround?

"Can you send my pictures to a few and see if they want to shoot?"

"I'll work on it." She answered her ringing phone. I looked along the wall for my comp card. Scanning rows of perfect features, I asked, "Nassar, do you have my comp card up yet?"

"Sure, babe, it's on the wall."

Five minutes later: "Uh, Nassar, where is it?"

He swiveled his chair around. "Lemme see. . . . Ah! There." He pointed at the lowest display rack, a foot off the floor, and there, almost hidden behind a filing cabinet, was my card. Well, you've got to start somewhere.

"Should I move it so it can be better seen?"

He shook his head. "It doesn't really matter where it is. I know it's there."

"Okay, thanks, Nassar." But I knew it did matter.

On my way out I decided to make Hilda, the receptionist, my rehabilitation project. I would make her smile one of these days. "Bye, Hilda!" I beamed.

"Bye," she said, bored.

I got into the elevator with one of the young-Brad-Pitt-look-alike male models. "You new with Prima?" he asked.

"Yeah, about a month."

The door slid shut. "What do you think of Fabriziou?"

I just smiled.

"Uh-huh." He nodded understandingly. "Do you live in his model apartment?"

I was told that when it quieted down from the rush of summer girls, the apartments—for female models only—were actually quite nice. Fab lived in the same townhouse and kept mostly to himself. No one ever really figured out if he was gay, straight, or bi. Fab sent a lot of cross signals.

"No, I have an apartment in Jersey," I said.

"Don't tell the agency."

"Why not?"

The doors opened and we exited into the lobby. "A lot of castings are on short notice, and they only send the models who live in Manhattan."

"But it only takes me fifteen minutes to get into the city."

He shook his head. "Doesn't matter. Your address is put into the agency's computer, and if it comes up as anything but Manhattan, they won't send you in case you're late. A lot of models live in Brooklyn, but we all give Manhattan addresses."

"Good advice. Thanks."

"No problem. See ya." We set off in opposite directions. Sure enough, Fab asked for my address soon after that. I got a mailing service centrally located in Manhattan and was never late for a short-notice casting.

The call Veronika had given me was located near the Hudson River. Hot wind rushed up the street of brick, personality-free buildings. I found the number and pressed buzzer number 2; an answering buzz, and I was inside. Dim, creaky wooden stairs and a musty smell greeted me. I climbed the stairs, noticing that the door to the second floor was open, darkness beyond. That was weird. My instinct told me to turn back; I was starting to, when the sound of girls laughing carried from beyond the door. Up I went. I walked through the door and stopped to stare. Some light filtered through windows at the far end of the huge room. Packing boxes, bubble wrap, and plastic covers for the furniture were everywhere. Six desks with lit-up computers were the only illumination. The effect was one of spooky chaos. Heels clicking on the hardwood floor, I saw two models talking together. One was my friend Allie. The other girl was pale, with black hair past her shoulders, restless dark eyes, regular features, and an on-purpose pout. About eighteen.

"Cheryl!" Allie smiled and gave me a hug. The ever-moving dark eyes of the other girl took this in, looking me up and down—comparison time—and then shot a cold, challenging expression. I was too old for this. I was also trying not to smile, because the girl was wearing a short denim skirt and ridiculous push-up bra under her tank top. New York modeling is all about sophistication, or at least the semblance thereof. Breasts and the tops of bra cups spilling from a shirt is not the idea.

Allie motioned at her. "Cheryl, this is Mandy. She's in the model apartment too."

"Hey, Mandy."

"Uhn." Ahh, ye old cold shoulder. I knew it well.

There were two women working on computers. The drill at calls is to wait until someone acknowledges your existence. Mandy couldn't keep still; she pranced around, talking about herself, to herself, in a loud, high-pitched voice. "So anyway, Fabriziou says I have a great look for catalogues"—she didn't realize that was a put-down—"and I'm, like, really, really gonna book well." Mandy looked immediately to me for a reaction. I figured nothing would annoy this girl more than being ignored, so I turned partially away to ask Allie, "How's it going?"

"I almost didn't come upstairs here—it looked scary."

"I thought so too." In my dramatic voice: "They were last seen entering—"

"Ha-ha."

"AND SO I'M, LIKE, PROBABLY GONNA BE DOING A SHOOT NEXT WEEK. PHOTOGRAPHERS LOVE MY LOOK!" Yup, Mandy hated to be ignored.

A short, fortyish man with an amiable expression and sandy hair emerged from a light-filled room; a redheaded model followed and exited down the stairs. "So who's next?" The man smiled.

Allie started to speak, but Mandy blurted, "Me!"

Allie shook her head with a half smile. Mandy bounced forward, sticking her chest out, and flirted, "Hii, I'm Mandii!" The man remained friendly.

I decided I actually liked Mandy. She was entertaining, and that beat dull and nice any day.

The sandy-haired man motioned around the room. "We've just moved our offices here—it's still a mess. So anyway, what we're casting for now is an underwear catalogue. Not like Victoria's Secret, more like Hanes."

Veronika never said it was for lingerie. I didn't even want the job; out of politeness, I remained standing.

He continued, "I'm taking pictures now. If you're comfortable, only if you're comfortable, we'll take a few in a bra and panties set."

Mandy chirped cheerfully, "I don't mind."

Allie said, "No," looking a little panicked.

"I'd rather not." I smiled.

"Sure, no problem," he said.

"I'll shoot Mandy now, then I'll take some pictures of you, and you, in the clothes you're wearing."

He and Mandy set off toward the well-lit room. She tossed a superior look over her shoulder to say I-know-how-to-undress-and-you-don't-nyah-nyah.

When the door shut, I grinned, and Allie rolled her eyes. "Mandy is such a pain."

"No! Really?" I feigned shock.

A tired smile. "Where were you yesterday?"

At the magazine shoot. "What d'you mean?"

"You know, the flyers," she said.

"Ah . . . no."

"Really? Fabriziou made all the summer models hand out flyers for his friends' business."

"What!" Had he no shame?

"Yeah, it really sucked. Mandy was my partner, and she just dumped all her flyers on me and went to Starbucks."

I had to laugh. What a girl.

Mandy emerged, triumphant, from the photo room, waved bye in an exaggeratedly adoring way, and departed. It was Allie's turn. "Cheryl, I'll give you a call and we can hang out."

"Great. Good luck." Although I thought the chances of booking this job without stripping were slim to none.

Three minutes later, Mr. Sandy Hair was looking through my book. Then I followed him into a large white room, with floor-to-ceiling windows letting sunlight glare in. I blinked rapidly, adjusting to the change.

"These are great pictures," he said, pulling a comp card out of the back flap of my book and laying it alongside a few others on a table.

"Okay." He motioned at the white background paper surrounded by hot lights. "Stand in the middle, a natural pose . . . good."

I did the standard "natural look," which is totally manufactured and unnatural: standing on one foot, the other crossed in front and arched, with one hand casually on the front of my thigh. This is the first thing photographers teach you. A model will repeat it so many times that she begins to pose for family photographs in this manner.

He shot some digital photos and then a few Polaroids. "Thanks, Cheryl."

And I was off.

Veronika called as I was walking up Seventh Avenue. "How was your first call?"

"It went well."

"Good. Get a pen, there's a couple castings tomorrow."

"Okay." I hurriedly extracted a broken pencil from my crowded bag and wrote awkwardly on a store receipt in the middle of a stampede of people. I really must organize myself—like the demigods who have itemized day planners and actually use them.

I went to the library and lugged some books up to my apartment. Due to my limited budget, a TV would have to wait a few weeks. . . . Did I even want a TV? I looked at the lighter square on my living room wall where a TV clearly used to reside. Tigger followed my gaze, closed one eye, and cocked his head, contemplating. I nibbled a nail. In a moment of rebellion, I decided NO! Very nonconformist. A good conversation piece . . .

"Did you see that new show?"

"No, dahling, I threw my TV out the window."

I stacked books where the TV used to be and stalked self-righteously into the kitchen.

Ten a.m. the next day. I yawned as the chrome-mirrored elevator shot me skyward to the seventeenth floor and my casting. It was for "showroom modeling," when a clothing company invites important buyers to their offices for a no-frills parade of models wearing their new designs for the season. It possesses none of the excitement or exposure of runway modeling. So they compensate by paying around a thousand dollars per show, whereas runway rates can be as low as two hundred dollars during Fashion Week. The doors opened; dark green marble and honey-colored wood in an elegant Asian design. Appropriate, since a Japanese clothing company owns the entire floor.

"I'm here to see Yuki," I told the receptionist, who could be either a boyish girl or a girlish boy. Impossible to tell.

"Your name, please."

"Cheryl Diamond, from Prima."

"You can go through there, thank you." He/she motioned around a gleaming wood corner. Prima book in hand, bag over my shoulder, I rounded the bend. Before me was a stretch of creamy carpet, one-quarter the length of a football field, floor-length windows revealing Manhattan until it was obscured by smog. A glass table. One man, one woman, immaculately dressed, regarded me expressionlessly. I extended my portfolio as a peace offering. They rose in unison, graciously accepted it, shook hands, and solemnly introduced themselves.

Perfect choreography.

I turned my smile off; seriousness seemed to be appreciated here. The man looked through my book with a practiced flick of his wrist.

Yuki led me toward several racks of stylish women's business clothes, built into the wood wall. She selected an above-the-knee tan skirt and flimsy coral silk blouse, then directed me behind a wood partition to change. I emerged in their clothes with my stilettos on and, as directed, stepped onto the foot-high, white-carpeted runway in front of their table. Eyes straight ahead, wearing an aloof I-am-so-cool expression, I walked to the end, posed for a beat, and returned.

"Very good, thank you."

I changed back, recaptured my book. Yuki said, "Bye," calmly holding one of my comp cards.

I returned to the elevators. As one of the three opened, a woman appeared at my side from inside the offices and got into the elevator with me.

"Which agency are you from?" she asked as the door shut.

"I've just signed with Prima." I had a hunch—from her air of quiet confidence and the way the receptionist jumped when she went by—that she owned the company.

"Ah yes, may I see your book?"

I handed it over.

She studied it carefully. "You have a very sophisticated look."

"Thank you. You have a very sophisticated clothing line," I said.

"So you know it's my company."

"I was pretty sure."

The doors opened. A few men in business suits entered and pretended not to gawk as we continued down.

"How do you like New York?" she asked.

"I love it." That had been true since I was fourteen.

We exited into the high-ceilinged marble lobby. She was looking through my book for a second time and stopped near the gold security desk.

"How old are you?"

"Sixteen."

"You're very mature."

"Only out of necessity."

Her eyes smiled a bit. "May I take one of your cards?"

"Of course. They're in the back."

She extracted a comp card and extended her hand for an extra-firm shake. "A pleasure to meet you, Cheryl."

"You as well."

She smiled, tucked my card into her Chanel purse, and exited into the sunlight.

Boy! That went well.

The humidity was like a steaming blanket smothering the city. Drinking a root beer from one of the corner vendors, I was hit on by a good-looking man clad in an expertly tailored pinstripe suit. He was okay, but I was focused on other things. Like, for example, conquering the world.

"Can I treat you to lunch?"

"Thanks, but I already ate," I lied.

"Dinner, then." Devastating smile.

Think fast! I didn't want to be mean. Having been turned down by agencies, I'm always reluctant to inflict blunt rejection on anyone.

Brilliant idea! "I have a boyfriend."

A mischievous grin. "So don't tell him."

Damn it, I didn't see that one coming.

Next brilliant idea. "I'm sixteen."

He didn't see that coming. "Jesus! Really?"

"Yup."

A shrug. "Well, all right, let's have dinner anyway."

"Really, I can't." Firmly.

A big sad sigh. "In case you change your mind, here's my card." He handed over a card with the Lehman Brothers logo on it.

I had to work on my antipickup technique.

"Hellooo, Cherilll. This is Fabriziou at Prima."

No kidding. I tried not to laugh at my cell phone.

"Hi, Fabriziou," I said, while walking down Sixth Avenue.

"Can you come by the agency now? I want you to meet the owner."

"I can come by in twenty minutes."

"Okey, okey, bye-bye."

A salute to Baaf, the security guard, who knew the drill by then and returned it. Dazzling smile to Hilda, who regarded me blankly. Into Fab's office. The formerly unmanned desk across from his was occupied by a dark-haired woman in her late thirties. As she rose, it was clear that she used to model. She was slender, and while her perfectly proportioned face showed a few lines of stress, she was overall still a knockout.

"Hello. I'm Raquel, the owner."

We did the extra-firm handshake routine.

She did a quick look-over of me, my hair, face, waist, hips, legs—measuring proportions—and back up again. She nodded, satisfied. "Yes, she has a very good look . . . great hair. Talk to Clairol about her," she said to Fab, who seemed humbled by Raquel's presence.

"Yes, yes, when I saw Cherilll, I knew—"

"Yeah, okay." She cut him off. I liked this lady. "How old are you?"

"Sixteen."

"Fabriziou says you're a dancer?"

"Yes, ballet an—"

"Good. Do a shoot with some dance poses, it'll work in your favor." She turned to Fab. "Did Veronika talk to Louis Vuitton about how many models they want sent?"

"Ooee, I don't know."

"Okay, I'll find out. Nice to meet you, Cheryl." Firm shake. And she set off purposefully down the hall.

A moment of silent reverence after her departure, then, "Sit, sit, please."

I arranged myself in the chair of pain.

"You see, I wanted to introduce you to Raquel because you are the most promising new model. And she likes you, that's good."

The real reason: He wanted someone else's reassurance that I was in fact a promising new model.

"Yes, very good," I said to comfort him.

"Yes . . . good."

I discovered that by slouching down in the chair and leaning my head back against one of the lions, it was actually bearable. Fab was thoughtful. He opened the top desk drawer. Out slithered the measuring tape. "I want to measure you again."

I stood reluctantly; he took waist and hip readings. Fab got a kick out of doing this spontaneously, without warning, to make sure you hadn't gained an ounce. The models dreaded his Surprise Measuring Tape.

"Hmm . . ." He scrutinized my waist. "Twenty-five . . . try to lose one pound, okey? No more, and do it healthy, okey?"

"Sure." After all the scandals about anorexia and bulimia among high-fashion models, agencies always add the "do it healthily" conclusion. As if I would think, *Aww damn, but I was going to let blood.*

"Do you like health clubs?"

"Health clubs?"

"Yes."

"Yes."

"Okey, I get you a free membership at one of the best clubs. They like our models to work out there. Wait, I make appointment for you."

He selected a business card from his gigantic Rolodex and dialed. Today we were buddies. Ours was always a mind-numbingly complex relationship.

He hung up and scribbled, in his odd, spidery hand, *Duomo Gym, 11 E. 26 St. 4th floor.* "See Sarah," he said, and wrote that down too. Circled it and underlined it. "This is who you see, okey?"

I briefly considered a career at Dairy Queen.

Madison Square Park stretched lush and green, a sparkling fountain in the center. Cute little kids scampered in front of my feet. The usual characters a park collects—homeless, a girl with tie-dyed hair, Goths—relaxed on benches, enjoying the green contrast to the surrounding concrete, metal, and glass. I hurried across the taxi-clogged street. Number 11 was green marble framing a glass door—unlike any health club entrance I had ever seen. In the gleaming elevator, a television screen imbedded above the door imparted the latest news. This place was going to be interesting. I was dressed in my model uniform of low-rise jeans, stilettos, and a plain black tank top. You can't go wrong with it.

The doors opened, and I concentrated on not saying, "Ohh, cool." It looked like an expensive modern café. No workout machines in sight. Behind the reception desk was a long bar offering smoothies, as well as carrot, celery, and wheat-grass juice. Black leather couches and glass tables were placed so you could enjoy the window's view while sipping drinks. Was I on the wrong floor? Who cared? I was staying.

I told the well-muscled receptionist that I wanted to see Sarah, then flopped appreciatively onto a couch to wait. A woman rushed toward me, hands aflutter, with a glowing smile. "Hii, I'm Sarah. Sorry to make you wait."

I had been sitting down for ten seconds. "That's all right." I smiled and stood up to shake hands.

She beamed up at me. "Ohh, you're really good-looking. Welcome, welcome."

"Ah, thanks." My life seemed to alternate dramatically between being treated like dirt and like a princess.

"Follow me, please." She half bowed.

I gathered that models prancing around in workout gear would make them look like geniuses at getting people into shape. Not to mention motivating legions of men to join. I tagged along to her office; we sat on opposite sides of her desk. She looked about ready to propose marriage. "We would love to sign you up for a complimentary membership." Was she blushing? "If you give me your ID, I can get you a membership card and then give you the grand tour."

I handed over my ID. She yelped. "Augh! You're sixteen!"

"Yeah."

"Omigosh . . . ahh . . . uhh . . . See, if you get injured here, we could get sued because you're underage."

"I don't plan on getting injured."

"Oh, ha-ha, you're so funny."

"It's a pity about my age. Thanks anyway." I stood.

She looked at my body as an expression of debilitating loss clouded her face. "Uh, wait. I'll talk to the manager and he'll contact Fabriziou, okay?"

"Sure."

"Thanks soooo much for coming. I hope this works out. A pleasure to meet you."

I absorbed and stored all this ego stroking. It might be awhile before I got any more. However, I wasn't enthusiastic about joining a club just to become a display piece.

Sarah escorted me lovingly to the elevator. A man in a business suit sipping a carrot juice entered with me. As we traveled down, he asked, "Are you joining?"

"Maybe."

"Oh, you'll love it, great juice bar!"

I called Fab outside to explain the age difficulty.

"Ooee, no problem, Cherilll. Just get a fake ID."

I looked at the phone, eyebrows raised. "Okay, where do I get one?"

"Just ask anyone. Make yourself eighteen, okey? We'll send you back, say you had a birthday."

My next casting was what models call a "cattle call." Meaning there are between fifty and two hundred models who are seen, instead of ten or fewer at more exclusive calls. It wasn't clear what this clothing company was casting for, in their expertly modern office. I stood among models carrying portfolios from Elite, Ford, and Next Model Management. They call themselves "management" companies so they can charge clients an additional management fee. Agencies, by law, are restricted to only a commission of models' earnings. We were each hurriedly ushered against a white wall, where a quick Polaroid shot was taken to make sure we looked as good in person as we did in our professionally shot pictures. Then a comp card was confiscated. "Thanksforcoming."

I got off the bus several blocks from my apartment and jogged the rest of the way in my flip-flops. Weight loss of one pound, definitely accomplished.

Ten a.m. the following day found me hauling a bag of groceries back from the local supermarket, answering my ringing cell phone.

"Cheryl, you need to go to a call." Veronika sounded fierce, a change from her usual icy indifference.

"Okay." I had nothing to write with; memory time.

"*Honey* magazine, 315 Park Avenue South, eleventh floor. See Janice." Her words were clipped with anger.

I was too busy memorizing to wonder about that.

"Cheryl, I'm very busy, so listen. You are *not* to talk so much at calls. Do. You. Understand. Me?"

"No," I said.

"Listen! I got a call from the owner of a company, who says they loved your look and were going to use you, but you talk too much. Got it?"

"What company, I don't unde—"

"Never mind, just remember to keep your mouth shut."

I was feeling slightly dizzy. "Was it that Japanese company?"

"Yes!"

Now I was mad. "She kept asking me questions! Am I supposed to not answer?"

Her voice became tired. "Cheryl, from now on talk as little as possible, or don't talk at all."

I squeezed my eyes shut and tried to figure this new betrayal out.

Then it clicked. "You mean from now on, play dumb, right?"

A sigh. "Cheryl, just go to the call." Bingo.

I didn't want to go to a casting. I wanted to find that woman and punch her for orchestrating a confrontation between me and the head booker. Not just any booker, the head one! What a bitch.

"All right," I said, my ambition taking over. "What was the address again?"

"Augghh!" Veronika repeated it.

"What time is it at?"

"Nowwwwww!" Click.

Ahh, this must be a short-notice casting.

I stood, jaw clenched, holding my grocery bag. This couldn't be real. The woman had asked for my comp card outside the elevator because it had my name and the agency's phone number on the back. This was all just a movie. I pounded up the stairs to my apartment. Humans are treacherous beings. I changed into a skirt, stuffed my book and stilettos into my bag, and chased the bus.

I sat very calmly on a white leather couch in the reception area of *Honey* magazine. I channeled my inner Aussie—"No worries, mate"—while fighting the urge to call my mom and tell her to calm down. A delicate-featured, auburn-haired model sat next to me and asked the question all models, all over the world, ask one another. "What agency are you with?"

"Prima. You?" I had recovered from my inner temper tantrum.

"I'm with Classique. They're really nice."

"Really?" I remembered Classique as one of the agencies that had been interested in signing me.

"Yeah, the owner's a great guy."

Hmmmm.

"Ladies, could you come back now?" a tanned young woman in a white pantsuit said. We were led into a conference room with a shiny mahogany table and muted lighting. Two women in suits looked through our books. I kept my mouth firmly shut.

They took a digital shot of me against the wall. I posed solemnly.

Snap.

"Thanksforcoming."

For the next week, things progressed in a now familiar cycle. Castings barked through the phone by Veronika, attending them closemouthed, getting lost on the subway, then hiding in a book at Barnes & Noble. In a way, I was enjoying myself.

I asked Veronika—who seemed to have recovered from her fury, returning to indifference—how it was coming with finding a good photographer for me.

"I'm working on it," she said dismissively.

It was late July, and I had found out that Fashion Week—when Manhattan's Bryant Park is taken over by gigantic white tents for top designers' runway shows—would be in early September. Meaning the castings would be starting very soon. But Fab was reluctant to send me out on those calls, due to the sorry state of my portfolio. Veronika couldn't get me shoots to improve my book, because photographers wanted to shoot models with more experience. I couldn't get more experience because I didn't have enough shoots for my book.

Catch-22. A recurring theme in the modeling industry.

At about eight in the evening, Allie called while I was wandering along Fifth Avenue.

"Hey, Cheryl, there's an industry party tonight. It's at a restaurant-slash-club, wanna come?"

"Okay." Cautiously, "What's an industry party?"

"Oh, it's entertainment industry people, producers, agents, models, actors, you know."

"Cool, where is it?"

She rattled off an address in Chelsea, and we agreed to meet inside at nine o'clock.

"Oh, hey, Allie, I'm in shorts and flip-flops, is that okay?"

"Who knows with these things? Just come anyway."

I stood across the street from the club/restaurant and sighed. There was a half-block-long line of well-dressed people arguing with the bouncer to be let in. Déjà vu. Mostly young people in their late twenties, the women wearing variations of the ever-present Little Black Dress. Across the street, I was stylishly dressed in khaki shorts with lots of unnecessary pockets, a white tank top, and my ever-present flip-flops. Recklessly I crossed the street.

Bouncers are the coolest people. A bomb could go off and they would remain calmly in place asking, "Are you on the list?" I walked up to a standard-issue bouncer who towered behind the red velvet rope.

"Hi. How long's the wait?" I asked.

He looked me over quickly with a practiced eye. "Are you on the list?"

"Most definitely not."

He grinned. "Well, most of the people in line aren't getting in tonight. It's full. But you're not most people, right?"

"Ha-ha."

"Which agency are you with?" Bouncers are trained to spot models a mile away.

"Prima."

"Like 'em?"

"Depends on the day."

"Ain't that the truth."

The club door opened, and another bouncer came out. Through the door I saw a glow of gold and shimmering orange. The door shut. I would rather have gotten a burger with Allie than squish though a crowded club. So when the bouncer asked, "Can I see your ID real quick?" I decided on honesty for novelty's sake. "I'm sixteen."

"Eeeeee." He grimaced. "I'm not supposed to let anyone in under eighteen . . . but you're a model, lemme ask the owner." He vanished inside.

"Hey, Barbie, you have to get to the back of the line!" a pointy-faced woman in the queue yelled.

I ignored her, thereby inspiring her friends to join in. They issued commands that had to be obeyed, unless you didn't want to be invited to their next *Sex and the City* rerun party.

"Get into line, stupid."

Then, in purposely theatrical whispers, "She's probably retarded."

"All models are brain-dead, you know."

I had, happily, reached a point in maturity where this only bored me.

The bouncer reappeared, dwarfing a small, slender man in his fifties with the pale skin of a nightclub owner.

"That's the model." The bouncer pointed.

"Really? No kidding," responded the owner with city sarcasm. He looked at me and sighed. "Let her in."

The bouncer unfastened the velvet rope, causing my fan club in line to go hysterical. "We've been here for forty-five minutes!"

"Do you know WHO I AM?"

As I passed the bouncer he leaned in and whispered, "Haven't you gotten a fake ID yet?"

I laughed, entering the club and taking in the dark, glossy floors; a long, creatively lit bar; and folds of orange and gold cloth on the walls. There were a few beautifully sculpted candlelit booths, but the rest was standing area. Good-looking young people crammed together like sardines trying to meet the serious-faced, impeccably tailored beings in their forties who were grouped together deciding the fate of our universe. The owner graciously cleared a path for me.

As I squished along looking for Allie—*Where's Waldo?* flashbacks—the women checked out my fashion statement, or lack thereof. I got a kick out of rejecting the dress code; my ease could be mistaken for being "cool." I'm not, just indifferent.

When we were centrally located in the room, the owner turned to me. "What do you think?"

"It's beautiful," I said honestly.

"Well, I hope you come back often. You're always welcome here!" Clubs adore models. Often they hire organizers to befriend and recruit models to show up.

"Thanks." I displayed my smile to him, and he disappeared into the crowd.

I was captured by a rush of pretty girls who were charging toward the far end of the club. In the shadows I discerned the outline of a man sitting at one of the coveted booths. Dark hair cropped close, a calm, watchful expression, his pale skin stretched tightly over the bones of his face. A crush of cosmetically blessed young women were crowded around his booth, all talking at the same time. He held slim hands up protectively, while his deep-set dark eyes searched for escape. "Ladies, please, not tonight. I'm trying to relax." Personally, I didn't see bliss in his near future; he was a wiry bundle of concentration. The girls continued to press forward, some waving eight-by-ten actor's head shots with their contact info on the back. I managed to separate myself from the madness and moved away.

"Hey, you."

The same voice: "Hey, blond girl!"

Half the women in my vicinity turned around and pointed hopefully at themselves.

"No, damn it. Her! In shorts."

I swiveled; the dark-eyed man stomped up. In flip-flops I was still a couple of inches taller. He let his breath out in a whoosh. "Wow, you're hard to stop." He smiled a surprisingly nice smile. "I'm Jacob." An elegantly engraved card was placed in my hand, identifying him as the managing partner in an acting/modeling agency whose name I recognized.

"What's your name?"

"Cheryl."

"Cheryl . . . what?"

"Cheryl Diamond."

"Good. Good name. How old are you?"

"Sixteen, you?"

He stared at me silently, then made a machine-gun sound—laughing.

"I'd like you to come by our offices for a meeting. Do you have pictures with you?"

"No." It's perfectly natural for models to always have comp cards on them, even at the gym. You never know who you'll meet.

"That's all right. What's your cell number?"

The girls with their eight-by-tens crowded around again as Jacob wrote my number down. My cell phone was of the grossly overpriced prepaid species. Therefore none of my personal information was linked to the number. Jacob clicked his pen and replaced it in his suit. "Please give me a call tomorrow, Cheryl, and we'll set up a meeting."

We shook hands. I set off in search of Allie, who was nowhere to be found; my legs were getting tired. I passed a booth of men in dark suits; three women were standing and batting their eyelashes at them. One man dominated the table: midfifties, a real tan, slightly overweight, with a gold Rolex and matching pinkie ring. He spotted me wandering by.

A sharp whistle. "Join us, please." It wasn't a wolf whistle, more a commanding tweet, the way you would summon a dog. I ignored him and continued through the crowd.

A big hunk of flesh suddenly blocked my way, I was looking at the knot of a black tie against a white shirt. Angling my head far back, I observed a classic goon. Directly out of the movies, blunt features and all.

We regarded each other curiously.

"Uh," he began eloquently, "my boss wanted me to ask if you'd like to have some dinnuh."

For some reason, the big clod inspired my motherly instincts. I said gently, "Tell your boss that I'm not a dog and so I don't obey when whistled at."

He stared at me. "Uh, are yuh sure you want me to say that?"

"Yup."

"Uhh."

"Verbatim."

"What?"

"Tell him word for word," I translated.

"Yes, ma'am." He lumbered off.

I felt like adopting the guy and teaching him English.

I stationed myself near the front door to await Allie. Surprisingly, the tanned man with the clichéd pinkie ring—in addition to a wedding ring—strode over. His slicked-back hair caught the orange lights. "My dear young lady," he boomed. I tried not to giggle. "My deepest apologies for my inexcusable actions." Wow, he must have had ample opportunity to perfect that speech. "Would you honor us with your presence at our booth?" It was too much; he actually seemed sincere. I burst out laughing. I really must learn to control myself. After a week of going around my calls in total silence, the prospect of actually being allowed to talk to a person was irresistible. Besides, these guys were funny.

"Okay."

"Ahh, wonderful!"

He shooed the other women away, and I plopped myself at the end of the booth and observed my tablemates. Mr. Pinkie Ring, who introduced himself grandly as Giovanni Lago. To the right, my goon, followed by an identical goon. Scrunched in the middle was a man who resembled a younger, thinner version of Giovanni. They all regarded the older Gio with awe/fear. Everyone was silent, probably trying to put me on edge. So typical. I gazed idly into the distance.

Gio leaned forward, smiling good-naturedly. "You always dress like that to go out?"

"Yeah. Do you always dress like that?"

He laughed delightedly, which everyone at the booth took as their cue to laugh. Gio stopped chuckling; so did everyone else.

"Whatta lady, huh?" Gio said to the other men, who all nodded dutifully.

"Would you like some sushi?" Gio asked.

Sushi is one of my main weaknesses. "Sure."

"My dear, pick anything you like." He handed over a menu.

Gio snapped his fingers—he was on a power trip—and a young waitress with short pink hair and a little black dress appeared magically. "Yes, Mr. Lago?"

Gio bowed his head toward me. I ordered; then he ordered half the menu. Gio gazed at me penetratingly. I tried to give it right back.

"Isn't modeling a somewhat brainless occupation?" Gio asked abrubtly.

"So is sitting around eating sushi." When accused, never defend yourself; it implies guilt.

"Ha-ha, that's good, isn't it?" His goons bobbed their heads dutifully.

I looked at them and asked, "How much do they cost per day?"

He raised his eyebrows. "You need protection?"

"Nah, but it would be cool to have three people agreeing with everything I say."

That really cracked him up. The sushi arrived on pale wooden slabs with the unavoidable fake grass sticking out of the wasabi. I once ate the plastic grass when I was five. It was pretty good.

The goons didn't eat, only Gio and his younger, mute clone. I dug my chopsticks in happily, and everyone stared.

"Why are you holding the chopsticks like that?" Gio frowned with genuine interest.

I had developed a unique way of holding them, with my hand on top instead of underneath, simply because I can't do it the other way.

"It works better, more control." I said.

"Hey look at that, she never loses food!" Gio exclaimed.

I nodded sagely. Yes, Grasshopper.

After consuming a couple of pounds of raw fish, we drank green tea and discussed crooked politicians and the modeling racket. I hadn't had that much fun all week. Actually being encouraged to talk! Weird.

"You're a very smart girl," Gio observed.

"Thanks."

"It's hard getting started in New York, and you're only sixteen."

"I'll be all right," I said, with all the confidence I didn't feel.

"Listen, I like you. You deserve a little help." Discreetly he extracted a clip holding hundred-dollar bills. Did everyone in Manhattan have these? I kept my face blank. The goons stared straight ahead—great poker faces, or maybe just low IQ. Gio unclipped the whole wad. About two thousand dollars, I calculated giddily. I needed the money, very much. Gio smiled. "Because we're friends. You don't have to pay me back."

The bills hovered temptingly above my knee under the table.

Sanity returned. "Thanks, Gio, but I can't accept it."

His eyes twinkled. "You're turning down free money?"

"Nothing's free."

"Hmm, really?"

"Yeah, sooner or later I'm going to owe you."

He leaned back, pocketing the money with a smile. "You're smarter than I thought. Never take money from a guy like me." He may have been watching a tad too much TV.

We smiled at each other in understanding.

"CHERRRYL!" Allie squealed, leaning against the side of the booth in a blue, summery dress, catching her breath. "Ohh Goddd, it took me half an hour to get in here, it's a circus outside—" For the first time, Allie noticed the other occupants of our booth. "How long have you been here?"

Gio eyed Allie calmly. He wasn't thrilled with the squealing newcomer. "We just finished dinner."

Allie gaped at me. "Did you bribe the bouncer?"

I turned to Gio. "Thanks for the sushi. I had fun."

"My pleasure. Can you stay for some after-dinner drinks?"

"Actually, Allison and I were going to hang out, but thanks." I was working on my gentle letdown technique.

A voice nearby said, "Bye, Cheryl, see you soon." Jacob was making his escape toward the exit, a group of annoyed eight-by-ten holders in his wake.

Jacob asked Gio, "Can we meet Monday?"

Gio considered. "Tuesday, two o'clock. You met Cheryl already?"

"Yes."

"Good."

Jacob smiled and headed for the exit.

Allie was looking back and forth among everyone with a confused expression.

"We're friends," Gio said to me.

"Ah," I said, although my impression was of Gio having the upper hand.

I got up. Gio rose with me; he lifted my hand smoothly to his lips and planted a kiss.

Eww.

Allie and I squeezed through the crowd. "Who were they? What were you talking about?"

"Nothing much." I didn't want to let on about another agency being interested.

"That guy at the table looked scary!" Allie thought everyone in New York was scary.

At the bar Allie sampled an apple martini, while I sipped a tiny glass of Diet Coke that cost one of the troupe of males congregated around us six dollars. Clubs are so happy to have models coming in that I have never heard of any of the obviously underage girls getting carded. I have also never heard of a model actually paying for a drink.

A watermelon martini was placed in front of Allie when she finished off the apple.

"You sure you don't want to try a martini? They're great," one of the men said.

"Nah." I was sure no one there was particularly interested in my well-being, and I wanted full control of my noggin. Allie was pretending to enjoy her martinis, but I could tell she didn't like the taste. After each sip she unconsciously wrinkled her nose and closed one eye while swallowing. I watched with a mixture of concern and amusement.

She leaned toward me. "Y'know, Fabriziou hasn't gotten any of the new models a shoot or comp cards yet." I decided to keep quiet. Must preserve harmony at all costs.

In an even lower whisper, she continued, "Cheryl . . . I think he's probably making money off the rent for the model apartments, with the girls who don't have a contract."

Old news. "Really?"

"Yes. But—ohh whatever, do you wanna get out of here?"

Our male following was deeply distressed. Yelping excuses, we plowed heroically toward the door. We gulped fresh air outside. I was tickled to see my female fan club still in line, scowls etched on their faces.

"I know a place," Allie declared.

"How do you know a place? We've only been here a few weeks."

She raised her eyebrows dramatically. "I know some people, who know some people . . . who know—" She started giggling with me.

Runway

At noon the next day I was regally summoned to another "new girl meeting," This one was promised to be short. I chatted pleasantly with an array of the girls from the runway show. A commanding click of heels and Mandy burst through the door, push-up bra firmly in place. "Hello, girls." She tossed her long dark hair and waited for applause. Dramatically removing her sunglasses, she leaned against unsmiling Hilda's reception desk. "I got that underwear modeling job." She waited for us to collapse weeping or commit suicide.

The girls were too polite to point out that no one wanted that job. "Ohh, cool," they murmured. I tipped my chair back against the wall and closed my eyes. This, of course, infuriated Mandy, who began preaching only to me. "From here, who knows . . . ohh, maybe Victoria's Secret," she said.

The girls shook their heads. "It's almost impossible to even get sent to a casting for them," said one.

Mandy glared at my half-closed eyes. "You never know!" she yelped.

Fab danced in. "Ooee, hellooo, girls."

I managed to avoid getting air kissed as we filed toward the glass table. Fab began his little speechie about various things coming up. It was pretty boring. He reminded us to take regular baths. I bit my lip to keep from laughing. After ten minutes, he threw out the finale. "Ooee and yes, I wanted to say how proud I was of all you new girls' behavior at our runway show last week. No one was drinking. That's very good. Okey, okey, that's all."

The other girls, in a daze induced by Fab's talk, got up and went to pester the bookers. I stared at Fab. *He* had encouraged Allie and me to drink at the club. In fact, he was tipsy! Fab and I discussed Fashion Week. He avoided giving straight answers to my questions by telling me that I had to develop patience, because there was always next year. My cell rang, and Fab said, "Pick up, pick up," eager to get out of further conversation.

"Hello?" I said.

"Cheryl. This is Jacob. When can we meet?"

"Ahh," I said, vaguely panicked to be in Prima while on the phone with another agency.

"How about today at two?" he asked.

I took a good long look at Fab and said, "All right."

"Excellent. Do you still have the card with our address?"

Fab was looking toward me. "Yes."

"See you then."

I hung up, trying to look relaxed.

Before leaving, I asked Veronika how it was going with finding a photographer; she froze me with a look. I exited past La-shawnda, who, from her scowl, may have been considering putting a hit on me. What nice people; they really inspired loyalty.

In my modeling uniform, I headed to my meeting with Jacob. It was at a white stone building in SoHo with gold around the doors. I got buzzed in and climbed the polished hardwood stairs to the second floor. The entire floor was open space, large shaded windows, a few sturdy desks, and a conference table behind a glass partition. The delicate buzz of phones, the click of computers, and subdued voices were the only sounds. It was more like a law firm than an agency. Jacob walked toward me from the far end of the room, dressed in a dark gray suit; it took him awhile to make it all the way. I had removed all my pictures from my Prima book so he could look through them without being aware of my agency.

"Cheryl!" He smiled. "C'mon, let's talk."

We began the trek to the ten-seat conference table, where he looked approvingly through my pictures. "Okay, Cheryl, I like your look. We handle acting as well as modeling. Have you ever acted?"

"Some," I lied.

"Personally, I think it's better for you to stick to modeling. Here's why: It's difficult to cast models without making actors look very short in comparison. Also, models aren't expected at acting auditions, and if it's a woman casting, you'll probably put her off."

"Yeah, I've noticed that."

He laid a single sheet of paper in front of me and said, "It's a one-year, nonexclusive contract." Meaning I would be free to sign with other agencies, a good deal. Technically, signing it would be a violation of my exclusive contract with Prima. Then again, I didn't think literally twisting a model's arm was in the Prima contract.

"I'll have to think about it," I said.

His eyes narrowed. "You've signed an exclusive with someone, hmm?"

I gave him my Bambi-in-the-headlights look, which seemed to amuse him.

"No matter. I'll send you on castings, you'd be great for Fashion Week. When you book a job, I'll take the usual twenty percent, no contract necessary for now."

It was perfect. "Okay."

He gave me a small roll of labels—like the ones with your return address for sticking on envelopes—with his agency's name, address, and phone number on them. "I'll make you some copies of your pictures, and you can hand them out with a sticker at castings until we make comp cards."

Pseudo-technically, I wasn't in violation of my Prima contract, and that was more than they deserved. The best part was that Jacob didn't try to air kiss.

The next morning Tigger was sunning his glorious self on the fire escape. He gave me a look of earth-shattering love because I had just fed him tuna. I was on a diet of Whatever's in the Fridge. My cell rang; the knock of opportunity. "Hello, gorgeous." Jacob rarely called me Cheryl. "I've got a runway casting for you today." He gave me the address. I hung up eagerly. Runway! Finally!

I had a casting for Prima to go to first. Cattle call. A digital picture was snapped, a comp card taken, "Thanksforcoming."

In a Starbucks, I switched all my pictures from the blue Prima book to my black portfolio and sipped water. Without Starbucks, I might never have lived to tell the story.

At Jacob's casting on Fifth Avenue, near Trump Towers, I stared with boredom at the now-familiar security sign-in sheet as the uniformed security guard handed me a pen.

Name:
Occupation:
Reason for visit:
Time:

The guard looked like a guy who could take a joke. With extreme solemnity, I accepted the pen and wrote:

Name: Ethel McGillicuddy.
Occupation: Bricklayer.
Reason for visit: I'm gonna build a big wall
through the lobby.
Time: It's all relative.

Pleased with myself, I returned the pen and glided elegantly to the elevators.

Three stern-faced women in black sat behind a table, a prime view of Manhattan baking in the sun behind them. In front was a long stretch of wood floor for the models to walk. Three male models and two female models stood holding books from Elite and Karin. They gave me small smiles of camaraderie, we're-all-in-the-same-boat-and-doesn't-it-suck. A disinterested man, also in black mourning clothes, took our portfolios one by one to the table with the three women presiding. They would look through the book, extract a comp card, and make the model walk. A blond model did his runway swagger, while the bored man took my book. He was used to seeing model after model every runway season, an endless parade of tall young people with hopeful expressions.

"Take off your shirt, please," said one of the stern women to the male model.

Accustomed to this, he pulled his shirt off while the women narrowed their eyes, gauging muscle tone. One whispered audibly, "Ohh, nice." The others giggled. Actually giggled! The model humored them with a well-practiced naughty grin. Male models often have to show their chests in open shirts during runway shows, so being inspected topless is common. The girl models were unimpressed by all the fuss, and we patiently waited our turn, although I did check out the model's abs. He pulled his shirt on, retrieved his book, and headed for the door. "Byeeeee," cooed the formerly glacial women.

"See ya." He gave them a big smile over his shoulder, then rolled his eyes at us on his way by.

"Okay, Cheryl, you're next." The women were solemn again as they looked at my picture, with my name and Jacob's sticker below it. I walked. They nodded. I got my book and left. The security guard caught sight of me in the lobby and burst out laughing. "That was the funniest thing."

I grinned proudly. It's good to be appreciated.

A few days later, Jacob called. "I've got another runway casting for you from two to three."

"Great. Have you heard from the other company yet?"

"Yeah. You didn't book it, but don't worry, you have to go to ten castings to book one."

So I arrived at my second runway go-see thinking, *After this, eight more to go.* I could tell the security guard, in a high-rise on

Fifth Avenue near Fifty-third Street, had no sense of humor. So I behaved myself.

Upstairs behind the table were two women and one man, dressed in black, awesome view behind them. They gave me serious-faced scrutiny as I joined ten other girl models. There was only the silence, the vast expanse of spotless white carpet, and the *thumpity-thump* of my heart. One woman tapped her black-framed glasses on the table, and the sound carried clear across the room. I idly wondered if I'd left the oven on. A harassed young woman with unruly brown hair, a pocket protector, and sensible shoes scurried up to us. She had "someone's assistant" written all over her. She collected the first five girls' portfolios and conveyed them to the judgment table. The elevator opened; out stepped two models. Oh, no! More competition. Suddenly a blast of sound shattered the silence. Someone's Assistant had turned on a high-fi sound system, and a throbbing boom blasted out to match my heartbeat. The judgment table had reviewed the first girl's book, and one woman yelled over the music, "Asia, please walk." Asia, a discouragingly beautiful, raven-haired, amber-eyed creation, glided across the carpet in a short denim skirt. Her comp card was kept, her book returned. Exit Asia. Eight more girls strutted in a parade of physical perfection, although a few had stiff walks, probably induced by nerves. We watched one another; modeling in New York is not a hobby, and all the solemn-faced girls were conscious of having to pay the rent. The damned elevator kept popping out more models—seven stood behind me, one was left in front.

"Jennifer!" one of the women called.

The blonde in front of me started walking. With a guilty pang of joy, I realized that Jennifer had a terrible walk. Elbows swinging out, stilettos stomping, chin thrust forward, she forged across the carpet. Anyone would look pretty good following that act.

The judgment table stared in mute distaste and returned her book without keeping a card.

"Cheryl!"

Butterflies attacked my unsuspecting belly. I posed, ready to walk, and realized with horror that I had never runway-walked on thick carpet before. My skinny stilettos wobbled alarmingly, and the music crashed around me. Within three seconds I was going to have a very premature heart attack. Oh, what the hell. Straightening my shoulders, elbows daintily at my sides, I took the first step in time to the beat. After that, everything seemed to be in order. I kept a steady, arrogant look directed at the table.

Suddenly my left foot jerked sharply to one side. I was actually going to fall. My life flashed before me. Not a bad life, considering.

A flash of seven years toiling in ballet classes, and inspiration hit.

Pirouette!

My left ankle was almost touching the carpet. I crossed my right foot over the left and did a swift turn, hair swirling, and continued to walk without breaking stride. While keeping the sullen expression on my face, I extended a telepathic thank-you to every sadistically bitchy dance instructor I ever had. I stopped to pose. The judges were exchanging puzzled, what-the-hell-was-that-move looks. I turned and walked back in a straight line, feeling their eyes burning into the back of my neck. One of the women extracted a picture from the back of my portfolio and laid it on the table along with the others, and the assistant returned my book. With forced calm, I passed the ever-increasing line of models, stepped into the elevator, and waited for the door to close. Then I let my breath out and started to giggle helplessly.

In the lobby I slipped into flip-flops and my light khaki jacket, then set off down Fifth Avenue doing my I-am-not-a-model walk. All models develop this stride to attract less attention on the street. Hands in pockets, no swing of the hips, efficient long steps, and occasionally a baseball cap pulled low. Basically, we resemble a bunch of escaped convicts on the lam.

Two hot, muggy days passed without word from the runway casting where I unexpectedly broke into dance. It didn't bother me too much, because I was so relieved not to have fallen splat on my nose.

Ring.

"Hi, Cheryl, it's Jacob. What's your bra measurement?"

Agencies often call with unexpected questions like, "Can you swim?" when casting a model for a company. When supermodel Tyra Banks was just starting out, she lied about that one to land a swimsuit job. She nearly drowned.

"Thirty-four," I said.

"Yeah, yeah I know. What cup size?"

"A or B, depending on the bra."

"Do you fit well in a B?" he asked.

"Yeah." That was a questionable truth.

"Can you come to the office now? It's important."

"Sure." I was already in Manhattan for a Prima go-see.

In the agency, Jacob narrowed his eyes professionally at my chest; models hardly ever wear bras. "Okay, fine," he said.

We sat at the conference table, Jacob serious as usual. "There's a closed call today. I want to send just you to it." A closed call is one to which very few models—just one each from selected top agencies—are sent. It's conducted in paranoid secrecy to keep the riffraff out. Jacob was writing the information down. "It's for elegant nightgowns,

the making of a model

from the beginning . . .

Showing my early aversion to Polaroid shots, age two.

Suited up and ready to race the neighborhood boys, age nine.

My very first swimsuit shoot, ooh la la! Age four.

The one, the only, Tigger Diamond.

Photos this page courtesy of Cheryl Diamond

behind the scenes . . .

1 p.m. Wednesday, arriving for my cover shoot.

David, makeup magician to the stars, conjures up a look.

Getting the hair just right.

Stiletto for the cover shot; bare foot for the balance.

making it . . .

© 2008 by Matteo Trisolini

© 2008 by Kevin Sinclair

© 2008 by Om Rupani

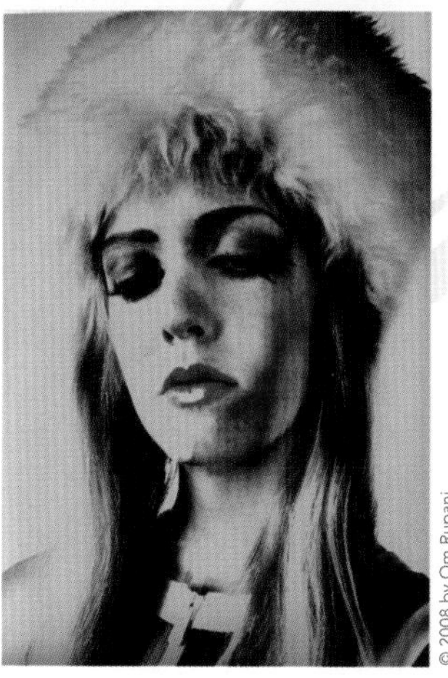
© 2008 by Om Rupani

Moscow chic, age seventeen.

Ninja Cheryl, age sixteen.

Shooting at Manhattan's Columbus Circle with Nan, who has an eye for how light can be used to fire up a picture. Age twenty.

Right: My attempt at a look of mystery, age seventeen.

Below: Vamping it up backstage at FIT, age seventeen.

Ho hum, another swimsuit shot. Age seventeen.

like negligees. You're a lot younger than the models they usually use, but let's try anyway. If they ask, say you're eighteen."

I nodded, processing the data.

He finished writing and handed me the paper: "VS Direct. Grace Building, Forty-second and Sixth. Fifth floor. See Claire Daves."

"You have to go over now," Jacob said.

"What's VS Direct?" I asked.

"Victoria's Secret."

Oh boy, oh boy, this would be one for the grandkiddies. The Grace Building is shaped like a giant curved sail. Forty-nine stories of smooth, gleaming pale stone and glass. In the massive lobby I was vetted by security at their circular gold desk, which resembled a spaceship's control panel. I stepped out of the gold elevator onto the fifth floor's completely white marble hallway. At the end of the hall were tall glass doors; a receptionist's desk, with a dark-haired woman presiding, was clearly visible behind them. She looked up and locked eyes with me. My heels made surprisingly loud clicks as I forged in slow motion toward the door. I pushed it open, having to use my shoulder for extra heft, and approached the desk.

"Yes," she said.

"Cheryl Diamond. I'm here to see Claire Daves." I was very pleased with myself for remembering not only my name but someone else's, too.

"I'll tell her. Have a seat, please."

No other models were present. I sat on one of the straight-backed chairs and inspected my surroundings. It went down as the most impressive company office I had ever seen: all marble, resembling an art museum, with twelve-foot pictures of supermodels Gisele Bündchen and Adriana Lima modeling bras lit on the wall. The receptionist returned along a seemingly endless carpeted hallway. "She'll be right out."

The walls across from and behind me were covered entirely in mirrors. I watched myself sitting there—black top, short jean skirt, portfolio in hand—and wondered what would become of me.

"Cheryl."

I got up. An attractive woman in her late thirties came forward for a firm, yet not bone-crushing, shake. We proceeded down the blue-carpeted hallway; I prayed not to have to pirouette again. The hallway opened up to a large room stuffed full with endless chrome racks of lacy, dainty underwear thingies. A faint aroma of Chanel No. 5 was in the air.

Claire produced a tape and took bust, waist, and hip readings.

"Where are you from, Cheryl?"

Clients always ask this puzzling question. I never know how to answer, not having stayed in one place long enough to brand it "home."

"Colorado." I've passed through the airport.

"It's beautiful there."

"Yes, great skiing."

"Mmm, can you try this on?" She held up a short blue nightie.

There was a row of white-curtained changing rooms along the wall. I stepped into one while she looked through my book. In the nightie, I assessed my reflection standing there barefoot, hair loose.

Oh, horrors! I looked sixteen!

No. No-no-no-nope-nix-nada-nein.

"Don't put your heels on with it," Claire called through the curtain, thereby burying my last hope of appearing older. I stepped out, and Claire looked me over. "You have gorgeous hair," she said unexpectedly.

"Thanks," I said happily. Clients never compliment you unless they really mean it. In fact, they rarely speak to you.

The negligee had the reverse effect of making me look adorable instead of devastatingly sexy. Curses on my age. Claire thanked me and kept a picture with Jacob's sticker on it. I managed not to trip on my way out. A definite success.

I walked along Forty-second, smiling giddily. Being at a closed casting for Victoria's Secret is quite the accomplishment at sixteen. Yeah, baby.

My cell rang immediately. "How'd it go?" Jacob snapped.

"Good, she was very nice."

"Did she make you try anything on?" If clients ask a model to try things on, it's an indication of interest.

"Yeah, one negligee, and she said I had gorgeous hair."

"Good, well done. If they don't book you this time because of your age, we'll send you back in six months or so."

"Okay." I was happy that he was happy. I was becoming an approval junkie. Feeling extremely hungry, I popped into the brightly colored, partially open-air Europa Café for a bagel. At a table I relaxed, preparing to savor the first bite.

Ring.

"It's Jacob again. Where are you?"

"Forty-second and Fifth."

"There's a runway show tonight. One model is sick, and they're replacing her now." He stopped briefly to breathe, "Get over there as fast as possible; try to make it at six p.m." He recited an address in the trendy West Village.

"Take the V or F train downtown from Forty-second," he said, and I was off. It was a difference from Prima. They expected models who had been in the city for only a week to know their way around perfectly. And they delighted in saying, "It's in Noho, west of that other place we sent you." Click.

It was 5:50. I sweated down the stairs to the subway and made a desperate dash for the rapidly closing F train door. I hurtled through the tiny gap and stopped my momentum by banging my hip into the centrally located metal pole. I pretended it didn't hurt and pondered where the nearest hospital would be.

"Wow, cool jump!" A young guy with an artfully crafted Afro grinned, holding his bike upright.

"Thanks." I sat down gingerly.

At the next stop a pale, scowling old woman, who reminded me instantly of that tight-faced witch in *Snow White*, boarded regally. She stood directly across from me and extracted an extra-large black plastic garbage bag from her Vuitton purse. She gave the entire subway car a shudder of intense disgust, flapped the garbage bag open like a beach towel, and laid it across three seats before sitting down. The young guy with the bike made the mistake of smiling. She turned on him immediately, fierce painted eyebrows joining in a frown. "Vat you looking at, azzhole?"

My eyes popped wide open.

The bike guy replied, Manhattan-style, "You, you crazy witch." He was still grinning.

I started to smile, trying desperately not to. The witch's eyes burned into mine. "Vat you smiling at, bimbo?"

"Jesus Christ," I said, bounding off the train at my stop.

Time: 6:07 p.m. I triumphantly entered the chilly, dark interior of the club being taken over for the runway show. It was even better than Club Vue, with more endless expanse of dark hardwood floors. The runway was dimly, almost eerily illuminated in the center. Someone's Assistant materialized ghostlike in front of me.

"You're late," she informed me, sour-faced.

Oh, sorry, maybe I should have taken the helicopter.

I gave her a big smile: Where have you been all my life? "I'm here to see Susan."

"Backstage," she snipped.

I climbed a few steps to the backstage area. It was even darker and colder, and goose bumps tickled my arms. Seven girl models were present, near the chrome racks of clothes. The models smiled nicely. There's actually a lot of camaraderie among models who are signed to an agency and on the casting circuit. A slim brunette with a manic smile appeared. I assumed it was Susan, the designer. She confirmed this by announcing, "Hi, I'm Susan. Can I see your books?"

Weighed down with eight portfolios, she staggered to a table and reviewed them. Miscellaneous people pounded around backstage, arguing about the wiring and lights.

Susan, seven comp cards and my picture in hand, instructed, "I'd like each of you to walk when I call your name." She skipped down the steps and stood on the floor in front of the runway. A black curtain shielded the cavernous backstage from view of the club; a small opening allowed models to walk through and onto the catwalk.

"Louisa!" Susan barked, reading from the back of a comp card.

Louisa walked the runway, posed, and returned. The silence was broken only by her rhythmically clicking stilettos. Four more girls were called.

"Cheryl!"

Shivering backstage, I jumped to attention. *Click, click, click*. The lone, faintly lit figure of Susan watched me, eyes narrowed. I posed, and returned. The remaining two models walked. Susan bit her lip, looking through our cards.

"All right," she said. "I'd like Louisa . . . Megan, and . . . Cheryl to walk again. The rest can go." The girls who hadn't been called back shrugged good-naturedly and gathered up their things.

The three of us walked again.

A silence.

Susan came backstage. "Thanks for coming. Cheryl, can you stay?"

Yay, yay, yippee, Geronimo! "Yes."

The models retrieved portfolios and were good sports, waving to me as they left.

"The show starts in two and a half hours," Susan said. "Makeup and hair should be here soon, so it's best if you stay, all right?"

"Sure."

She vanished to discuss wiring.

I sat on one of the white designer lounges, staring up at the runway in rapture, and dialed on my cell. "Hi, can I speak with Jacob, please?" I told the secretary.

"May I ask who's calling, please?"

I always have the urge to reply, *No, you may not*. "Cheryl Diamond." I was being so well behaved. Muzak invaded my ear. Lah-de-dah-dee-di—

"Gorgeous?"

"Yeah, hi, I got the runway show!" I whispered giddily.

"Well done. The pay's just four hundred, that's standard. I've been invited to the show anyway, so I'll bring a payment slip for you."

We hung up. Bored in the dark cave, I discovered a stack of the club's business cards and proceeded to draw Tigger on the back of one. He ended up looking like a spoon with legs.

The first model arrived. She dropped onto the lounge across from me, brushing short auburn hair out of green eyes. "Hey, I'm Lottie. It's sooooo humid, I had to, like, swim here."

I smiled. "I'm Cheryl."

"Is that French?"

"Yeah, *chérie* means 'dear' or 'beloved.'" Curious that most people seem to loathe me.

"Cool, cool."

She saw the doodled-on business card. "What's this?" She pointed at spoon-face Tigger like an art connoisseur.

"My cat."

"Does he really look like this?"

"No, he's normal." We both started giggling.

"Are makeup and hair here yet?" Lottie asked.

At that moment a short, slim man exploded into the room, swaying designer-blue-jean-clad hips. With bleached blond hair spiky from gel, he trailed a large black bag. "Hiii, ladies." He waved daintily at us; we wiggled our fingers back.

"Makeup! Hi!" Susan declared, obviously stressed.

"Makeup, my name's Makeup?" He pretended to be mortally offended.

"Raul. Hi."

"What-ev-er, too late, I'm not friends with you anymore." He tossed his head and sashayed backstage to set up. That guy needed musical accompaniment.

Susan massaged her temples and gave her mean assistant drink orders for Starbucks.

The hairstylist, a slight, ponytailed man, glided in. "Hiii, I'm Fugi." He wheeled his huge black bag backstage. I frowned. "Isn't there a mountain called Fuji?"

Lottie nodded solemnly. "I do believe you're right."

Three more models arrived simultaneously, all dressed in worn jeans, loose tank tops, and flip-flops. Once you've booked a job, the model-client relationship resembles that of an older married couple. Dressing up? Why bother?

A woman with short, brightly dyed red hair and multiple piercings rolled in her black bag. The second makeup artist had arrived. In the gold-flecked black marble bathroom, I washed my eye makeup off. Susan intercepted me outside. "I need you to try outfits on." She thrust a short green silk dress at me. Once I had emerged with it on, she circled me, one eye nearly shut, contemplating.

"Mmmm, no." She shoved her nose mere inches from mine. "Damn it! Your eyes are blue, not green." She managed to make it sound like my fault. "That won't work with this dress!" she yelped. An endless stream of dresses followed. Susan was getting more and more agitated, beginning to yell at the lighting and sound guys for no apparent reason. They pretty much ignored her. I returned to the bathroom and slipped on a mid-thigh-length, ultraclingy, black spaghetti-strap dress.

"Yesssssss," Susan hissed through clenched teeth when she saw me. A long, dark blue dress with a très risqué slit was my second outfit for the show.

"You will wear these shoes." Susan dangled a pair of silver Jimmy Choo three-inch stilettos.

"Ah, these are a size eight, I'm a ten."

"You'll manage." She whirled and stomped off.

Nice.

Now all I had to do was chop off my big toe.

Fugi wielded a straight iron. Raul was deeply absorbed in intricate eye makeup, while the pierced woman applied foundation to another model. All twelve models for the show were lounging backstage, trading industry anecdotes. Assistant returned from a successful voyage to Starbucks and dispensed drinks. *Has she poisoned mine?* Oh well. I took a big sip. Life is full of risks.

The models traded résumés: how long in the business, which agency, are they any good? I was the "baby" of the show, since all the other girls had reached the ripe old age of nineteen or twenty. One of the models, twenty-four-year-old Vera, looked out of place. She was about two inches under the minimum five-nine height requirement and, by unforgiving modeling standards, ten pounds over fighting weight. It didn't take long for Vera to bug everyone with her prima donna attitude.

"Get me some champagne," she commanded Lottie, in her thick Russian accent.

Lottie sighed. "Get it yourself, okay?"

How had Vera and her ego slipped through the ultracompetitive casting process? Fugi, misting gloss onto a model's hair, was slightly distracted by Raul giving him the eye. They held each other's gaze through a haze of Citré Shine.

With great ferocity and concentration, I played Space Dude on my cell phone, which was low on minutes and reduced to only taking messages. When my thumbs cramped up and people were giving my feverish face weird looks, I called a temporary truce with my galactic enemies.

"I looove your makeup," Fugi gushed to Raul, admiring a model's completed face.

"Ohh, stop!" Raul blushed. Cue a romantic song. . . .

When the moon hits your eye like a big pizza pie . . .

An hour later, Susan was in a state of mild hysteria, trying to organize her assistants—there were three of them scurrying in all directions, their feet messing up the wiring. Guests were beginning to arrive in impeccable tailored suits, with fashionable crewnecks underneath, instead of a conformist tie. The women were attired in attractive fake tans and jewelry. Almost everyone was a good twenty-five years older than me. I peeked out from behind the curtain and yawned. A strange reaction, since I was excited and more than a little nervous. All the charging across Manhattan to castings in the sweltering heat was getting to me.

A posse of squealing women—friends of Susan—came backstage toting Cristal champagne. Pop went the cork. Vera made sure she got the first glass. Susan's friends raised their glasses. "To the show," they said, giggling.

I cautiously dipped my tongue into the glass to see if I liked the taste any better than a year ago, when my dad and I had methodically, daintily, sampled beer, wine, champagne, and vodka. We considered this educational. We consider everything we want to do to be educational. Don't tell Mom.

I balanced my still full glass, looking for a place to get rid of it. Vera snapped, "You drinking zat?"

"No, but I put my ton—"

She grabbed the glass and drained it.

I wrinkled my nose, smug with the knowledge that she now had my cooties.

A short, roly-poly man in his midfifties, real tan, skipped backstage on the balls of his tiny feet. The gargantuan security guards let him through. He waved at Susan, who ran over and leaned down to hug the butterball. Vera looked up from her chair. "Darlink," she said.

He planted a sloppy kiss on Vera's thin lips. "I've got a surprise, kid."

"Vell, vell." Vera appeared completely bored by him; he, condescending toward her.

"It'll be here soon, kid." He patted the top of her head like a dog and wandered off. She went back to flipping through *Vogue* as if nothing had happened.

Outside the curtain, the place was filling rapidly, guests talking animatedly in groups while sipping creatively decorated drinks. The makeup woman hurried over to me. "Hi. I've got to get your makeup done, the show's soon."

We headed for her chair.

Susan stopped us. "These are my friends." She motioned to a giggling, already made-up trio. "They'd like you to work some magic, mmmkay?"

The makeup artist shook her piercings. "This model and Lottie haven't had hair or makeup done yet. We're cramped for time."

Susan turned bitchy to show off. "I don't want Cheryl's hair done; I like it natural. I'm paying *you*, mmmkay? So fix these ladies up first, and I want my face done too."

A tense silence.

The makeup artist opened her eyes wide. "Mmmkay, Susan."

Ohh, yeah.

Butterball was staring at me from across the room. He winked saucily.

I pretended not to have seen that.

Lottie whispered discreetly in my ear, "Cheryl, check him out, against the wall."

After a few seconds, I casually scanned the backstage area. Leaning confidently against the wall was what mothers like to call Trouble. Tall, well muscled, blond, dressed all in white—slacks and a short-sleeved white shirt. The all-white look is hard for guys to pull off, but he managed.

"Doesn't he look just like that guy in *The Fast and the Furious*?" Lottie asked.

"Exactly."

One of Susan's friends, a painfully thin brunette, now professionally made up, sipped champagne and sighed. "Omigosh, isn't that guy over there just a hunk! He produces television. . . . Sexaaayyy! Haw-haw."

She was so embarrassing.

Select photographers were being let backstage to snap the models preshow. The other girls were all fully made up, with dark, dramatic eyes. Both Lottie and I had washed our faces clean. I thanked God I was having a good skin week and smiled prettily at the photographers. I moved across the room to ask the makeup artists when they would be done with Susan's endless stream of friends, relatives, Sunday school teachers, etc. True makeup artists won't be hurried. Once they start on someone's face, even if they don't want to be doing it, they will not stop until it's perfect. It's a matter of pride. Raul and the redheaded woman were deep in concentration, making intricate additions to Susan's pals. Without asking, I knew it was going to take awhile. I was heading down the hallway toward the clothes racks when Susan yelped, "Where are you going, Cheryl?"

Clients are always paranoid about letting a model out of their sight, lest she meet a cowboy and elope or something. This would force the client to do a last-minute recast, a horrifying thought. So they shepherd the models adoringly. After the show, they wouldn't care if I took a flying leap into the Hudson River.

"Just stay nearby, mmmkay, honey?" Susan panted.

"Okay."

She plopped into Raul's vacated makeup chair. "I want a really dramatic lip." Raul wielded a dark red lipstick, caught my eye, and shook his head in disbelief.

A hand on my arm. "Hi, beautiful."

I turned to face the blond man in white.

"I'm Steve." He smiled.

"Hey." I avoided eye contact and looked at Lottie across the room. She opened her mouth and eyes wide, the internationally recognized signal for "Omigosh."

"Do you by any chance"—he widened the grin, cue the *Smooth Operator* song—"have a name?"

"Cheryl." Lottie was mouthing confusing instructions to me.

"'Dear,' right? My mother's French," he said.

"So's mine."

"I hope it's not the same one."

I frowned. "I seriously doubt that."

"Aww, come on, just kidding."

"Gorgeous!" Jacob marched unexpectedly up to me, looking spiffy in his suit. He gave Steve a look of deep distrust, typecasting him as a cowboy who might steal his model.

"Hi, Jacob," I said. "This is Steve. Steve, this is my agent."

"Yes, we've met before," Jacob acknowledged.

The modeling/entertainment industry is a very small world. They shook, holding eye contact.

"Nice tie," Steve said with a grin.

"Cute T-shirt," Jacob said in a straight-faced monotone.

I said nothing. Sometimes I know exactly when to shut up. Having established that they each resented the other's presence around me, Jacob and Steve seemed at ease with one another. They actually began discussing whether I would "translate well onto the screen." They agreed that yeah, I would, and plans were hatched. Then Steve was torn away to get hit on by a blushing friend of Susan, whose skeletal hand massaged his arm. He kept an amused eye on us. Jacob extracted an envelope from his suit jacket and gave it to me. "Payment slip," he said. Payment slips are a carbon copy slip the size of a check. The client's name, amount of payment, and model's name are written and signed on the slip. One copy goes to the model, one to the model's agency, and one to the client.

"I'm going out there," Jacob said, referring to the lounge, "to talk to some people. See you after the show. Do well."

With that he was gone, leaving me to contemplate the consequences of tripping, falling off the runway, and squishing several VIP guests. I had told him that I possessed vast runway experience from shows in Paris. It had sounded so good at the time.

Immediately Steve reappeared next to me. "How long have you been with him?"

"About a week."

"And you're already doing a show. Nice going."

"Darlink!" Vera summoned Butterball to her side. "Vat time is it?"

"Time to get a watch, kid. Har, har."

Steve observed them, obviously entertained. I lifted my chin in Butterball/Vera's direction and asked, "What's the deal there?"

"Oh, it's a good one. The Russian bitch—don't smile, she is—married him to be able to stay in the U.S."

"They're married!"

"For about three days. This is the honeymoon."

I laughed. "Does he know the reason she married him?"

"Sure, I mean, why else, right? But he's loaded and connected . . . one of his connections happens to be Susan. He put some backing money into this show, and so Susan let Vera model in it."

That explained everything.

Steve shrugged. "It's pretty common. That's how rich kids get into modeling." He moved in closer. "Listen, Cher—"

"Oh, I've got to get my makeup done. See ya." I escaped. He looked amused.

Makeup was still busy. Lottie bounded up. "What'd he say? Are you going out with him?"

I shook my head. "He's twenty years older than me."

"So? This is New York."

"Why does everyone keep reminding me which city I'm in?"

"GET DRESSED!" Susan dashed down the hall. "We're starting soon!"

I managed to corner her. "Susan, I haven't had my makeup done, and neither has Lottie."

"Shit! Why not?"

I looked at her, amazed at how people can forget facts when it's convenient for them.

"RAAUUUUUUUUUUUUUUUUUULLLL!" she yodeled. He looked up from one of her friends. "Yeah?"

"Well, don't bother with her, get the models done, goddammit!"

Raul's mouth opened and hung there.

Susan's arms flailed like a traffic cop. "Lottie, go to makeup now. Cheryl, put the blue dress on and then get your makeup done. . . ."

She paused to suck air in. "Raul, go light on their foundation, just do eyes." She ran off.

I jogged into the bathroom, cradling the long blue dress. Vera was hunched over the black marble counter, snorting a line of coke through a fifty-dollar bill. She raised her head to say, "Hi," then sniffed calmly.

"Hey." By then nothing surprised or shocked me; I headed for one of the stalls.

"You vant some?"

Not stopping, I shot back, "Nah, I like my brain cells."

I changed and passed her again to leave. "Freak," she muttered.

I turned and grinned. "Welcome to America."

She smiled predatorily into the mirror.

All hell had broken loose outside. The guests had been cleared from backstage, leaving the models and assistants free to go nuts.

"What's the order?"

"Seen my shoes? They're black."

"Move. Move, move!" from Susan.

A few models had stripped and were changing in front of everyone, a practice that has always mystified me. Half-naked but fully made-up, Lottie hollered at me, "Rauuuul's ready!"

I squished my protesting toes into the high heels. Oh, the pain. Holding a palate of eye shadow, Raul worked frantically on me. Runway shows always start a fashionable half hour late, but we were already forty-five minutes behind schedule and the guests were becoming restless, seated expectantly on either side of the runway.

"Line up!" Susan commanded all the models.

Raul followed me into the queue, trying desperately to match my eyes to the other girls'.

The lounge lights shut off.

Excited whispers.

Powerful lights snapped on above the runway.

A horde of ten photographers were crowded on the floor at the end of the catwalk, waiting for the shot.

I began to panic slightly.

"Wait here, I'm getting the lip gloss." Raul charged off.

My heart pounded. I felt cold and hot at the same time. The music started, and the first model stepped onto the runway.

The next girl stepped out; two models remained in front of me. Could I even walk in these shoes? I was in mild shock, biting my nails.

Mommmmmmy!

In ten seconds it would be my turn. Rows of people watching, photographers waiting to capture it on film. Yikes!

"Open your mouth," Raul whispered.

I opened it, and he brushed lip gloss on.

Susan, at my elbow, looked me in the eye and hissed, "Don't fall."

That was the absolute worst thing to say to a model about to walk. And Susan knew it. Perverse.

It made me angry. I had survived Jersey City, open calls, and Fabriziou! In comparison, this was a piece of cake.

"Go!" Raul said urgently.

I set my jaw. The fierce expression I had stepping onto a runway for the first time was no fake. The photographers' powerful flashes unexpectedly blinded me. White circles swam in front of my eyes long after each picture was snapped. Strangely, I was calm, all the apprehension faded—no worries, mate. This was fun.

An appreciative "oohhh" emanated from the audience as I kept walking. Then I posed; there was a flurry of flashes as the photographers jostled one another for the best angle. I gazed at them with hostility and returned down the runway, passing an advancing stoned-eyed Vera. She swung her arms wildly, almost hitting me as we passed. It wasn't even intentional. I passed the curtain to backstage and almost ran into Lottie. "Wow, Cheryl, friggin' phenomenal walk." She grinned.

"Thanks!" I was extremely relieved and pumped.

"Change!" Susan said, as one of her assistants handed me the short black dress. I pushed the bathroom door open.

"Change here!" Susan shrilled.

There was no way I was stripping in front of everyone, including her male assistants. I pretended not to hear. Ten seconds later I reappeared and handed my blue dress off to an assistant, making it a point to say thanks. I would not be following in Hillary's angry stomping footsteps. I ran back into line and lifted my knees, high-stepping onto the runway. This time went as well as the first, maybe even better.

Almost as soon as it started, the show was over. All the models walked single file onto the runway and lined it on either side. The audience clapped loudly, then stood. Susan walked out, the picture of serenity, to acknowledge the applause. She beamed sweetly, and all the models smiled and clapped dutifully. Then we filed off. Sighs of relief all around.

I entered the makeup area and was confronted by a large, intricately decorated chocolate cake. Butterball presided proudly over it, knife in pudgy hand. Steve was watching him, trying not to laugh. I teetered in gingerly on my stilettos with the other models, all fresh off the runway. Vera smiled, showing her fangs.

"Ohhhh, cake, yessssss," all the girls said.

Champagne was popped. Steve raised his glass to Butterball/Vera and actually said, "A toast to the happy couple."

Butterball brought a piece of cake over to me. "You were stunning, absolutely *stunning.* Would you like to have dinner sometime?"

"You're married." I grinned, for lack of anything better to do with my face.

"In name only," Butterball pronounced solemnly.

"I have a boyfriend." He was so useful.

"Get rid of him! Har-har."

What a doofus.

Steve walked up. "I think Vera wants something," he told Butterball. Butterball looked over at Vera and shook his head. "Three days married and already a nag." Then to me, "So dinner it is?"

"I really can't." I really, really don't want to.

He sighed and went to Vera, who seemed extremely coked out.

"You were by far the best," Steve said, appearing sincere.

"Oh, thanks." He might have been lying, but I decided to believe him because it made me feel good.

I opened my mouth to take a bite of cake. Steve leaned in. "Can I walk you home?"

"Uh, I live a long way from here."

"So we'll go to my place."

"Ha. Ha. Ha." My nervous laugh. Activated in situations when I'm in over my head and just want to leave.

"So?" he asked.

"No."

"Why?"

People crowding around; the smell of champagne; loud, squeaky voices; too much perfume—I started feeling queasy.

"I'm sixteen, an—"

"You're what? You shouldn't tell people that," he said.

"Why?" Payback.

He grimaced at me.

Susan called for attention. "I'd like the models to circulate outside a bit, please, mmmkay?" I was relieved to escape Steve and clicked down the stairs and past security into the lounge.

Lottie caught up with me. "I think you lost him." Her eyes were wide.

"What?"

"That Steve guy, he started talking to another model."

"Really?"

"Yeah." She looked concerned. "I hear he's a playboy anyw—"

"Great! I really lost him, huh?" I said, relieved, and looked for Jacob.

"You're really unique, Cheryl, you know?"

"You mean I'm weird."

"That too." She laughed.

Lottie and I circulated through the room. Everyone swerved to come over and congratulate us as if we'd just scaled the Himalayas.

"How long have you been runway modeling?" a woman asked, looking up at me in awe.

"A few years now." I never admit being inexperienced at anything.

"I could tell. I said to my friend, 'Look at her, she's the most professionally experienced one.'"

"Well, thank you."

The men charged. I sidestepped, smiling and nodding at everything. How did I fall into this mad world? Oh, right, it all started with an open call, and I went voluntarily.

A middle-aged man beamed. "Bellissima!" He kissed his fingertips. "Would you like to come for a party on my yacht?"

"Ha. Ha. Ha."

I eventually bumped into Jacob, who was looking at me with an expression of respectful scrutiny. "You really know how to handle people, very in control all the time."

I was deeply flattered. "Thanks."

He waved his hand dismissively. "Two things: First, you made me look very good tonight; second, you booked the other runway show."

My jaw dropped. The one where I did a pirouette!

"Life is very strange," I said.

"So young, so wise," Jacob smirked.

Various guests came up to Jacob, asking who I was. "Cheryl Diamond!" he replied, as if shocked that they didn't already know. I went backstage and changed into my jean skirt and flip-flops. Red blisters were already forming from the too-small stilettos. Susan signed all the models' payment slips. She had retuned to human form.

Lottie and I agreed to e-mail each other. I threaded through the lounge, getting invited to various after-parties, which I avoided because everyone just gets drunk. I handed Jacob his copy of the payment slip and began in a businesslike voice, "Can you advance the money before the client pays?"

Clients usually take three to four months to pay the model's agency, which is a real drag.

"Sure, no problem, you can come by the office tomorrow and pick up the check."

That was shockingly easy. I told Jacob that I was heading home. He told me to get some rest, for Chrissake. I told him I would, goddamn it. He patted my back proudly and I left.

Limos were lined up outside. Butterball and Vera were boarding a black stretch. "Sharon!" Butterball hailed.

"It's Cheryl," I said.

"Right! We're going to Club Suede, coming?" He pointed into the limo.

"No, thanks. Have fun." The thought of having more contact with Vera was chilling.

I stood on the sidewalk. So much had happened. Victoria's Secret, my first runway show, and booking my second, all in one day. A phone booth beckoned across the street. I ran to it and dropped in a quarter for one minute of calling time, anywhere. Raul and Fugi passed, hand in hand. *Ring, ring, rin—*

"Hello?"

"Hey, Mom! Now just CALM DOWN!"

The Monkeys

Gazing out my window, I observed my hood sleepily, still hungover from last night's runway extravaganza.

There is nothing like the almighty dollar to get my weary leggies in motion. I presented my hopeful self to Jacob's non-plussed secretary and pocketed my much-needed check. Then I scurried down a few blocks to Prima. Hilda recognized me but still refused to crack a smile. I stocked up on my comp cards from their invisible perch behind the filing cabinet. La-shawnda regarded me with intense hatred; I had given up analyzing her, knowing a lost cause when it bared its fangs.

"Hey, you!" Veronika barked.

I turned, recognizing my name.

"There's a casting for Zang Toi." She scribbled the address, handed it to me indifferently, and locked gazes with her computer.

I was headed out of the "No models allowed" booking room when Veronika's voice stopped me.

"You really have to do something with your hair." I turned to face her. Veronika narrowed her eyes at me. "It looks like shit." She went back to her computer.

That hit me between the eyes. I quickly arranged a grin on my face. "Thanks, Veronika."

She looked up, surprised at my reaction. I could understand that Veronika was stressed, organizing her army of models, but the verbal jabs seemed oddly calculated. Considering it in the elevator, I realized that the comment had its intended subconscious effect.

Doubt.

I nibbled a nail. It was becoming a habit.

Threading along ultra-high-rent West Fifty-seventh Street off Fifth Avenue into Zang Toi's building, I went through the usual ritual of a casting.

TGIF. I collapsed on my couch, prepared to lick my wounds over the weekend. My traumatic down-and-out experience had faded into Fact. Like stubbing your toe, it hurts like hell when it happens, but afterward all you can remember is the fact that it happened, not the pain.

I spent Saturday morning in worn jeans under a tree in Central Park, attracting babies and brooding about Prima. Babies are amazingly intelligent—they can sense which people like kids and present themselves with gummy smiles directly in front of me. I stuck out my tongue and crossed my eyes at a redheaded toddler. He giggled. Why had Prima become so negative lately?

"Micholly." He patted the front of his dungarees.

"Hi, Charlie." I'm fluent in baby-speak. "Me Cheryl."

"Hi, Cwewl."

"So, what's up?" I raised an eyebrow as if speaking to an adult.

"I'm twee."

"I'm sixteen."

"That's ooold."

"I feel old, Charlie."

"Reawy?"

"Yes, my friend."

"I go to pweschool."

"Learn anything there?"

"Nope."

An irate mother appeared. "Charlie, you naughty, naughty boy! I couldn't find you!" She shot me a suspicious look and removed Charlie from my corrupting influence. Charlie looked over his shoulder and waved apologetically while his mother baby-talked to him. I have never understood people who converse with children as if they are imbeciles.

Having developed a light tan, I exited the park at 79th Street and climbed white marble steps to the gigantic Museum of Natural History. An expensively dressed woman in her eighties was carefully descending. "You're very tall," she observed.

"I had knee implants."

"Oh! How funny." She leaned toward me. "I'm going to let you in on a secret."

"What?" I affected eagerness.

She adjusted her Coach purse, relishing the moment. "They charge seven dollars and fifty cents admission." She motioned at the museum, and her eyes unexpectedly took on a scheming glint. "But the small print says it's only a 'suggested admission.' You can just give them a dime." She grinned. "I come every week."

This kind of insider information has always interested me. "Cool!"

Having safely passed on the secret of the universe to the younger generation, she waved good-bye.

I kept a watchful eye on a three-story-high dinosaur skeleton that presided near the ticket counters. Feeling generous, I handed over a quarter to the bored woman behind the counter. I was genuinely awed by the museum; the life-size blue whale suspended invisibly from the ceiling and the endless gem room have always been my favorites. A few more toddlers hit on me.

On Sunday, midday light filtered through the blinds. I balanced groggily on one foot to adjust them and plopped limply back onto my darkened bed. Tigger lay on his back near my pillow, playing dead. My cell rang.

Prima's number appeared on caller ID. I frowned. Agencies aren't even open on the weekends.

"Hello?"

"Helloo, Cherilll, this is—"

"Hi, Fabriziou."

"Yes, where are you?"

"Home."

"Can you come to the agency right now?" Some of his fake accent was fading.

"Yes, why?"

"Clairol is here!" he hissed. "A representative from Clairol is casting for models and he *requested* to see you."

"Okay, I'll be there in forty minutes."

"Hurry, Cherilll, this is very important."

A "request" is when a client asks to meet with a specific model, instead of the usual selection an agency sends over. Out of bed—why is this such short notice?—pulling on a jean skirt—a model is usually told about requests in advance—black tank top over my head and brush the teethies. Without further ado, I brushed mascara on, charged out the door and down the stairs, and banged the side of my head against a devilishly low ceiling beam.

"Arrrgghh."

When I emerged, panting, from the subway near Prima, my cell rang immediately.

"Cherilll, where *are* you?"

"I'll be there in five minutes."

"Okey, okey, hurry."

I stepped off the elevator on Prima's floor. It was strangely quiet, no models rushing in or out, and blessedly no Hilda at the reception desk. The booking room was deserted, the computers showing little fishes swimming back and forth to save the screens. Fabriziou and a tall, slender, dark-haired man were sitting at the glass table. I rounded the glass corner and they stood. Fab gave me a halfhearted air kiss in the vague vicinity of my shoulder and introduced me to Michael as we shook.

"Well, it's good to finally meet you." Michael smiled without sarcasm.

"Yes, we were waiting here alone for an hour," Fab chirped.

There was a massive pile of Prima comp cards on the table, each of a different female model. Michael looked through my book. He seemed genuinely nice and straightforward, a rarity in the industry.

"Is this your natural color?" Michael asked.

"Yes."

"Yes," Fab confirmed, "Cherilll's hair is very healthy."

Michael gave Fab an ill-concealed tired look. I was amazed that he was still sane after an entire hour in solitary confinement with Fab.

"For the show we're having at Clairol headquarters," Michael said, "we'd like to demonstrate a new highlighting method for blond hair. Yours is already very light, so you won't see much difference."

I paused, thinking it over.

"We wouldn't highlight all the hair, just two pieces near the face."

"It's okey," Fab assured me. "Brad Jones is doing it."

Brad Jones, the acclaimed hairstylist with a salon in Trump Towers and a great rep.

"All right," I said.

Michael kept my comp card, along with a few others, and told Fab that he would phone on Monday when they'd decided which models to use. Michael exited cheerfully.

Fab and I faced each other in the deserted agency. "Good." Fab nodded. "We'll see who he chooses tommorow. You have maybe a fifty-fifty chance."

Air kiss, and I left.

Monday afternoon. I stood near the color copier in the booking room while Veronika made prints of some of my other pictures to keep in addition to my comp cards. I wondered if she summoned me to the agency with these excuses so she could criticize me, while La-shawnda murdered me with her eyes. Veronika shot mild put-downs: "You have to wear more eye makeup. You look too blond, like a freaking albino."

I didn't react, except to nod with amused detachment in the hopes of annoying her. Veronica watched me carefully; when she sensed I was shutting down against the barrage, she tossed a compliment. "Almost no one is this naturally blond and tans well. It's a good seller."

I regarded her warily, although the compliment was oddly very reassuring.

Nassar, in usual mourning apparel, was discussing lunch options with Amy while ridiculing a girl who had come to the open call.

"She was like Miss Teen America, all cutesy, you know?" He winced with distaste. There is a potent disdain in the modeling industry toward beauty pageants and their contestants. Nassar began mimicking the delicate-hand-flapping-in-front-of-fakely-tearful-face-as-crown-is-accepted routine, while everyone snickered. "Pageants, it's where wannabe models go to die," he snapped, and picked up his ringing phone. "Prima. Nassar."

Amy looked up and smiled at me, an action that threatened to short-circuit my brain.

"But Cheryl!" Veronika declared, making another copy. "Don't ever tan deeper than you are now. High-fashion clients hate that."

"Okay," I said, wishing she would leave me in peace.

Fab breezed nonchalantly into the booking room, handed some papers to Nassar, and saw me. "Hellooo, Cherilll, you booked Clairol." He patted my arm and exited.

I grinned and turned to Veronika. "Clairol! That's great."

"Uh-huh," she said.

I felt a jolt of anger but didn't let it show.

The news of my landing Clairol had an interesting effect on the bookers. They regarded me, heads cocked to one side, with newfound curiosity. Like a teenage boy who just discovered that girls had another purpose besides being fun to terrorize.

I set off happily to my last casting of the day. Entering the company's twenty-fourth-floor office, I spotted Lottie demonstrating a yoga position to the other models. She stood straight on one stiletto, the other foot crossed above her knee, hands in a praying position, eyes closed, face serene. I laughed.

One eye popped open. "Hello, Cheryl." She smiled calmly. "I'm demonstrating the art of meditation."

"Ahh," I said profoundly.

A secretary entered the room. Lottie hastily abandoned the art of meditation, and we followed the secretary to try on clothes.

"Cheryl, do you wanna get something to eat after this?"

"Sure."

We blinked at the sunlight on Sixth Avenue. "Let's go to the Olive Garden!" Lottie squealed.

"The Olive Garden? Jesus."

"Oh, I know it's lame, but it's so lame that it's kinda fun."

As we walked, Lottie began talking about the sorry state of our environment. For a moment I thought she was referring to the modeling industry.

I've never been a big fan of the Olive Garden, but Lottie managed to make it fun. Later, full of pasta, we walked toward Lottie's apartment in Hell's Kitchen. Lottie shoved open a building door with a bullet hole in it, veins of shattered glass extending from the point of impact like spider legs.

"I'm in apartment Three-C. You have to drop by sometime."

I regarded the wounded door.

"It's not that recent," she said.

Veronika e-mailed me the information on the Clairol job, held at their New York headquarters. I was actually expected to appear at six-thirty a.m.

Obscene!

But, I was getting paid seven hundred and fifty dollars for the half day, so I decided to become a morning person.

One week later, Sunday, 5:10 a.m. The alarm buzz on my cell phone went off. I resisted the urge to murder it, drank coffee, and dressed all in black as instructed by Prima: black mid-thigh skirt, elegant black shirt. I looked very Manhattan.

I trudged through eerily deserted Times Square as the sky began to lighten. A very recognizable NBA player emerged from the Marriott with a gorgeous bleached blonde on either arm. At least someone was having fun.

I managed to slip on an almost evaporated rain puddle and fall flat on my back. I spent some time lying there, contemplating the giant Cup Noodles cup that spewed imitation steam over Times Square. Do they use dry ice or what?

My tailbone throbbed. I could just lie here until someone called my parents to pick me up. But that would be chicken.

Bwaaak, b-b-bwaak, bwaaak, I chanted in my head for motivation. I rose, pretending it didn't hurt, and brushed my clothes off. Maybe this is why New Yorkers wear black; you can have a near-death experience and it won't stain.

The lobby of Clairol's building was two gleaming stories high. The sleepy-eyed security guard directed me up an escalator to the second floor, and I made my grand entrance. White marble, mirrors, and the exact same hairstyling stations that high-tech salons have. It was not open to the public and used only for inside promotions. One model, who looked identical to Gwyneth Paltrow, relaxed on a black leather chair while a trio of slender, attractive women in their late thirties had an intensely focused conversation. Everyone was dressed entirely in black; I blended in nicely. The women welcomed me with open smiles and intelligently told me immediately where the coffee machine was.

My kind of people.

I sat next to the Gwyneth look-alike. She yawned covertly and introduced herself as Sandy, twenty-four, also with Prima. I mentioned casually how short notice the casting had been. Sandy frowned. "C'mon, Cheryl, since when is a week short notice?"

My turn to look puzzled. "Is that how long you knew about it?"

"Yeah, you?"

I avoided answering while trying to figure it out.

A breakfast table was laid out with the usual assortment of muffins, fruit, croissants, and bagels. A male model in his late twenties entered, finger-brushing his long blond hair and checking out his reflection in all the mirrors. Sandy caught my attention and rolled her eyes. He placed his magnificent self on a chair and nodded regally at us.

It was obviously a festival of the blondes, as a very slim girl model with a short, asymmetrical haircut entered. Definitely "editorial" or "edgy," she had a grave expression and guarded eyes.

Karen.

Hers was an unhappy story, told to me while the other models were eating. Her mother had been diagnosed with cancer only a few weeks after her family had let their health insurance run out. So here was Karen, barely eighteen, alone in New York, never joining in on the jokes, only staring straight ahead with grim determination. She had let her shoulder-length hair be chopped off for a show that paid two thousand dollars. There is often a disturbing undercurrent of sadness and desperation among young models.

The room buzzed. Brad Jones was in the building. Michael—the wonderful person who booked me—came over to say hello and ask how I was faring at this ungodly hour.

"I shall survive," I declared bravely.

He smiled. "C'mon, I'll introduce you to Brad."

"Brad!" He caught the hairstylist's attention. "This is Cheryl, the natural blonde I was telling you about."

Brad was about forty-five, tan, in good shape. Shoulder-length blond hair and absolutely no ego. He gazed adoringly at my hair, ran his fingers through it. "Unbelievable," he said.

The other models looked slightly jealous. Then Brad looked at me and said something I'll never forget: "A gift from God." At a time when everyone was giving me hell, that was so nice coming from a person with no ulterior motive.

An elegant woman burst in. "I left my purse in the cab coming from the hotel!"

"Uh-oh," everyone said.

"My passport, credit cards, lots of cash, everything!"

"How much cash?" Brad asked.

"A thousand."

"Uh-oh," everyone said.

"Cancel all your cards," Brad advised.

"Right! Oh God, oh God . . ." She disappeared.

Forty minutes passed.

The woman appeared, glowing. "You'll never believe this! The next passenger in the cab found my purse and called my cell number." She indicated the phone clipped to her belt. "I got it all back. I love New York!"

Sandy and I stared at each other; we were too cynical to comprehend such honesty. The male model gazed lovingly at his reflection.

Nothing much happened for an hour—these events are slow starters. Sandy instructed me, "It's 'hellouii'—put more inflection on the *U*."

"Helloui?"

"Better."

The male model tore himself away from himself. "Hey, are we impersonating Fab?"

"Yeah." Sandy grinned.

"Check this out." He cleared his throat. "The call eis tommurrow, duu youi remember? Guud, okey, okey, okey, okey, bye-bye."

He was by far the best.

Karen was taken to a chair while her hair was prepped for total bleaching; she didn't seem to care what anyone did to her anymore. Brad explained the treatment in detail and then tried to entertain Karen, who gave small, forced grimaces. Sandy was living in Fab's model apartment and made fun of fellow resident Mandy—the push-up bra supporter—who was fast developing a rep for being constantly drunk and sleeping with anyone who might conceivably further her career.

It was good to know that everyone was enjoying their summer.

Michael summoned me to a chair, saying he wanted to trim just the tips off my hair. Keeping his word, he snipped off an eighth of an inch all around.

"So . . ." He looked at me in the mirror while working. "That Fabriziou, he's an interesting guy."

We caught each other's eye. I was careful in my reply to a client—you never know what gets back to your agency. "Mm-hmm."

He wasn't buying the stupid act and grinned at my reflection. "I thought it was strange that you have the best hair at your agency, and we asked to see all the blond models, but you weren't there."

I fixed my eyes on my lap so he wouldn't see how interested I was.

"Fabriziou had all the female models come, actually. I had a giant pile of comp cards."

"Oh, was this on Sunday?" I said lightly.

"Yeah, the same day I met with you. But after I'd seen all the other models, I told Fabriziou that I still hadn't found one of the models I wanted, and I asked if there was anyone else. . . ."

I stared at my knees.

"He said I'd seen all his models."

I felt my jaw begin to clench.

"You know how I found you?" Michael asked good-naturedly.

"How?"

"I actually had to make him open the booking room so I could check the comp cards on the wall, while he kept saying I'd seen all the girls."

I desired an Uzi assault rifle and some ammo.

"Also, Cheryl, your comp card is practically hidden behind a filing cabinet. You might want to get them to move it. So luckily, I found it and told Fabriziou that this is the girl I want to see. He said that you were probably not available. I had to practically force him to call you."

Michael finished trimming my hair and watched my angry expression with some concern. I pulled myself together, stood up, and nodded. "Great trim, Michael, thanks." I walked into the empty black marble bathroom and stomped around in furious circles.

When I exited, the models were being taken into a large room around a corner to hide from the arriving guests. They were top hairstylists and salon owners from across the United States there to observe Clairol's new hair products and make a massive order if they liked the look. This makes hair shows almost identical to runway shows.

Brad Jones took me aside, knowing I was nervous about any change in my hair color. He squinted at my head. "You know, Cheryl, I don't think it can really be improved on. I'd rather not lighten it at all."

"That would be great." Fabriziou, you bastard.

"Okay, here's what we'll do." Brad's eyes twinkled mischievously. "We have to apply the treatment in front of the audience, but then I want you to leave the room and Michael will wash it off immediately."

This sort of naughtiness delighted me.

Brad continued, "It'll lighten it a bit, but that will fade—and you definitely won't have any roots. Deal?"

"Deal."

Karen's short, ash blond hair was covered in foil, getting bleached white blond. The acidic smell of peroxide hung heavily in the room as I played Space Dude. It was time for the show to begin. The male model and I were being shown before and after, while Sandy's and Karen's hair would already be treated when shown.

Michael stood with me in the hallway outside the large modern showroom, where Brad was speaking to the guests assembled on black leather chairs, dressed completely in black.

"Okay, go!" Michael said with an encouraging smile.

I glided across the marble floor in my stilettos. Brad spoke into his microphone: "This is Cheryl's natural color." An amazed "ooooooh" from the audience. "We're going to make it even better."

I sat on a high black leather stool. Brad's assistant handed him a bowl of white goop, and he applied it carefully to a small strip of hair on either side of my head.

"This is usually left on for about ten minutes," Brad declared, and then whispered in my ear, "Go!"

I sashayed quickly out of the room. "Thank you, Cheryl," Brad said to my back, and everyone clapped.

Michael was posed like a sprinter outside. I tottered on my high heels after him, passing the other models relaxing on chairs. "Go, Cheryl!" they cheered.

I reclined comfortably while an assistant washed my hair, always my favorite part, unless they get shampoo on my forehead. My hair was blow-dried; I squinted inches from the mirror and tried to see the difference. The models assembled behind me, attempting to do the same. "It may be a tad lighter," Sandy declared with confidence.

We all nodded, being good sports.

Karen still resembled a tinfoil alien on a bad hair day while the bleach worked. There was a break for lunch, after which we would display the end results. Sandwiches, wraps, and dozens of unusual cakes and chocolates were laid out. Sandy and I raided the food. The male model, showing a very considerate side, brought a plate to Karen, who was rendered immobile under a hair dryer. As we all ate, I caught him looking in the mirror again and laughed. "One of these days, man, you're gonna run smack into your reflection."

Sandy giggled. "Oh, but what a way to go!"

The male model shook his head. "Immature, so very immature."

"Cheryl, you're on again in about twenty minutes," Michael called from the doorway.

"We should go clubbing together," Sandy informed me.

I mentally revisited my two past nightclub experiences and couldn't summon much enthusiasm for the idea.

"Or we could do something different," I said.

"Don't you like clubbing?" she asked sharply, suspicion written on every feature.

"Not really."

"You're an idiot," she stated with the confidence of someone eight years older, and therefore superior to me.

"Gee, thanks."

Suddenly her nose was almost touching mine, her giant face eclipsing everything behind it. "Do you see wrinkles?"

The answer was yes; she had abnormally deep creases under her eyes, making her appear older than twenty-four. I hesitated, curbing my natural vice of being brutally honest. Just as suddenly her face retreated, her eyes darting back and forth in New York fashion. "Let's go out for a cigarette," she chirped. I needed a break from the bleach fumes, so I agreed.

"Be right back," we told Brian, and slipped out of the building.

Outside in the sunshine, Sandy shook her cigarette pack in my direction. "Want one?"

I was permanently traumatized after my dad had a good laugh watching me try to smoke a cigar at age eight.

"Nope." I leaned against the building and people-watched.

"It's okay, I won't tell anyone, really."

I laughed. "I just don't like the taste. Relax, it's not weed."

She smiled and smoked her way through two wrinkle-inducing cigarettes while informing me that she could quit anytime—really, anytime.

"I'm worried about my wrinkles, though," she said. "Fab's riding me about it and so are the bookers."

I shrugged. "Maybe it's all that clubbing."

"You bitch!" she said, grinning.

In the industry, this passes for an ultrafriendly conversation. We rode the escalator back up. "Hey, Cheryl, quick, what's the square root of one?"

I frowned.

"Ha-ha, you moron! It's one!" she hollered triumphantly.

Michael hustled me back into place for my second appearance. Karen walked by, her hair a translucent white. Brad had agreed to dye it back to a more natural shade after the show.

"They're going to be like monkeys," Michael said.

I stared at him. "Who?"

"The guests, just watch. Now go."

I floated into the room. Brad Jones smiled into his microphone. "And here is Cheryl; see how her hair color is brightened with sunny highlights."

The guests oohed and ahhed, seeing the difference they wanted to see. I did my runway walk as instructed, and Brad boomed, "Thank you, Cheryl."

As I exited, some of the esteemed guests jumped up and surged forward. They surrounded me, lifting sections of my hair, touching my head, like . . . monkeys. Their eyes were strangely glazed over. Surprisingly, I didn't feel panicked; instead I watched their faces with academic interest, studying this phenomenon. And here, ladies and gents, for your viewing pleasure, is a prime example of overpassionate hair executives. None of them made eye contact with me, or showed any interest in anything but my hair. I gawked at them in fascination before stepping out.

"How did you get so wise?" I asked Michael outside.

"Experience."

I had to get me some of that.

After our payment slips were signed, we bid a fond farewell to Clairol. Sandy and I sauntered down sunny Madison Avenue. "I will call you, and we will go out," she commanded me.

"Yes, sir."

She waved, walking off, and I dialed Fab's cell phone, because even though it was the weekend, he had asked me to report on whether or not I had screwed up the Clairol job.

"Hellooooooooo?"

I frowned. This was even more extreme than usual. "Hey, it's Cheryl."

"Oooeee, Cherrrrrillll."

"Umm, right, the Clairol job went very well."

"Goodie, goodie!"

The penny dropped: He was high.

I couldn't restrain a chuckle. "Bye."

"Bye-bye."

It was semicommon knowledge that after a rough week of messing with his models, Fab liked to chill a little on the weekends. I resolved to take some time and decide how to deal with the fact that the manager of my own agency was sabotaging me for standing up to him. One thing was for sure: I hadn't a shred of loyalty left.

Monday noon—the day after Clairol—found me marching dedicatedly up Sixth Avenue on my way to a call, past a shish-kebab stand where a bunch of overheated New Yorkers crowded around, shouting their orders as the owner viciously chopped an unidentifiable species of frying meat, his sharp knife reflecting sunlight. My cell rang; Veronika.

"Hey, Cheryl," she said casually. "I've got a shoot for you."

This stopped me cold. She had spent the last month ingeniously avoiding even discussing this with me.

"It's going to be at FIT tomorrow morning."

"What's FIT?" I asked.

"The Fashion Institute of Technology." I could picture her rolling her eyes at my ignorance.

Veronika continued, "I'll give Je'mere, the woman who's organizing it, your number in case she needs to phone you. Be at Twenty-seventh and Seventh Avenue at ten a.m. You'll be met at the security desk." Click.

This was a direct result of Clairol. It's interesting the effect that proving you're a bookable model has on an agency—they actually start trying to book you.

My call was for a high-fashion wedding dress designer. He greeted me in his large, all-white showroom, dressed all in white with a deep tan and an attitude. I introduced myself.

"Hello," he sniffed.

Three other models, two of whom I knew were with Prima, gave me cool looks. The longer models are in the biz, the more likely they are to adopt the mood and manners of the client they are in the company of.

The designer selected one of a hundred pouffy-yet-elegant wedding gowns and handed it to me, the sixteen-year-old he was considering to model it. I was directed to one of a series of white-curtained changing rooms. Inside it, more gowns were hung, protected by plastic. I was struggling to reach the buttons on the back of my dress when I heard faint whispers from the other side of the adjoining curtain. Two models had wisely opted to change together for speedier buttoning and zipping purposes. I heard them murmur and caught the name Cheryl. Immediately I abandoned buttoning and put an ear near the curtain to eavesdrop.

". . . yeah, that's her. She's weird. Allie told me all about her."

"Isn't she in the next changing room?"

"No, the next one over, she can't hear."

"So . . . what about her?"

"She got shoots before anyone else did—she's not scared of Fab—and she, like, lives in the ghetto!" That's what I got for mentioning Jersey; but it was pretty much true.

"No!"

"Yes! And guess what?"

"Shhhh . . . not so loud, what?"

"She's in the Mafia!"

I was fascinated. I had no idea I was so interesting.

"No way!"

"Yes way! Allie met her at a club once, and Cheryl was eating sushi with a big Mafia guy and he was really, really scary. He owns one of the top escort services—Allie checked."

This also turned out to be true; Allie had been busy.

"Is Cheryl . . . like, dangerous?"

"Yessss." A giddy hiss.

I smiled. I was positively delighted. This was a fabulous rep to have among the models. Perhaps it was time to purchase sunglasses and a pinkie ring.

"I think she can hear us," whispered one.

"No, she can't."

"Maybe she can." Frightened now.

I leaned closer in my wedding dress and whispered, "Yes, I can."

Their shrieks pierced the perfumed air, and then came a massive clatter as they knocked over the dress rack in their room.

The designer hollered, "What?! What?!" as I flung my curtain aside and stepped out, buttoning the last button. An assistant immediately began salvaging the scattered dresses while the designer glared at the two models, who fled soon after.

I twirled in front of a mirror, the dress fanning out around me. The only thing missing was Brad Pitt. I did a more subdued version of my walk, trying to look less mercenary than I really am. I didn't end up getting the job, but the casting was one hell of a good time.

I wanted to have a serious talk with Fab—if such a thing were possible—about the tricks he pulled to try and keep me from landing the Clairol job. I used my dwindling comp card supply as an excuse to storm the agency.

Hilda still refused to return my smile, but I was undaunted and complimented her on her choice of mud-colored polo shirt. She grunted. Eagle-eyed Veronika raised a hand to summon me to the booking room. It was buzzing as usual. "You look overheated. Are you sweating?" Veronika asked in horror.

"Glowing, Veronika, always glowing."

"You're sweating."

"It's a hundred degrees."

It had taken me a few months to figure out the compliment/put-down strategy that Prima used to keep their models in line, and I was tired of it. I felt constantly on edge, walking the thin line between acceptance and rejection. Models are the most insecure people I've met, due to this treatment at a young age. By the time you claw your way past these petty conversations, you've been thoroughly humbled.

"The photog for the FIT shoot is really enthusiastic about you," Veronika said. The compliment.

"Mm, good." I put some cards in my portfolio.

Fab entered the booking room with some papers and flinched slightly when he saw me.

"Hiya," I said.

"Hellooo." He was trying to figure out if I knew, decided that yeah, I probably did, and said, "Cherilll, let's have a talk."

His jaw was tight, his accent wavering, but it wasn't because he was worried; he just seemed angry. I remembered a girl model telling me that Fab would sometimes slam his fist on his desk to freak a model out. I had a sense this was to be our showdown. Feeling slightly reckless, I followed him to his lair.

We faced each other, me in the torture chair, Fab on his therapeutic cushions.

"Well . . . ," he said.

I smiled thinly, imagining a sagebrush rolling between us.

"How is everything?"

"Pretty good, considering everything. I noticed with Clairol that I've been informed of calls late." This was putting it mildly.

"Cherilll, you must understand, in New York—"

"Everyone else in New York was told a week in advance."

He pushed his glasses up and focused his fury on me. "You are a very rebellious girl!"

I was secretly pleased—a rebel, *moi*? I spoke very calmly so as to annoy him more. "Really, how so?"

"You do not take orders! You are a rebel! You don't live in the model apartment!"

"Is that mandatory?"

"No, it is not," he said through clenched teeth.

"Well, that's one down. What else?"

"This! This!"

"What?"

"You talk back!"

"Forgive me," I said earnestly.

Fab's face was turning bright red; I was deviating from a model's usual response, and he no longer had a script.

"My only concern," I said, "is that I meet as many clients as possible, which is in your interest as well—"

"Yes, yes!" he barked.

"Are you going to do that?"

"Of course! You have booked Clairol now!"

I tried to wrap my mind around his logic.

"When you came here, Cherilll, you were nothing." He flapped his hand. "You were dirt. But now—"

"I was *never* dirt." I fixed him with a furious look.

"Okey, of course," he backpedaled. But I never forgot that line.

"Cherill, now you are our most promising model, booking shoots, and Clairol told me they were very impressed with you. But you must obey us!" His fist was moving, and I was ready for it when he smashed it full force onto his desk. There was a loud clap, like lightning, and everything on his desk jumped. But not me. I sat in the chair, giving him a blank look. My lack of reaction startled him and he lost his train of thought, staring back at me openmouthed.

A good ten seconds of silence passed.

"How's the hand?" I inquired.

"Ooee, good, good, thank you."

His bag of tricks exhausted, Fab spent ten minutes assuring me that he would get me shoots and go-sees with top clients. I believed him for one simple reason: It really *was* in his interest. I stood up. Fab scurried around his desk to hug me, then searched my face, almost as if looking for approval. I smiled. Turning the tables is always fun.

Heading past the booking room, I noticed all the bookers covertly watching me. Veronika, her curiosity overwhelming her, waved me in. The modeling industry had toughened me up. A few months ago, a meeting with Fab would have left me in shock. Instead I was feeling mischievous and triumphant; a risky combination. Plopping myself into a vacant chair next to Veronika's desk, I grinned at her. She seemed surprised that I wasn't crying. It was not unheard-of to see a model leaving the agency in tears after a meeting with the Fab.

"What's up?" she asked.

My naughtiness took over, and I leaned forward. "I have just come from a fascinating tête-à-tête with Fabriziou in the war room. We discussed things of global—possibly universal—consequence! I have learned many, many things."

Veronika raised an elegant eyebrow. "Really?"

"Yup, I've been enlightened. I've seen the light. No more independent thinking for me! No siree Bob!"

She was smiling full on. The other bookers were straining to hear, but I kept my voice down. "I'll toe the line. I will be a good duckling. I will work tirelessly for the good of the state."

"Oh, Jesus." Veronika laughed. "Where did you come from? You're usually so quiet."

"I'm a deceptive little bitch."

"Yes, you are," she said with a hint of pride.

"There's a point to this outburst," I said.

"I would hope so."

"I don't want to have to fight with you every time I come through the agency. So could you save the energy of trying to give me a nervous breakdown and channel it into giving one to someone else?" I was fed up with Prima and their games, so I was pushing a lot further than it was wise to. In a way, I was hoping they would tear my contract up. It was not to be. Veronika was having a great time.

"Well, well, how do you know I won't tell all this to Fabriziou?"

"You can if you want. But you won't, really, because he annoys you and I can be sort of entertaining."

She thought it over and nodded her agreement.

Outside in the blistering heat I caught my breath, feeling like I had just taken an extremely steep hill on my Rollerblades and narrowly missed an oncoming car. Blood pounded in my ears and my fingers tingled. What a rush. I walked for a while. My upper lip began to feel wet, and I wiped the sweat off with my fingertips. They came away red. I leaned forward and fat droplets of blood spattered onto the baking asphalt.

It was a gusher. I fumbled some Starbucks napkins out of my giant purse and pressed them to my nose. Passersby ignored me. It wasn't painful, or even uncomfortable, and it would repeat itself when I was under a lot of pressure.

I stood still, waiting for it to stop, and gazed across the street. The logo of one business looked familiar; then I recognized it from an envelope I had seen in Fab's office. It was the place he sent models' pictures to be printed. I jaywalked across the street, napkins against my face, and entered. The owner did not seem disturbed by the blood. It was, of course, New York.

"Can I help you?"

"Yuh," I wheezed. "How much is a den-by-dwelve laser print?"

"A ten by twelve? Are you with an agency?"

I was pleased that even with a nosebleed he identified me as a likely model. "Yuh."

"For models, it's ten dollars a picture. If you print more than five, it's eight dollars."

Not twenty dollars? Fab was in expense-padding heaven. I danked him and headed to a phone booth.

I managed to draw a few clear breaths through my nose and dialed.

The owner answered, "Classique Models, Philip speaking."

"Hi," I said. "This is Cheryl Diamond. I came to your open call a few months—"

"Yes, I remember you. How are you?"

"Good. I'd like to come in and meet with you."

"Great. How about today at four o'clock?"

We sat on either side of an oak desk in his nicely decorated office near Bergdorf Goodman. His was a boutique agency, with twenty models and a sweet, wisecracking booker whose name I could never pronounce correctly. Philip told me he had once been mobbed by misguided fans who mistook him for Tom Cruise when he was lunching at an outdoor restaurant in Manhattan. He was puzzled by it, since he was six-one, bald, and not prone to leaping on furniture. We talked for a while and came to an agreement. He had intuited that I didn't want to sign a binding contract, since technically, I was already bound. This is by no means a novelty among new models. I once met a male model with seven agencies.

Hey, all's fair in love, war, and the modeling biz.

Don't Smile

FIT. A sprawling concrete building spanning several blocks, where hopeful students go to learn how to be the next superstar designer. Young people swarmed about, intent on showcasing their nonconformist fashion ideas, with sometimes disastrous results. A girl wearing neon leggings—one green, one orange—and a Goth-black dress raised a pierced eyebrow at me. I didn't know what to make of that and entered the lobby past a girl who made me immediately hate everything I was wearing.

"Cheryl!" An attractive woman launched herself away from the security desk and zeroed in on me. It was the photographer. She hugged me in delight; the show was on.

"I'm Tina," she said with a smile as I followed her down an endless white hallway. We made a turn revealing another identical corridor; a trip down some stairs produced a similar result. I was convinced we were lost for all time when Tina threw open a door and we entered a cavern. At least that's what the massive backstage area of FIT's auditorium resembled. The air was cool with a faint smell of paint, the walls were exposed brick, and it was dark except for the powerful lights being set up for our shoot. A wave of smiling people converged on me. Je'mere, the coordinator/stylist of the shoot, shook my hand warmly.

The makeup artist, Nicole, was setting out her magician's tools as the hairstylist, Brian, looked on. "Who says a straight black man can't style hair?" he joked.

Tina's assistants—three young girls who seemed somewhat in awe of the flesh-and-blood Model before them, and a blond, dreadlocked guy—moved lights and connected wires. The metal door smashed open, and on the pathway of light cast from the hallway, in walked a man. Small, slightly round, and white-haired, he advanced with total confidence and dignity. I immediately liked him.

"Professor Di Di!" Tina, the photographer, squealed.

"Yes! It is me!" A French accent, naturally.

Professor Di Di marched up to me, stared intently at my face, then spread his arms wide and boomed, "Beautiful woman! Beautiful woman!"

My ego was delighted.

He whirled and stalked toward the circle of lights assembled like Stonehenge on thin metal poles. "Move this one!"

The assistants snapped into frantic action as Di Di patrolled the area.

Nicole applied foundation, her shiny brown curls bobbing up and down. *Don't pull one, don't pull one,* I cautioned myself. This impulse to pull a curl is shared by most straight-haired people. Looking into the makeup mirror, I could see Tina taking light readings as Di Di appeared through a different door, a high-tech camera in hand. This wasn't a shoot, it was a production.

My eyes were partially closed as Nicole brushed on eye shadow and Brian lounged in the corner, when a bright flash enveloped the makeup area. Tina stood triumphantly behind us, camera to her eye. "That's a great shot!" And it was.

When I was primped, Je'mere handed me an extra-short dress with a dungaree-like top and a black skirt. She paired it with pink shoes, and we were off. I walked onto the set; the assistants scattered, wide-eyed. Tina, camera around her neck, bravely climbed a rickety ladder so she could shoot downward.

I positioned myself on a stool Di Di brought, and a spotlight was directed at me. The first shot was fired. "Good," Tina said from her perch, checking the photo on her digital camera's small screen. "A little more light, Numi."

I had learned a commonly used trick from studying more experienced models' comp cards at Prima. It's simplistic, but if you watch, it can be found in nearly every ad campaign. The model dangles one hand between his/her legs. If you don't figure this out yourself, photographers will pose you this way. It's a little marketing device of the industry, like always setting the watches in ads at 10:10, making the clock's hands form a smile.

I changed outfits and makeup before being directed to the top of the unstable ladder, where I clung on for dear life. Tina snapped away. I was focused down on her camera when a confusing flash went off on my other side. I looked left. Di Di was in the photographer's stance—one foot in front of the other, knees slightly bent—snapping pictures. A flash from my right; I looked back at Tina's camera. A burst of light from Di Di's corner and I snapped my head back to him. I had never been double-teamed before, a confusing experience at best, and my neck was beginning to hurt.

Di Di sensed my bafflement and delivered a classic line: "Look at Tina's camera. She is the photographer; I am just the pain in the ass."

I hung on to the swaying ladder while laughing.

During our break for lunch, as we ate delivered sandwiches, Veronika called.

She sounded warmer since my monologue of the previous day. "I've got you another shoot."

"Awesome."

"I'll set it up for a few days from now."

"Thanks a lot, Veronika," I said, meaning it for once.

"Yeah, yeah." Click.

The next couple of days were spent pounding Manhattan's sweltering pavement, sprinting up and down stairs, getting lost, and trying on countless items of clothing.

The casting circuit. Hard to get in. Exhausting to stay on.

Frantic interludes were spent in the lobbies of designers' buildings, switching my pictures from Prima's book to my black one for Philip's or Jacob's calls. Occasionally I almost forgot which agency I was supposed to be representing.

Veronika seemed to have adopted me as her pet project, which sounds a lot more charming than it really was.

"Cheryl! Where are you?"

I hauled myself through the humidity. "Downtown, Varick and King."

"I need you uptown! What the hell are you doing downtown?!"

"You sent me here on a call."

"Jesus, Cheryl!" It was obviously all my fault. "Get uptown now, Fifty-sixth and Sixth. . . . Don't be late. And don't forget your shoot, eleven a.m. tomorrow."

I saw the entrance for the uptown 1 and 9 subway and ran.

Later that day I met with a beaming Tina, who gave me a disk from the shoot with one of my pictures on the cover. She never asked why I didn't want it messengered to the agency, as is customary. If Fab had gotten his paws on it, I would have been paying twenty dollars a print to pad his wallet, since he regularly confiscated disks. Veronika wanted to review my new pictures, so I moseyed over to the agency, and we brought it up on her computer. Luckily, Fab was sequestered in his office.

"You photograph well," Veronika said, narrowing her eyes at the screen. This was the equivalent of another person doing a spontaneous cartwheel. She wrote down the numbers of the pictures she wanted printed. There were eight, a huge number for her to want in my book from just one shoot. Usually it's about three, if you're lucky. I was worried about whether I could budget all the prints; it's easier to be overcharged as long as it goes on your account. The method to Fab's madness.

Veronika leaned close as she ejected the disk. "Don't let Fabriziou print these—he gets a kickback."

"Yeah, I know."

She gave me one of her rare grins. "I like you."

I was floored. "What's this going to do to your rep?"

"Get the hell out of here," she said, laughing.

I waited for the elevator. It opened, and Allie stepped wearily out. She saw the photo disk in my hand and the leftover smile on my face.

"Hey," she said, avoiding my eyes. Obviously she had heard about the wedding dress fiasco.

"Yeah, hi." I stepped past her into the elevator and pressed close. It didn't disappoint or even annoy me that she had been gossiping behind my back. Probably as a consequence of my nomadic childhood, I'd learned to be independent and not get too emotionally attached. I'm not exactly distant, just guarded.

There were weeks as a model when very little would happen. A few calls and not much else. Then an avalanche of activity seemed to engulf me. As soon as I waved bye to Baaf, my phone rang and Philip informed me that he had scored a shoot. "It's tomorrow at six p.m."

The shoot Veronika had arranged was at eleven a.m. With luck and good running speed, I could make both.

"He's shooting another one of my girls and an ID model as well, so you'll have company."

"Great," I said, although I have always preferred to be in the exact center of all possible attention.

I rode the bus back to Jersey and got off at my stop to see a familiar little head peeking out from the bushes. I had begun letting Tigger into the neighbor's tiny, overgrown backyard to play while I toiled in the great metropolis. Tigger, being street-smart, had figured out where I got on the bus, and that by leaping over a few fences he could wait in the shrubbery to ambush me as I returned.

"Hey, my man." I scrubbed his head.

"Meow," he said profoundly, and trotted down the sidewalk, leading me home.

The owner of the corner ninety-eight-cent store—a shiny-shirted, blinged-out Trump wannabe—wiggled his unibrow and leered at me. I made a mental note to start frequenting the ninety-nine-cent store directly across the street from him.

As I opened the door to my apartment building, a wave of overly loud rap music invaded my ears.

It was 1C.

I was cautiously hateful of Apartment 1C.

They were a clan of indeterminate number: large-muscled, wild-eyed music and beer enthusiasts. Which means they would swig beer on the front steps and crush the cans against their heads, or throb the floor of my bedroom with salsa at two a.m.

No one in the building dared confront them. I was hoping for a unified revolt. We would rise up, arm ourselves, kick down their door, and slaughter their stereo equipment.

It never happened.

At eleven o'clock the next morning I entered a gray concrete block of a building on the Lower West Side. My tired muscles were already protesting as I climbed the stairs. You can imagine my reaction when the photographer, Derek, opened the door to his studio and snarled, "Veronika tells me you're a dancer."

"Yeah."

"You any good?" he snapped.

"Are you a photographer?"

"Of course!"

"There's your answer," I said.

Derek bared his teeth. "Little girl, I'm going to have fun with you."

A crazy woman wearing gigantic pink bunny ears on her head hopped around the two-story, all-white studio.

"I'm a hippy, hoppy bunnieeeeeeeee!" she squealed, molding her six-foot, reed-thin body into a rabbit leap, curly black hair flying, pale skin flushed.

"You're craaazy," trilled a five-foot-tall man dressed exactly like a mime, with white gloves and a black beret pulled low. The hippy, hoppy bunny giggled hysterically, bounded toward the mime, and leaped onto him, wrapping her legs around his waist. Predictably, they fell in a heap to the floor. I debated using my cell to call the mental ward. They jumped up, seeming refreshed, and Derek introduced me:

Bunny ears was Sarah, the hair/makeup artist.

The mime, Jacques, was handling styling. Help me, God.

"And this," Derek said, pointing his finger at my face, "is Blondie."

"Cheryl," I corrected.

"Cherry," he chirped insolently.

I sighed.

"He's fucking with you," said a spookily disembodied voice. I searched for the source: A dark-haired, ghostly pale girl of twenty was curled in the corner of a black leather couch, staring at me with yellowish eyes.

"He's a sick bastard, aren't you, Derek?" she rasped.

"The sickest," he declared proudly, and they exchanged cold smiles.

My survival instinct fought with my need for pictures.

The pictures won.

I sat in the makeup chair. "I've been thinking of becoming a porn star," Sarah said, a rabbit ear jabbing the side of my head as she applied mascara.

"Nothing but the bunny ears?" I asked.

"She's funny, Derek!" Sarah hollered.

"Will it make up for her lack of personality?" Derek asked sweetly.

I rolled my eyes.

"You smudged the mascara!" Sarah wailed.

My hair was slicked back into an elegant ponytail, and Jacques' white-gloved hand gave me a short wraparound black dress.

"Where can I change?" I asked Sarah.

Derek pointed to the exact center of the studio, "Right there."

I shot him my carefully cultivated hard look.

"The restroom's back there," said the emaciated girl on the couch.

I headed toward it. Derek capered around the studio, keeping his tone jokey. "Aww, Cherry's shy. Cherry's shy."

I turned around. "Why don't you strip, Derek?"

"What?" He was shocked.

"Right there." I pointed to the center of the studio, praying he wouldn't.

"You just wanna see me naked!"

"I'd rather have a root canal, but I think I've made my point."

Everyone giggled; I had a sense that they all disliked one another intensely.

"We want photos of you doing dance leaps," Derek declared a few minutes later, adjusting a light reflector. This played into exactly what I needed for my portfolio. I decided not to tell him, since he would probably change his mind just to annoy me.

"Strrrrretch your muscles," Sarah sang, as I propped my leg on a windowsill and leaned forward.

"You're not gonna throw your back out, are you?" Derek barked.

I ignored him, and he continued popping off light readings.

I ascended the shooting platform that Derek had rigged specially so I could get some extra spring on jumps. A foot off the concrete floor, balanced precariously on a metal frame, was a large wooden board, painted white. If I stood in the center, there was some give. I was glad to have taken Veronika's advice and brought the model's staple of both skin-colored and black underwear. The first for light-colored clothing; the second for if the dress flew up.

"So, let's see if you're any good," Derek commented cynically, popping a final light reading off in front of my nose. He retreated to his shooting position, and we glared heatedly at each other. Sarah, Jacques, and the couch girl all leaned forward expectantly.

"On the count of three," Derek ordered. "One . . . two . . ."

I jumped into the air, one foot bending behind me to head level, the other pointing ahead. I landed, the board reverberating in a satisfying way.

"Wow," Sarah said.

Derek stared and then shouted, his brown hair standing on end. "You preempted the count! I said on three!"

"Really?" I asked innocently.

"You did it on purpose!" he screamed, but he was obviously enjoying himself.

"Again, on three," I said.

"Okay, Blondie!"

I leaped again; he snapped a picture and checked it on his screen. "Keep your face relaxed—don't look like you're jumping."

I jumped over and over, the vibrations of the board on its metal frame echoing around the studio.

The shoot brought out the worst of both Derek's and my personalities. We hurled fiery insults at each other, our faces flushed, grinning madly.

Derek checked his camera's screen. "I'm a fucking fantastic photographer, Blondie!"

"Will it make up for your lack of intellect, Brownie?" I asked smugly.

"Arrgggh," he growled, and I leaped for the ceiling once again. Upon landing, we both burst into hysterical laughter.

"Don't smile!" Derek bellowed.

The rest of the crew cowered on the couch as we vented our various frustrations on each other. Soaked with sweat and nearly mad, we broke for lunch.

I collapsed on the couch next to the scarily skinny girl.

"Thirty-seven," she said flatly.

"What?"

"How many jumps you did. I was counting."

She was creepy. "Oh," I said.

As we waited for the veggie wraps to arrive, Derek felt compelled to pontificate about the cadaverous girl.

"Lola's a model. She's supposed to be shooting today, but she's not feeeeeling well."

Lola stood up to get a bottle of water, and I got a shock. She was a skeleton, my height, with an oddly green tinge to her skin.

"You gotta eat," Derek said.

"I do eat," she whined.

"She weighs less than a hundred pounds," Derek informed me.

Lola sat down and complained incessantly about everything. The daughter of a well-off family, she had her parents paying for a permanent suite at the Hilton. Derek & Co. ran into her on the club circuit and, sensing a trust fund, had befriended her. The food arrived; Sarah took away half my veggie wrap and began coaxing

Lola into eating it. There was a reason for this coddling; Lola's mother would later help buy an even larger studio for the crew in return for them putting up with Lola's grumpiness. Sarah and I were eating Hershey's Kisses for dessert when Lola tottered into the bathroom and we heard her throw up.

That was half of *my* veggie wrap.

I did a few more jumps, Derek smiling genuinely. "These are fantastic."

There was a furious knocking at the studio's door. Sarah opened it and a slender, sensitive-looking man entered. "There's this incredible pounding on the ceiling of my studio. It's like someone is jumping up and down in here."

We all exchanged guilty looks.

"It must stop. I'll inform the authorities! I'm trying to paint!"

I stepped off the platform and padded barefoot across the studio, working on summoning a genuine smile.

"Hi," I sparkled at him.

"Uh, hi."

"We're creating history. Derek, show our friend one of the pictures."

Derek obeyed, holding the camera screen at the artist's eye level.

"Wow," he said. It appealed to his creative nature. "Would all of you like to take a field trip and see my paintings?"

"Ooooooh," I squealed, and clapped my hands. We trooped after him.

"Very nice," Derek whispered.

The painter's studio, one floor directly beneath Derek's and just as big, was full of nude oil canvases. They were somewhat obscene, a lot of full-hipped women and tousle-haired young men. I considered it an educational experience. We raved about the artist's talent and stomped back upstairs, with the assurance that we could set off an atom bomb without him informing the fuzz.

Sarah caught up to me on the stairs. "He wants me to ask if you would pose for him."

"No!" I yelped.

"It's art," she scolded.

I changed into a long black evening gown for some nondance shots while Sarah met with some models they were considering for their next shoot. This gave me a unique opportunity to hear what people say at castings *after* you've left the room.

It was brutal.

"Her hips were too big," Derek said over his shoulder.

"That last girl looked like a pretty boy in drag," Jacques supplied.

"That girl's ass really was fat. We should call her agency so they can put her on a freaking diet," Sarah decided, flipping her comp card over for the agency's number. The girl was a slender size four.

At about four p.m., Lola roused herself from the couch, bitching and moaning, to declare that Her Highness was ready to start shooting.

"If it wasn't for her parents' money, I'd wring her neck," Derek muttered to me.

Lola did something I wish she hadn't, since I've never been able to get the image out of my mind. In the middle of the studio, she stripped all her clothes off and shot a challenging look at Derek's profile. He ignored her. It was clear that they had, at some time, been sleeping together. Her hip bones jutted out like shelves, her knees were the thickest part of her legs, and only loose skin remained where her breasts had been.

I felt like eating a pizza.

Instead I took a water break on the couch. Lola strolled over, still naked, and kneeled near me to snort coke from a plastic Baggie off the coffee table. I had begun to both feel sorry for and dislike Lola. She was one of those people who mope through life, making excuses for themselves and blaming everything on others. Before she snorted another noseful, Lola confessed to me that her agency, who also repped Naomi Campbell, had given her an ultimatum: gain ten pounds or they would drop her. Proof that the heroin-chic look was definitely on its way out.

Lola decided not to shoot after all and spent the remainder of my time there wrapped in a bathrobe. I made Derek burn me an unedited disk before I left, which sparked another snarling match between us.

"Don't you trust me to messenger it to your agency?"

"No," I said.

"Fine!"

After being lied to 3,681 times, I had developed Trust Issues, Paranoia Issues, Sarcasm Issues, and Tolerance Issues. Basically, I'm a big ball of angst.

While the disk burned, I washed the makeup off and changed. Checking the time on my cell, I prepared to rush for my next shoot. Grabbing the disk and hollering, "Bye, thanks, it was fun," over my shoulder, I dashed eagerly out the door. Freedom was so close. As I headed down the hallway, Derek leaped out of his studio behind me. "Where the hell are you from, anyway?"

I thought about it. "Jersey."

"Well! That explains everything!" He reentered his studio and slammed the door.

I began speed-walking east, since there aren't any crosstown subways in lower Manhattan. Derek actually called Veronika to complain about me, a conversation that Veronika gleefully relayed to me:

"You sent me this smart-ass kid who was mouthing off the whole time!"

"Okay," Veronika said, nonplussed. She knew Derek's rep as a hellion.

"She stuck her tongue out at me!" he yelled. It was true.

"Fine, I won't send Cheryl anymore."

"What? I'm calling to book her again."

Veronika asked me if I would do it.

"Tell him I fled the country," was my response.

"No-no-no-no-no-no," I pleaded while jogging in circles around the Village, completely lost. I'd been instilled with an automatic feeling of horror at the mere thought of being late for a shoot. It simply wasn't done. Gargoyles and vampires would emerge to suck the very life out of my fledgling career. Fab would have been proud that some of his conditioning had worked. I vented my panic by making mad dashes in random directions that looked promising. I was finally rescued, near tears, by the aforementioned fuzz. Limply I followed directions to a large-windowed building. Thirty minutes late, I climbed a steep flight of hardwood stairs to the studio, which occupied the entire second floor. Loud, somewhat catchy rap music leaked through the door. I hesitated, nibbling a nail. Would I be yelled at? Given a lecture on punctuality? Tarred and feathered?

I had exhausted my day's supply of fighting spirit on Derek and opened the door with a martyred expression.

No one noticed me.

It was a party: Everyone was moving their heads to the rap while they styled hair, applied makeup, or just boogied down. I snuck in, put my bag down, and tried to look like I'd been there since six.

The walls were painted a warm orange, with overstuffed white couches grouped around. Rolls of background paper—one white, one black—extended from their ceiling-level rollers and along the floor. On the black backdrop posed three young men, bling around their necks, chins thrust forward, in fashionably baggy clothes topped off with do-rags.

"Rap stars," said a skinny, strung-out man who was arranging a red fox fur coat. "I'm JoJoba, the stylist."

"I'm Cheryl. Isn't JoJoba a kind of oil?"

"Yes, I *love* it. You're with Classique, right?"

I mentally calculated which agency had booked me this shoot. "Yes."

"The rappers will be finished soon. Hair and makeup's still working on the other two models, so you can chill if you want."

Relieved, I immediately slouched sleepily into a couch near the open bay windows, sniffing the warm evening breeze. Smog, car exhaust, and a slight essence of garbage. I sulked. My legs were sore, I missed my parents—unbelievable, I know—and I had stubbed my toe on the way over.

"Yo! Don't look sad, don't be mad, you too lovely to be down, baby."

The rappers, on break from shooting, had formed a concerned triangle in front of me.

I smiled. "I'm fine, thanks."

They kept a worried eye on me, sitting on the windowsill and pouring shots of Johnnie Walker Black into clear plastic cups.

My head felt heavy. Slowly, inexorably, it tilted toward my shoulder.

"Hey, honey, do you want some?"

The rappers had decided to take action to resuscitate me. One poured a cup half full—or half empty—of Johnnie Walker, while another opened a tin and extracted a plump joint. I realized that they were genuinely trying to help—though the medication would probably be counterproductive—and I started giggling.

"We won't tell anyone, don't worry," said one.

"Thank you, it's very considerate. But if I shocked my system with that"—I indicated their offerings—"I would—"

"Feel better!" he chirped.

"Yeah, probably, but I'm enjoying feeling sorry for myself."

"Hey, that's cool, we gotchu."

They lit up joints and asked about modeling. "What's it like?" they chorused.

"Have you ever spent all day banging your head against a brick wall?"

"Hey, sounds like the music biz."

We all giggled, while I inhaled secondhand marijuana smoke.

Their agent, a balding man with pale New York skin and a five-thousand-dollar suit, checked me out. "Ever thought of rapping?"

I looked at him.

"Nah, I guess not." He sipped Red Bull.

I was called to the makeup chair. A model getting her black hair styled next to me complained about Bob, the manager of her agency, ID Models. I had met with him once, and he'd said in his trademark staccato voice, "Modeling is the most subjective business in the world. Any model on the casting circuit can be a supermodel."

"Could I?" I asked.

"Of course. But I'm not going to sign you. You're too young and inexperienced, and I don't think you'll take orders well." He shoved my book across his desk.

A fourteen-year-old flame-haired model from Classique had brought her mother. This was usually accepted in an industry that employs barely teenage girls, but her mother was instantly rude to me. I was competition, at her daughter's very own agency!

I was styled by JoJoba in a white suit and elegant gloves and positioned in front of the photographer, who was confusingly chipper and friendly. The rap stars, still puffing away, shouted encouragement and some profound thoughts—which once examined, made no sense. A large fan was directed at me, blowing my straightened and glossed hair in a way that I hoped resembled the carefree girls in allergy medication commercials. I was instructed to look mischievous as I pretended to remove a glove one finger at a time.

"Excellent!" The photographer checked his screen. "You pose well."

The red-haired model's mother looked as if she was about to kill me.

A half hour of shooting later, I was sent to change outfits, while the Classique girl began shooting. The rap stars left, but not before attempting an extremely complex handshake with me and cautioning, "Don't let the haters getchu down."

We nodded at one another solemnly; fellow travelers in the murky fishbowl that is the entertainment industry.

My hair was being tied up and bloodred lipstick applied, while the photographer was imploring the redheaded girl, "No, no, no, look *natural.* Why are you doing that? Don't do that. Jesus!"

Her mother was contorting her fingers in a series of complex, prearranged hand signals that served to completely stress her daughter out.

JoJoba watched the girl sagely. "She just doesn't have It."

No one can define what "It" is. But it certainly exists—the difference between one model being able to light a picture up and another coming off flat.

The ID model had It. She prowled fiercely in front of the camera, clad in an animal-skin jungle-themed outfit, a large predator's tooth hanging around her neck, and somehow made it all work.

I shot four more looks, until I was barely able to stand. The photographer called Philip the next day to tell him that I was his favorite model from the shoot, adding that I had "strong presence" in front of the camera and a "calm attitude." Little did he know I was sleep-shooting. He also added that Philip's red-haired model was dead in pictures. This is proof of how subjective modeling is; at the same time Philip was hearing praise about me, Veronika was being informed that I was impossible. The shoot ended at midnight. A disk would be messengered to Philip.

I stumbled onto the dark street and headed for the PATH train. By the time I arrived at the dreaded Journal Square, no more buses were running. Walking would be borderline suicidal, so I approached the line of cabs and drivers congregated outside. They surrounded me—I had pulled on a shapeless sweatshirt and baseball cap, my technique for safe passage. I haggled for a while before agreeing on five dollars.

We drove off, past graffiti-decorated storefronts and hulking, shadowy figures on the street corners.

"Where're you from?" the driver asked, eyes aglitter in the rearview mirror.

"Bosnia."

"Oh." He leered at me. "Are all the girls from there so pretty?"

"No. I'm the only one."

I had him drop me off a good two blocks from where I really lived.

"Twelve dollars," he said.

"What? We agreed on five."

He held up a laminated card with "zones" and the price for each one you crossed.

"See! Twelve dollars." He pointed at it.

I was beyond fed up. "Don't you have the capacity to remember anything that happened more than five minutes ago?" I am strangely articulate when angry.

"It says here, twelve dollars," he repeated with fake stupidity, making the mistake of holding the card too close to our connecting window. I grabbed it out of his hand and hurled it out the open window like a Frisbee.

He was shocked.

"You are ridiculous and transparent!" I hollered.

"Lady, okay, just give me whatever."

I viciously flung five dollars into the front seat and walked away with my nose in the air. I hope Tigger appreciates how I risk life and limb every day to put tuna on the table.

A couple of days later found me gazing forlornly across the big lawn in Bryant Park. Fab's comment about my walk needing work had spread into the booking room. Veronika stubbornly refused to go out into the hall with me so I could demonstrate otherwise. So I wasn't being sent on any castings for the upcoming Fashion Week. It's scary how a rumor becomes unimpeachable fact so quickly. In two weeks the great white tents would go up, the celebrities would flood in, the runway would be strutted, and I wouldn't be a part of it.

A small, fluffy white dog went *yip*, *yip* and bounded gleefully in the grass around my legs. I bent down to scratch his ears, and he fell over on his side in paroxysms of joy.

"Winston has admirable taste in women."

I looked up to see a distinguished white-haired man in a tweed suit and fedora looking at us from his seat at a table where he was playing chess. He eyed his opponent, moved his bishop, and said, "Checkmate."

I was completely impressed. I had seen a movie about Bobby Fischer.

"Would you like to play?" he asked.

"Yes!" Winston and I leaped up and approached the table aggressively. The defeated opponent fled in the face of our youthful enthusiasm.

"I'm Vincent." He rose from the chair and doffed his fedora. "How are you at chess?"

"I'm Cheryl and I suck."

"Ah, good. I like winning." He grinned.

"Why is your dog called Winston?" I asked, sitting down.

"After Winston Churchill. A great man."

I tried to assess if he was being serious; with adults, you can never tell.

"Why was he a great man?" I'm so insolent.

Vincent thought a moment. "Here's an example. He was at a very exclusive dinner party when he got into an argument with Lady Astor across the table. She said, 'If you were my husband, I'd put poison in your coffee.' Mr. Churchill replied, 'Madame, if I were your husband, I'd drink it!'"

I laughed. This sort of dark humor appeals to me.

We began playing. My dad had taught me the basics. After about five minutes, Vincent said, "On guard."

I jumped, looking behind me, expecting to be mugged. Vincent was amused. "It means I've put your queen in check."

"Oh," I said nonchalantly, trying to slow down my heart. How bad a position was this?

He had me checkmated in two more moves.

I was tight-lipped; I hate losing at anything. He saw my reaction and made me a deal: He would help me with chess if I would stop being such a type A personality for a few minutes.

Vinnie—I was the only one who got away with calling him that—and I became good friends. I would walk by the park when in the area and stop for a few games if he was there. Many pleasant hours were spent beneath a spreading tree, sunlight filtering through the leaves, me getting brutally thrashed at chess.

My forced exclusion from Fashion Week didn't completely prevent me from walking a catwalk. The show I had booked through Jacob, by doing a pirouette at the casting, was that night. I wasn't even excited; it was a job. The gloss was rubbing off the modeling industry pretty quickly.

I arrived in my uniform of jean skirt, black top, and flip-flops. In the back of the cavernous lounge/club, models were assembled, all playing games on their cell phones. I had been to enough runway shows by now that I could predict exactly what craziness was about to unfold.

1. Deceptive calm; a polite designer.

2. Makeup and hair nearly attack each other over differing styling opinions.

3. Designer morphs into Joan Crawford.

4. New models are terrified; the experienced ones smirk knowingly.

5. Chaos rules; the show will never be brought off.

6. The show is brought off.

Hair and makeup were shouting at each other. "We're supposed to be going for the natural look!"

"Red lipstick can be natural!"

"No, it can't!"

"Yes, it can! The lights will wash them out otherwise."

"Do you have *any* experience?"

"I have studied my craft for many years!" The makeup guy thrust his hips to the side.

"Girlfriend, please!" the hair guy trilled.

The designer, dressed all in black, her hair tied tightly back, broke them up and vetoed red lipstick. "Go with something peachy!" she snarled, an inch from the makeup guy's nose. In fairness to designers, they don't just accept applause at the end of the show; they have to produce and manage the entire event. The best strategy for a model is to remain invisible and not get involved until you actually walk the runway.

A half hour before the show was due to start—which meant fifty minutes before it really did—Giovanni arrived. He was mysteriously allowed backstage with the Goon I wanted to adopt, and zeroed in on me. I sensed our meeting there was no coincidence, although he put on a show of being surprised at my presence.

"Look who's here! It's Cheryl!"

I was immediately wary. No one is ever *that* happy to see me.

"Hi, Gio." Perversely, I was also somewhat pleased to see him. I have always gotten along well with nonconventional people. We understand each other. Life is too brutal to go through it being politically correct and obeying all the rules. Of course, once you're established you can affect staunch morality and fleece people in a socially acceptable manner. Like taxes, campaign donations, and toll booths. I desperately want a toll booth.

A select few expensively dressed men and women had been allowed back to commune with the models. They were drawn to Gio, who thumped a man on the back, making him choke, and pointed to me. "You know what this girl is? Street-smart!" This was obviously a high compliment in Gio's mind. The show was about to start, and Gio fixed me with a frighteningly intense look. "We'll talk after."

"Uh-huh," I said, thinking, *Uh-oh.*

I began rethinking the wisdom of hanging out with a guy who ran a high-end Manhattan escort service and God knew what else. Gio basically bossed Jacob around, though, and Jacob was booking me well.

It wouldn't hurt to be polite.

I stepped out onto the runway amidst the throbbing music in an asymmetrical black dress, and when the spotlights hit I remembered why I liked modeling. The video cameramen trained their lenses on me to feed the projection screens. My eyes were becoming accustomed to the flurry of bright white flashes from the pack of photographers camped at the end of the runway; they no longer blinded me. I posed, gave them a final withering look, spun, and returned down the runway, watching the back of me on the projection screen. I was having fun.

My next outfit change—an asymmetrical blue dress that I was sure

I had put on wrong—went just as well. The designer was applauded by one and all, and everyone backstage apologized for their previous stress-induced behavior.

A woman backstage was talking pompously about her antiques.

"What's the difference between antiques and used furniture?" I asked, genuinely curious.

She was horrified and pronounced me "uncultured."

I changed back into my clothes down a hallway in the spacious bathroom. One of the models, about my age, was standing at the sink crying. It wasn't an unusual occurrence and I had enough problems of my own to worry about, so I patted her on the back and let her be. She splashed water on her strained face and left.

A few minutes later I followed out the door and came face-to-face with Gio. His entire demeanor had changed; he seemed intensely menacing. Women are far easier to intimidate than men. Not because we lack courage, but because we have overactive imaginations. To scare a guy, you have to smack him around and explain in detail how you are going to flay him alive. You only have to give a woman a scarily cold look and we assume that our entire family will be butchered. Pets included.

I hoped Tigger was hiding in the bushes somewhere. My parents were hundreds of miles away and therefore safe. Or were they?

Gio had a really perfect intimidating look.

"Get your things," he said. "The limo's outside, we'll go for dinner."

I glanced pretend-casually down the deserted hall. The Goon was standing at the entrance, blocking it, his back to us.

"Dinner . . . hmmmm . . . Oh! I'm kinda busy tonight. Maybe some other time."

He put his hand on my waist, and the hallway suddenly seemed very narrow and stuffy. "I want to talk to you tonight," he said firmly.

"Uh . . ." My brain was stalled. I wanted to run away or hit him, but the Goon was there, and he was very large.

"Can't tonight," I said stupidly, trying to get his hand off me.

He replaced it gently. I began to feel queasy. "You've got to start thinking about your career, Cheryl." *What else did I ever think about?* "You have a lot of potential, and if you want, you can be very successful. We'll go talk about that now."

"No." The hallway was closing in with amazing speed.

"You don't want to be successful?" He took his hand off my waist.

"I can do it on my own!" I said proudly.

He threw his head back and laughed at me. The Goon resolutely faced the opposite direction.

"Cheryl, Cheryl, Cheryl . . . you're just a little girl alone in New York. You've got no connections, no money, no backup. You're nothing."

Twice in one week! First the comment by Fab and now this! I was furious.

"I'm nothing?" I asked coldly. "What are you?"

His face darkened. "Watch yourself."

"I'll leave that to you; you seem to be so good at it."

"You won't last six months," he said.

I had a horrible feeling that he was right. "I'll last six months easily, and in the meantime, Gio?"

"What?"

"Just leave me alone." I walked away as quickly as possible without running, toward the small pinpoint of light that wasn't blocked by the Goon's body. Ducking and plastering myself against the wall, I slipped out under his arm.

I broke into a run—through the lounge, where civilized people sipped drinks—and burst through the door onto the sidewalk. It was dark, and Gio's limo and driver waited for him. I sprinted in the opposite direction, my flip-flops slapping against the pavement. I was terrified of being shot in the back of my head, "execution-style." I had been reading too many crime stories in the *New York Post*. Three blocks away, I developed a charley horse and my nose started bleeding again. Perfect!

I knew this would likely finish my relationship with Jacob's agency, and I was right. I never heard from him again. Things were not going according to my grand scheme.

I had my life all planned out when I was four.

First: international acclaim as a prima ballerina. Second: marriage to the ultrahunky Marlboro Man. Third: an idyllic life spent riding horses, roasting s'mores by a campfire, and being generally adored. Of course, I couldn't be a ballerina because I grew so tall and my legs are too long. S'mores are fattening, and the Marlboro Man died of lung cancer.

Reality bites.

Fire!

A squirrel began hanging out on my fire escape. Tigger detested it. He would crouch, growling, on the window-sill, hoping I would open it wide enough for him to spring out and beat up his bushy-tailed rival. Instead I would slip my hand out and leave the squirrel—I named him Nuts—some almonds. Fab interrupted this tender moment with a phone call.

"I have booked you a shoot!"

"A shoot?" No way.

"Yes, yes, tomorrow at two p.m. with Yao."

I sat on the puke-colored linoleum of my kitchen and copied down the address on an overdue utilities bill. I routinely ignored these until the company sent me threatening notices printed all in red. Next I got dressed, tiptoed downstairs with Tigger bringing up the rear, and slipped out of the building. I was a week behind on my rent, and the landlady had begun making sad puppy eyes at me whenever we encountered each other. Tigger followed me to the bus stop, saw me off, and vanished into the bushes to patrol the hood.

In Manhattan I dodged irate honking cabs and made my way downtown to a printing place Philip at Classique had recommended. The disk from the rap star shoot still hadn't been messengered to Philip and would prove harder to extract from the photographer than a tooth from a live shark. But I still had my other disks.

The photo place was intensely hip, resembling a white and chrome spaceship interior with bright red and yellow couches. Comp cards that they printed for all the top agencies lined the walls, and a secretary with pink-highlighted hair gave me a cool look. I was willing to put up with some bitchiness, since they printed pictures for models—signed to an agency they had an account with—for only two dollars.

I scanned my competition's comp cards while waiting.

Twenty minutes later a large, curly-haired woman emerged verrrrry slowwwwly from the back offices.

I was raring to go. "Hi, I have some pictures to print."

She produced a long, detailed form for me to fill out. "I'm Gretchen," she said with satisfaction.

It was the beginning of a torturous relationship.

A gorgeous, dark-haired male model was sitting near us, checking his newly minted comp cards. When Gretchen strolled leisurely back to give my disks to the technician, he leaned over. "They're evil," he whispered seriously.

"Why do you come?" I asked.

"They're the best."

In what would become a tradition, I strolled through deepest Chinatown nursing my bubble tea addiction and getting used to the smell of raw fish in the outdoor display bins. Slimy-looking scallops and octopus tentacles were laid out on ice, flies buzzing around. The scene held a bizarre fascination for me. Then I would hustle down the street to slurp noodles in a place where I had never seen a non-Chinese person; perhaps because of the headless roasting ducks in the window.

In Jersey I crept stealthily back to my apartment, Tigger flinching at the music downstairs, and enjoyed my usual dinner of cornflakes.

At one a.m. my cell went off. I got out of bed too quickly, was overcome by dizziness, and flopped back down. By the time I reached my phone, there was a message. I accessed my mailbox and listened.

Pounding music sounded in the background, and then Giovanni's distinctive deep voice said, "Cheryl!"

Eeeek.

"How're you? . . . and . . ." Some of his words were garbled. He sounded tipsy and unhappy.

This made me happy.

"I'm at Suede, we've got a table . . . great fun . . . come down."

Landing a table is always expensive and therefore cool. Gio mumbled some more and eventually stooped to begging me to come.

This impassioned plea was repeated the next night at two a.m. The early-morning hours seemed to cause Gio to develop a conscience. I ignored both messages and considered yelling at Jacob for obviously giving my number to Gio. But I abandoned that when a check for the full amount I earned at the fateful runway show appeared at my mail place.

Noon dawned, and I got out of bed for the shoot Fab had arranged. Breakfast was Rice Krispies, for their entertainment value.

As I closed in on my Upper East Side shooting destination, my mother called.

"I'm on my way to a shoot," I said importantly.

She was suitably impressed. "Are you eating healthily?" she asked.

"Yup." Corn and rice by-products are good for you, right?

Yao was in his midtwenties and resembled a young Fab. He knew this, but it didn't stop him from immediately making fun of Fab's made-up accent. I struggled to keep a straight face. Yao and Fab were actually friends, and everything would probably get back to him.

The stylist was a bouncy, dark-haired woman, and the makeup/hair artist was named Om. Om had bleached-blond hair, a good fake tan, sequined jeans, a pink top, and a fantastic personality. I just couldn't tell what gender Om was, though I analyzed him/her the whole time.

Space was cramped, so Om did my makeup next to a window in the tiny kitchenette.

"You should marry an ugly guy," Om informed me point-blank.

"Why?" I asked worriedly.

"He'll be more appreciative, and the kids will still be good-looking because of your genes."

I nodded, slowly processing the information. Maybe it was time to stop ogling male models.

"Just a theory," Om said.

Om had a theory for everything, and soon we were having so much fun that she/he decided to put water on the gas stove for tea.

Om teased my hair up into a subdued Mohawk. "Oh, water's boiling." Placing calming chamomile tea bags in cups, Om wrapped a dishcloth around the pot's handle.

"Ahhhh!" Om yelped as the cloth caught fire. She/he totally freaked out, flinging the blazing cloth onto the counter. I had a vision of burning to death, which spurred me into action. I bolted off my makeup stool and turned the sink on. Yanking out the spray nozzle attached to a hose, I pressed it and aimed at the flames. Om was hyperventilating, trying to open the kitchen's eighth-floor window with the intent, I guess, of jumping out.

My feeble arc of water seemed to be having an effect, and eventually all that remained was a soggy, blackened cloth. Om abandoned the now open window and enveloped me in a bear hug.

"Omigosh! I love you!"

We heard Yao and the stylist approaching, talking to each other. This time Om sprang into action, grabbing paper towels from a roll and wiping the water and singed cloth into the sink. We both stared down at the sooty dishcloth in horror: the only remaining evidence. Just before Yao rounded the corner, I pitched it through the open window.

"Hi," Yao said.

"Hey." Om and I nodded, leaning against the counter.

"How's everything going?"

"Great!" I chirped.

"Oh, you're making tea. Make sure you use a dishcloth on the pot handle so you don't burn yourself." He went away.

Om and I gawked at each other, then deliberately poured the hot water into cups and gulped the calming chamomile tea.

Despite that rocky beginning, the first two looks went well. Yao was aiming his camera at me, snapping away, when I saw one of the light poles start to fall. "Behind you!" I yelled.

Yao leaped around just as the pole crashed to the floor, shattering the bulb.

"Okay," he said. "Let's break for a sec."

We ate pretzels in the kitchen and sipped more calming chamomile tea while Yao changed the bulb. Yao appeared and grabbed a pretzel. "Bulb's fixed. I had an idea for a picture."

We all raised our eyebrows encouragingly.

"Cheryl would be lying on her side in that thin dress outside a door, and there would be blood seeping out from under the door. Like she just had an abortion. It would be a cool shot."

The reaction was immediate. "No!" we all yelped.

"Are you sick?" Om asked.

"We wouldn't use Cheryl's blood," Yao protested. "I have a recipe for fake blood."

We vetoed his suggestion but never really relaxed after that.

The pictures turned out great, and in the year that followed Yao became quite the successful photographer. The field in which he excelled? Shooting for teen girls' magazines.

I listened to my Rice Krispies in the morning while Tigger eyed them suspiciously. I got a call from a designer, Esther, who knew someone who had seen me walk in the last runway show and got my number from someone.

This is how the industry works.

Would I be available for a runway show? I picked up some of my overdue notices and shuffled them near the phone—checking my busy schedule. Yes, I said.

It would be at Capitale. I had heard buzz about Capitale—a massive, stone-columned building that used to be a bank but was converted into an exclusive club. It's where Bill Clinton held his inauguration party. The rascal. And it was strangely situated in the middle of Chinatown. Esther gave me the standard info, and I was booked.

No agency fee!

Before heading out to my daily castings, I held an almond invitingly out the window. Nuts was becoming increasingly bold and actually had the courage to grab the nut off my hand. Next I would tame grizzly bears.

Lottie phoned me as I headed into a call for Max Mara. "*Please* do the club circuit with me just once!" she squealed. Out of curiosity, I agreed. The club circuit is not really a circuit; it's West Twenty-seventh Street, where most of the coolest clubs huddle together like an exclusive clique.

After night fell—the air alive with chatting and laughter—Lottie and I met up outside Suede. She was wearing a short green wraparound dress and silver hoop earrings; I was still in my model uniform with heels. The bouncers were smart, so there was less drama than usual when we cut the line and someone, of course, shouted, "Do you know who I am?"

The inside was a modern, rectangle-shaped area, the white walls and floors seeming internally lit from a mysterious concealed source. Orange and white-cube shaped lounges and tables lined the walls. Suede was minimalist in the way that appealed to models and celebs, making it the hot club of the moment. It was a place to commune with the beautiful people, watch everyone boogie down, and quite possibly get jiggy with it yourself. I nervously made sure Gio wasn't holding court at one of the tables. All clear.

Lottie and I set off purposefully toward the bar, our heels clicking, making heads swivel. After a day of being given bored looks by clients, the attention was salve for our bruised egos. A faceless man bought us drinks: designer water for me, because I was parched, and a bubble-gum-pink drink for Lottie. She offered me a sip; it tasted like candy with a very high alcohol content. These concoctions must be designed with the sole intent of getting underage models drunk quickly. I shook my head to get rid of the buzz. A Brazilian model next to us, her breasts vying to escape a silver dress, asked, "Don't you like it?"

"I don't really drink," I said.

"Why not?" She was appalled.

"I'm actually a recovering alcoholic."

Lottie tried not to laugh.

"Really?"

"Yup."

The girl frowned. "Do you go to the, like, meetings?"

"We prefer to call them get-togethers." I sipped water.

"Are you being serious?"

"No."

"Omigosh! I couldn't tell!"

"Thank you," I said.

A green-eyed male model from Lottie's agency came over to say hi. His name was Alex, and he possessed a uniquely naughty personality. Lottie began worrying about the Iraq war. "It's sooooo necessary for freedom, but I'm sooo worried." Alex and I shrugged at each other. Lottie was upset by our lack of reaction. "I have friends in the army!" she lied.

"Oh, really?" Alex asked. "Which army?"

Lottie smacked him on the side of his head and he retreated, laughing, to the end of the bar. A high-strung woman in her late forties immediately pounced to Alex's side.

"A cougar," Lottie whispered to me. The nickname was given to older, well-off women who pursue guys barely out of their teens. We knew who the woman was; she had connections to the modeling and fashion industry. We inched closer to eavesdrop. Her back to us, she tipsily cooed baby talk at an amused Alex. "I would *love* to help with your career. You could get a lot of jobsies; you have such a strrrong look." She rubbed his bicep.

"Hmm." Alex frowned. "How many jobsies are we talking about, exactly?"

We snickered.

People around us became increasingly drunk. Lottie and I were invited to one of the tables, where we were fawned over. I found the attention confusing and somewhat unsettling. Like the majority of young models, my only party experience before New York was standing around in some kid's basement, holding a can of Dr Pepper and making awkward conversation with a group of self-conscious teenage boys, while the kid's mom baked us Pizza Pockets upstairs. From that to being the most sought-after commodity at Manhattan's wildest clubs—it's no wonder so many of the shell-shocked models start taking the free drugs we're offered.

Every model I have met was teased for being extremely gawky between the ages of eleven and fourteen. We were lanky, skinny kids, with overly large hands and feet and knobby knees.

Modeling: the revenge of the string beans.

We soon decided to switch clubs. Out in the street, Lottie bravely led the way past a young girl throwing up on the curb, into a cab, and on to another club with pulsing lights and deafening music. The purpose of clubs has always eluded me. They seem like large rooms filled with people lying about themselves, drinking until they pass out, and screeching into one another's ears to be heard. It was interesting the first time I went, like observing an unusual habitat at a museum, but I didn't fit in.

We ran into Mandy—in her push-up bra, as usual—hanging on to a guy who resembled a wet noodle. Wet Noodle, a man completely devoid of personality, had a large trust fund, and Mandy had appointed him her sugar daddy. She was decked out in some very nice designer duds and was drunk out of her mind.

Lottie and I had fun, decimating velvet ropes, celeb sighting, and infiltrating all the clubs we had heard gossip about. But having seen it, I henceforth, posthaste, quit the club circuit.

It was noon by the time I extracted myself from bed and tried to remember what the hell I was doing that day. I am unique; I don't have to drink to be hungover. I sifted through some scribbled reminders near my bed. A casting for Versace at one o'clock!

Springing into action, I hurled my clothes in all directions, trying to find something clean and unwrinkled. I was seriously considering phoning my mother to ask if she would mind making a nine-hour drive to do my laundry and cook me a decent meal.

Nuts was on the fire escape, waiting for his daily almond. I proffered it on my hand, and Nuts advanced eagerly. Suddenly he pounced and sank his teeth and claws into my middle finger.

"AAHHHHHH!" I shrieked, trying to shake him loose. Nuts clung on tenaciously as I flapped my arm, screaming. Finally he came loose and catapulted through the air, landing in the middle of my kitchen. Nuts charged into my bedroom. There were thumping sounds, a crash when my lamp fell, and Nuts reappeared with Tigger hot on his tail.

I did what any sensible girl would and cowered in the corner while Nuts launched himself back out the window and onto a faraway tree branch. Tigger stood growling on the fire escape; I yanked him back inside, shut the window, and assessed the damage.

My finger was red, but surprisingly, there wasn't any blood. I poured peroxide over it, affixed a Band-Aid, and wondered if I had rabies. How would I be able to tell the difference from my regular personality?

Halfway to the Versace casting, Veronika called to reroute me to a different address—"The freaking dumb-ass intern made a mistake"—and to tell me that she had booked another shoot. In the space of the next weeks my modeling experiment, which had seemed erratic at best, began to actually pay off. Money from the work I had done came in, my landlady started smiling at me, and I upgraded from cereal to gourmet frozen dinners.

Brightly colored lanterns with interesting symbols were strung up in Chinatown as I headed for Capitale. I actually passed it several times, dismissing it as a very large bank, until I remembered it used to *be* a bank. I spotted the unmistakable figure of a bouncer and hustled up the red-carpeted outdoor steps.

"Name?" he growled, looking like a Secret Service agent with his earpiece.

"Cheryl Diamond."

He checked the list—I was actually on it, for once—and stepped aside. "Upstairs to your right."

It was very lavish inside, the kind of place that makes you feel important just for being there. An exceedingly cheerful, slender woman introduced herself as Esther, the designer. She vibrated with excitement, brown curls bouncing, while a quiet, solemn version of her—later identified as her sister—oversaw operations. Since no guests were due for another ninety minutes, we were using the area where the show would unfold as a staging area. Backstage, we later discovered, was roughly the size of a shower stall. Eager photographers were already circulating, sucking up to us models so they would get good preshow pictures. These photos, published at the end of each *Harper's Bazaar* and *Vogue* issue, show models smiling ecstatically, arms around one another, eyes aglow. Joy!

It's a pity the stressed designer in the background, arms flailing, shouting, "Move it!" while hair and makeup threaten to decapitate each other, is never shown. I talked with an eighteen-year-old model called Sacha, who informed me happily that her boyfriend was coming to watch the show.

I expressed appropriate enthusiasm.

"Yeah," Sacha said. "He's not Mr. Right, you know? He's more like Mr. Right Now. Actually," she mused, "he's kind of annoying."

We devoted ourselves to trying on various rocker-chic fashions featuring safety pins, sequins, and short skirts—the type of thing I always pondered wearing to the mall, without ever managing to summon the courage. Dark purple eye shadow was applied with ink-black mascara and looked cool instead of strange. Sacha and I posed for the photographers while two massive, black-clad bouncers talked into their earpieces and "secured the area."

Showtime approached like a runaway freight train. We were hustled backstage with our outfit changes—I had two—and they promptly got mixed into a giant pile with others. The doors were opened, the lights dimmed, and guests rushed in, securing a glass of overpriced wine from the tuxedoed barkeep.

The bouncers stood backstage in the half-light, looking out at the well-mannered guests suspiciously, flexing their jaw muscles, protecting us from nothing. Sacha rolled her eyes at me.

"Five minutes! Five!" Esther struggled through the ten cramped models toward the jumbled-together clothes pile.

"Uh-oh," she said, looking at it.

I was searching for a place to change into my next outfit that wasn't in full view of the bouncers. Sacha was obviously thinking the same thing when she whispered in my ear, "Come check this out! Bring your outfit changes."

I followed her down a couple of steps, farther backstage, to a plain wooden door. Sacha yanked it open and we snuck in.

We found ourselves on a smooth white marble walkway that led to a wide arc of stairs. I peeked over the marble balcony to see where the stairs went and felt slightly dizzy. Far below was what used to be the main lobby of the bank. Wall-to-wall polished marble, a glorious unlit chandelier, and completely deserted. . . .

Oh, the havoc we could wreak.

But there was a runway to be walked. We stashed our outfits, opened the door, and snuck back out. The show had just started; I found my place in line and put on a straight face. I had become accustomed to the pounding music and disorienting lights, but I always enjoyed the *oooooh* I got from the audience for putting more boldness into my walk than most new models. I lifted my knees higher, tossed my head, and stomped forward. I do walk like a horse, and strangely, it works. A few people even clapped; if only Fab could see it.

Sacha and I passed each other as I headed back after a snowballing from the photographers. Sacha was a bit shy and kept her head slightly down and to the side as she advanced. We met up hurriedly behind the secret door to change.

"How was I?" she asked worriedly.

"Awesome!" I fudged.

We bolted back out into the chaos.

"You can't change back there," snarled one of the bouncers.

"Why not?" I hollered over the music.

"It's not allowed."

"Not allowed by whom?" I inquired snootily.

He seemed ready to throttle me; it's really a miracle I've survived this long.

When I stepped out again, the audience actually remembered me and applauded in a sophisticated way. I made sure not to get so excited that I would trip over my stilettos. It was a recurring nightmare of mine. Sacha and I passed again; she seemed more confident this time, her head held higher. When the show ended, we high-fived and tiptoed away to retrieve the clothes we had strewn around during our ten-second change.

I closed the door behind us and, kicking my heels off, ran for the long marble stairs.

"Nooooo, you can't!" Sacha whispered urgently.

I kept going and flew down the stairs. Naturally, Sacha followed immediately, giggling with excitement.

In the middle of the bank lobby—preserved teller's windows looking emptily at us—we spun in circles under the chandelier. For a brief moment, instead of high-fashion models expected to be adult at all times, we were teenagers again. I got bored with that pretty quickly and raced Sacha back upstairs in our bad-girl rocker outfits. We put our stilettos on again and were escorted by a fuming bouncer to the VIP room. There we mingled in the final, and coolest, outfit we had worn. A select few photographers had been let in and snapped photos.

A nicely chubby woman in her forties rushed up to me. "Omigosh! You were great!"

I grinned.

"Pleeeeaseee tell me how I can order this outfit you're wearing. I just loooove it!"

I visualized her stuffed into my short wraparound skirt and partially belly-baring sequined top. I threw my moral obligations away and directed the poor woman to Esther for ordering information.

Sacha hurried off to finagle her boyfriend in to the party. They appeared soon after, and I was introduced. I had expected him to be slightly dorky after what Sacha had said, but not totally crazy. He was dressed in skintight silver bike shorts—it was a formal event—proudly displaying pudgy white legs and grinning maniacally at me. He stepped way too close and threw a meaty arm around my waist to be included in a photographer's shot.

I was horrified.

It was bad enough to be pawed by him, but to have it recorded on film! Action needed to be taken.

I disengaged myself and hurried away, trying to get lost behind people. A different photographer spotted me, smiled, and raised her camera. Just before the flash went off, Bicycle Shorts threw his arms around me and squeezed. This heartfelt moment was captured for all time.

He didn't seem to comprehend that the photographers were shooting only the models to showcase Esther's clothes. The photographers were annoyed, I was beyond angry, and Sacha was tugging Bicycle Shorts's arm, trying to pull him away from me.

He was infatuated. He wouldn't be deterred, and bounded after me wherever I fled. One of the photographers notified a bouncer I hadn't alienated yet, and Bicycle Shorts was escorted out to the regular-people room.

Sacha came over. "He's sort of hyper tonight." She shrugged.

When the photographers had their fill, I changed and headed resolutely for the exit, deflecting men whose manners were becoming obliterated by alcohol.

Bicycle Shorts actually had the chutzpah to make Sacha phone me the next day and ask if I would go see a French "art" movie with them. I declined.

I settled into the casting circuit. Weeks went by and the air developed a slight nip.

The issue of *Dance Magazine* with my spread in it hit newsstands. My father bought an alarming number of copies. My mother had the whole thing laminated. And they called me to point out that I was featured in more pictures than either of the other models. We were triumphant. This was obviously a turning point and we discussed what to do about school. My parents had always believed that real world experience was a large part of a good education. And I was certainly getting experience! We decided I could safely put my formal education on hold for a year to see if I could build a career in modeling.

I hurried past the gaping hole where the World Trade Center used to stand. Sad little memorials were painted on tiles and hung along the fence surrounding the area. It's one of the few places that can make you sad just walking by. I was late for a shoot and jogged down a quaint street to the photographer's studio. He was a solemn man, in conservative clothes, named Om Rupani.

"Would you like some POM?" Om Rupani asked.

I was fascinated by the walls of his studio, which he had papered entirely—floor to ceiling—with high-fashion magazine ads that he approved of. Ralph Lauren, Calvin Klein, and Versace models were everywhere; it had a distinctly mind-boggling effect.

Taking my openmouthed silence as a yes answer, Om Rupani

poured POM juice for everyone. He poured Perrier over the juice, and we toasted to a successful shoot. The makeup artist, Zelda, tucked a lock of blond hair behind her ear and went to work on me—in multiple ways.

She had just finished with foundation and was lining my eyes when she told me that she had recently "converted to lesbianism."

I blinked.

"Don't blink!" she said. "I felt I was at a time in my life when I wanted to pursue a more spiritual path. Have you ever thought about experimenting?" Zelda asked. The clothes stylist's eyebrows shot up.

"Nope," I said nervously.

"Well." Zelda straightened up. "In about three years, when you're twenty, you'll have realized that men are essentially predators. They don't do it on purpose, of course. It's biological; they can't help it. They conquer and leave!"

I was sitting morosely on the makeup stool when Om Rupani, a man, came to rescue me. "Is Cheryl ready? The light checks are good."

I really think the male population of the world should get together and hire a good public relations agency to rep them. They're taking a beating.

The theme of the shoot was fashions from the sixties and their comeback. I was given a black minidress with a white zipper on the front. A white fur hat—the kind Russian women wear in movies—topped it off.

Having hacked through the issue of our sexual orientations, Zelda and I began cheerfully trading industry anecdotes, since she had been a model. Om Rupani marched along, pointing out ads on the wall and lamenting the recent preference for masculine-looking female models and feminine-looking male models. I agreed heartily; this fad was the reason clients would sometimes deem me "too pretty" and hire a girl who resembled her own brother.

I stood on the dark green background paper and we went to work. As I directed my serious, challenging look at the camera, Om Rupani and Zelda engaged in a well-known game of Crack the Model Up.

Zelda said, "So this dog limps into a bar and says, 'I'm looking for the man who shot my paw.'"

I started to giggle.

"Don't laugh! We're shooting!" Om Rupani scolded.

"It's her fault!" I protested self-righteously.

"Who, me?" Zelda asked innocently.

We shot a few more looks before I had to dash out, makeup still on, to a five p.m. casting.

I popped up from the subway at Rockefeller Center and passed a homeless man holding a cardboard sign:

need money for drugs/hooker/booze. please help.

I walked a few steps past him, stopped in my tracks, turned back, and gave him a dollar.

Honesty must be rewarded.

Soon after, Veronika sent me on a high-fashion couture showroom casting at the inhumane hour of ten a.m. The day was gray and chilly; I disapproved of it. The designer's company took up an entire floor on West Fifty-seventh Street near Philip's agency. It was starkly white, with painful-looking modern furniture and severe people dressed in black. I joined two other models and gave my book to a panel of appraisers seated behind a table.

Two men, two women: equal-opportunity doomsayers. I was handed a red silk dress.

"Where can I change?" I asked.

"Here," said the pale-faced woman flatly.

The blond model next to me didn't hesitate to strip down to panties, her eyes immediately focusing on something far away. The rest of the panel gave her a cold reptilian look and then ignored her.

"Can I change there?" I asked, indicating what was obviously a vacant changing room.

"No," the woman said coldly, "you have to change here."

I handed the dress back to her. "I'd rather not. Thank you."

What a sucky day this was turning out to be. I retrieved my book from the glaring judges, who had already removed a comp card so they could call Prima and complain. Even the other two models were shooting me dirty looks for, I suppose, being "rebellious."

I tottered out of the building, feeling thoroughly disliked and uncool. This scenario was repeated on me about once a month. It's another step in the "breaking in" of a model that I elected to avoid like the plague. The main cause of young models falling apart, I found, are these cold and unnecessary examinations. It would be better if the assessors would leap up and, salivating, chase the model around the room. At least they would be displaying a human emotion, instead of giving a naked teenage model the fish eye.

It began to drizzle. Of course I didn't have my umbrella with me, since I only carry it on days when it remains sunny. I took a subway downtown toward Prima and got into a fight with a self-righteous guy who insisted I had bumped into him on my way to sit down.

"You bumped me!" We were sitting back to back, and he tapped my shoulder annoyingly.

"Stop touching me," I snapped.

"You have to apologize! You bumped me."

"I did not." It was true.

"I'm going to punch you!" he threatened.

He was a skinny, uncoordinated guy, and in my fury I decided I could take him.

"Okay, punch me!"

I really wanted an excuse to attack someone.

"I'm totally going to hit you!" he screamed.

"Go ahead," I said insolently.

Men and women in the subway car stared resolutely at their laps. The New York policy of minding your own business applies in *every* situation.

My stop was approaching.

"Say you're sorry!"

"You've said it enough for the both of us."

A man near the doors snickered appreciatively as I got off.

Fuming, I trudged through the cold drizzle to retrieve my disk from Om Rupani's shoot. Veronika had begun diverting mine out of Fab's greedy hands.

Damp and shivering, I entered the agency—and Hilda smiled at me!

I nearly had a heart attack.

"Cheryl!" she sang. "Aww, you're wet!"

I recovered and beamed at my successful experiment. "Hilda! You look lovely. How're things?"

"Good, good."

In a daze I headed for the booking room, and Veronika waved a disk at me. We sat together and studied the pictures.

"They're good." Veronika nodded. "By the way, I got a call earlier today."

"Ugh," I said.

"Well, they said you refused to change into their dress and stormed out."

"I refused to change in front of six people and thanked them before leaving."

"Yeah, that's what I thought. I blah-blahed and got rid of them."

"Thanks."

"But Cheryl, this is the modeling industry, and eventually you're going to have to get used to being nude in front of a lot of people."

"Why?"

She frowned at me. "It's the modeling industry."

"So what? I model clothes. It only matters what I look like in the clothes, not without them, right?"

"You'll lose jobs," she said matter-of-factly.

"How many out of a hundred?"

"Ten."

"Okay, then."

Rain pattered against the window, and we contemplated the computer screen.

"It doesn't really mean anything, the nudity," Veronika said.

"If that doesn't mean anything, what does?"

She thought about it and said for the first and last time, "You're right."

"Ooooooh." I grinned.

She smacked my shoulder. "Take your disk, that's what you're really here for."

Leaving the booking room, I glanced at the wall of comp cards. In the very center was mine.

Fab intercepted me near Hilda's desk and asked for a meeting in his office. We assumed our positions. I waited for him to impart wisdom into my dumb-blonde head.

"Cherilll, were you disobeying a client today?"

"Yes."

He blinked. "Don't do that!"

I'd really had enough of him. "I don't want to be scolded anymore. Let's cancel the contract." I had been thinking about it.

The air left the room. Fab recovered quickly and leaned forward. "That is a bad idea, Cheryl." His accent was faltering. "Lawyer fees are very high, and other agencies won't want to hire you when they hear about your attitude problems." Or the ones he would invent when he called around, blackballing me.

"But Cherilll, I don't mean to scold you. We can work together, okey?"

It didn't seem like I had much choice. I was aware that he had withheld another important casting from me, but Veronika had taken control of my booking schedule, and she wouldn't listen to Fab even if he yelled "Fire!"

"'Kay," I said.

He bobbed his head happily. "Ooee, good, good! We like you here, Cherilll!"

I restrained myself from rolling my eyes, and we shook hands sweetly.

Hilda had found a spare umbrella for me so I would be "dry and varm." We smiled nuttily at each other.

Outside, I opened the umbrella and splashed to a good pizza

place nearby. I wasn't being contrary at castings on purpose, or even because I wanted to. It just seemed that, as a culture, somewhere along the way to being "with it," "modern," and "cool," we lost the magic.

Within the first six months of a model's career, a mini nervous meltdown usually occurs. Mine arrived, conveniently, in the middle of an important casting for Louis Vuitton.

A model is supposed to learn how to budget her time, energy, and stamina. Instead I tossed all caution to the wind and stormed ahead, thinking activity equaled productivity. Ten a.m., a shoot for sportswear. The photographer stormed by. "Got a call from the designer, need camera-ready a week early, get undressed, makeup! Let's go, hurry!" The shoot was tense, and we snipped at each other. One p.m., no time for lunch, I dashed for a *Newsweek* cattle call. Two p.m., I was seeing dots and rushing for the subway. Three p.m., almost impaled by a cab while jogging from another casting to Louis Vuitton.

Their headquarters, in a high-rise off Fifth Avenue near Trump Tower, were big enough to host a football game. Two-story-high floor-to-ceiling windows surrounded me. At the far end, only four chairs, facing two chairs, broke a vast expanse of cream-colored carpet. The four Louis Vuitton execs were actually quite friendly, and only two other models were present. I had been specifically requested to appear, and Veronika had high hopes.

They were casting for a highly anticipated showcase of their trademark—and much copied—bags. I was instructed, along with a pixie-cut dark-haired model, to start at the far end of the football field. We were to "glide" forward, pick up a two-thousand-dollar satchel in the middle of the room, and continue advancing before breaking in opposite directions and then crossing each other in the middle.

I was confused and sleep-deprived, and I hadn't eaten since my Rice Krispies.

The execs sat and nodded encouragingly. The pixie-cut model counted to three under her breath, and we began runway-walking forward.

"Oh! No, no, no," said one of the seated women. "This is for a showcase. We'd like a more subdued walk, please."

That was a problem: I don't know how to be subdued.

We walked again, trying to break our runway training, and were stopped once more.

Next try: We sleepwalked forward, bent our knees—without stooping—to pick up a bag, and then stumbled around in circles, trying to remember the intricate walking plan.

The windows spun slightly, and my head became fuzzy.

Then we sat knee-to-knee with the execs on two facing chairs, and they began asking the dark-haired model questions.

How much experience have you had?

Which runway shows have you done?

Do you have any dance training?

The model answered smoothly, smiling at times, but serious when she was listing her experience. I listened approvingly while staring vacantly over the assessors' heads and out the window. I had been proud of my ability over the preceding months to take borderline traumatic experiences and stuff them away into brain compartments for review when I wasn't so busy. As the compartments spilled over and I contemplated my encounters with Fab and Gio, it never occurred to me that I would, of course, be expected to answer the same questions as Pixie Cut.

All four execs simultaneously turned eager faces toward me and raised their eyebrows hopefully. It would have been normal to be intimidated by sitting in a vast, empty space with four high-powered interrogators. But my overstrained brain was busy watching a bird fly by. It angled to the side and disappeared.

"Okay . . . ," I said profoundly. "I've, ah yes, done runway shows and have eight years of dance training. So, lots of experience, yeah."

I had managed to come off as stupid instead of completely nuts, which was the best to be hoped for. The execs smiled in an overly cheerful way. "Okay! Cheryl, Vanessa, thanks so much for coming, we have your comp cards."

I weaved onto the sidewalk outside and called Veronika.

"How'd it go?" she asked.

I didn't have the heart to tell her. "Fine, I think."

"Good."

"I'm taking tomorrow off," I announced.

"Okay." She never asked why, and the models hardly ever told.

I managed to maneuver myself home and into a warm bath, where I read the shampoo bottle. The next day was spent sprawled on my couch eating Doritos. I was in the throes of intense self-pity, and it felt pretty good. Dramatically, I contemplated what people's reaction would be if I really was impaled by a cab, for example.

Fab would wipe away a fake tear and say I was a "good kid."

Hilda would holler, "She was a damn fine *Mädchen*!"

La-shawnda would smile for the first time in her life.

Veronika would say, "Fuck!" and go back to working the phones.

Gio would fling himself to the ground and wail, "How dare she die without sleeping with me first?!"

I grinned at the ceiling; my meltdown was passing. In the evening I was sufficiently recovered to attend a movie and watch bad actors murder a good script. In the morning, refreshed and quite frisky, I rejoined the casting circuit.

You Tarzan, Me Jane

The news spread quickly among Prima's models: Paris was coming!

Fab, in a long-standing industry tradition, had headhunted a super-booker from a rival Paris agency. His name was Paris. Fab was overjoyed and agreed to let Paris pick two of Prima's top male models and one female model for his own personal "stable." These models would, guided by Paris, go boldly forth and vanquish New York. It sounded like bullshit to me, and I forgot about it until Fab called.

"Cherillll!" he squealed. "You have been chosen!"

Grudgingly I neared the agency. Paris had requested audiences with me and his two chosen male models. I didn't want a new booker; it had taken me months to get Veronika on my side. I returned the borrowed umbrella to a beaming Hilda. "Oh, Cheryl! You are so honest!"

Into the booking room I went and found a situation that could quickly turn lethal. Fab was informing all that Paris would now be head booker. Veronika was pale with fury, her lips a thin line as she hammered computer keys.

Paris was sitting, leaning close to Ryan, a nineteen-year-old, tousle-haired blond model. Paris was tall and trim, with a fine-boned face waiting to be impressed while knowing that it never would be. He leaned closer to a tired-looking Ryan and began massaging his knee. Ryan gave him a sleepily exasperated look and started coughing. Amy was hiding behind her computer, eyes wide. I was seized by an exuberant Fab, who trilled, "Paris, this is Cherilll! The girl you chose! Cherilll, Paris is an expert on runway. The best."

Paris seemed far more interested in Ryan, but gave me a thorough twice-over and offered me his seat while he got water.

I sat across from Ryan. "Hey."

"Hi, Cher—" He descended into another coughing fit.

It turned out he had been up until two a.m. filming a cigar ad. With all the retakes, Ryan had smoked his way through five cigars. I made eye contact with Veronika and raised my eyebrows, searching for advice. She shook her head sharply and went back to the computer. Not only had she been arbitrarily demoted from head booker, but Paris had stolen me, the model whose book she had been developing for months.

I couldn't demand that Veronika be my booker. As head booker, Paris now decided which models were assigned to which bookers. He came back with water for Ryan, who quickly blew out of the agency.

Only La-shawnda seemed smug. She enjoyed chaos.

Paris focused his attention on me and flipped through my book. "You have a marketable look. I want to see your walk."

Was it possible that Fab hadn't told Paris that he didn't like my runway strut?

Apparently, yes.

I put my stilettos on and we passed Hilda into the hallway. Paris stood in front of the chrome elevators, looking jaded. Thirty feet away, I faced him.

"Okay," he said, nonplussed. "Let's go."

I locked gazes with him and walked like a horse. Two feet away from Paris, I stopped and glared at this arrogant bastard who had taken my booker away. I whirled around and stomped back.

"AHHHHHHH! OH MY GOD! THAT'S THE FUCKING BEST WALK I'VE EVER FUCKING SEEN!"

My jaw dropped. Paris's face was flushed. He advanced, waving his arms around and screaming. The entire agency heard and congregated at Hilda's desk, looking cautiously into the hall. Only Veronika wasn't present.

"Everything okeydokey?" Fab singsonged nervously.

Paris sprang into the agency and everyone flinched. "Everything is okey-fucking-dokey! I've got GOOSE BUMPS! That girl can WALK!"

We all stared, openmouthed.

Fab was the first to recover; his face lit up with a chipmunk smile. "Yes, yes, that is one of the reasons I signed Cherilll! I saw right away what a good walk she had."

My mind short-circuited.

Amy rolled her eyes.

"GOOSE BUMPS!" Paris shouted.

Hilda, Amy, Fab, La-shawnda, Paris, and a UPS guy crammed for space near the elevator as I walked again. Paris wiggled his hips and chanted, "Walk the walk!" like a maniac.

Fab applauded the loudest. "Soo good! Oh, Cherilll!"

"Too bad we missed Fashion Week," I said peevishly.

"You didn't send her to Fashion Week?!" Paris, the runway expert, shrieked.

I went into the booking room to retrieve my portfolio. Veronika was refusing to acknowledge anyone. Paris burst in. "Okay, Cheryl, here's what we gotta do. You need an asymmetrical haircut. I know a salon. I want them to cut uneven bangs and take length off!"

My stomach tightened. When people are excited in the industry, they get the urge to chop hair. Someone else's, not their own.

"Not a good idea." Veronika spoke for the first time. "Hair companies love her. She's gonna land a lucrative contract soon if we leave the hair long."

Paris ignored her. "Call me at nine a.m. tomorrow, Cheryl, and I'll set up an afternoon appointment in between your castings. We'll go together."

"I'd really rather not cut my hair," I said.

"You have to. That's the way I want you to look."

"I don't want to."

"I won't book you otherwise, okay? Call me at nine."

"Mm," I said.

There was great back patting, but before leaving I looked over my shoulder and winked at Veronika. Paris would not be getting a call from me at nine.

For a week I heard nothing from Prima and went on Classique castings exclusively.

To pry the disk from the rap star shoot out of the photographer's death grip, I went to his studio and camped there while it burned. He was embarrassed.

Philip was proud of my initiative; he had given up on ever seeing the pictures.

After seven days of silence, a very chipper Veronika phoned me to relay some castings.

"How's everything?" I asked.

"Very nice." She almost giggled.

"What about Rome?"

"He's gone."

"Gone where?" I said.

"I can't tell you, but he's not coming back."

"Have you murdered him? Tell me the truth."

"No. Good idea, though. He resigned." She burst out laughing.

We had driven Paris out. I wasn't the only model to resist his drastic look changes.

"Whoooooo's the head booker?"

"I am!" she said.

We were back in business.

I passed the leering owner of the ninety-eight-cent store on my way to the supermarket. He had developed the disconcerting habit of rushing from his store and recounting to me exactly what I had worn on the day before.

"That white sweater and blue jeans were very nice. Oh, you have the same handbag today."

I restrained myself from adding that he was still wearing yesterday's unibrow.

Since food shopping is about as interesting as watching paint dry, I studied my fellow shoppers' food choices. They bought more non-frozen stuff than I did. Which I respected.

I also noticed the mob of women in the yogurt section fighting over the last cup of mixed berry. And yet I've never seen a man buy yogurt. Why not? Don't they like it?

I want some government money spent on researching this.

Veronika went back to work and booked me a shoot. The theme was Tarzan in the City, and the clothes, black Armani. Veronika was proud of me, since after the photographer had chosen a male model from Ford as Tarzan, she had scoured five top agencies searching in vain for Jane. Prima was the fifth agency; she saw my comp card and said I looked "angelic."

Veronika and I had a good laugh about that.

My cell number was given to the photographer, Malika, so she could reach me in case of a change in schedule, since the shoot was on Sunday. Malika took this as license to phone me and have ten-minute conversations about her "vision" for the shoot. I said "uh-huh" and hinted that she could discuss her visions with the male model, who was probably dying to hear them.

"His booker didn't give me his cell number," she said.

Smart booker.

The great day rolled around, cold and sunny, with scattered clouds. Malika and I had also discussed the reliability of weather forecasts, since we were doing a "location shoot." Meaning outdoors.

I jogged up four flights of stairs to her Village studio at ten a.m. The entire team was present. A mischievous dreadlocked stylist, Julian, was arranging all-black Armani duds while a preppy guy neatly laid out makeup and waved hello. Malika flung herself at me, clad in an army-green flight suit with military badges on the shoulders and candy-red four-inch heels. She hugged me as if I were an ailing, rich relative, and we air-kissed.

No one actually kisses in the world of New York modeling; everyone smooches the air. Adapting to my environment, I halfheartedly kissed air. Air loves me. I need Air. It's a very codependent relationship.

Twenty minutes later, as I was having my makeup done, the male model still hadn't arrived. The shoot would be a story of Tarzan and Jane on the run in Manhattan; so some dark brown eye shadow was smudged on my face, and my hair was artfully mussed.

Ten forty-five, still no male model. We gave up on him and were preparing to shoot me solo when he strolled in, smiling.

It was amazing how much alike we looked. Same eye color, exact same hair color—though his was chin-length. We could have been siblings. Malika's pale cheeks flushed, and she squealed, "John!"

"Hi," he said with a Brazilian accent. "Sorry I am late. I lost my way."

You slept in! I thought.

Malika was delighted with John and encouraged him to sample some of the designer strawberries and cheese she had laid out.

It turned out that John didn't delay the shoot, because—being perfect—he didn't need makeup, and his hair was already mussed. The makeup artist smudged some eye shadow on his forehead while John happily ate strawberries. Malika handed me a thin, mid-thigh-length dress to change into.

I thought of the cold outside. "Will I be wearing a coat?"

"No," she declared, "and you'll both be barefoot, just like Tarzan and Jane!"

We spilled out onto the quiet, tree-lined street. Me in a tiny black dress, my famous sneakers, and my bulky blue jacket. Malika in her belted flight suit, red heels, and military jacket, camera around her neck. Julian, the stylist, lugging countless cellophane-encased clothing changes, dreadlocks flying, in a neon green windbreaker. The makeup guy toting his magic tools, dressed in pink with a pink fur collar. John, in black Armani slacks and sweater with his red Converse sneakers, carrying folded light reflectors and offering us strawberries he had taken with him. Even in Manhattan we drew stares.

We piled into Malika's black Lexus. I was in the backseat, flanked by John and the makeup guy, whose fur collar tickled my nose. Malika, behind the wheel, turned to us. "I hardly ever drive. I'm really not very good at it!" She smiled.

In the backseat we exchanged worried looks, as Malika hit the accelerator and we zoomed to our first location.

Village scenery raced by.

"Red light!" Julian shouted in the front seat.

Malika slammed on the brake, and I flew helplessly over the divider. John and the makeup artist screamed, lunging forward to grab an arm and haul me back.

I was grinning; it had been fun.

"Omigod! Are you okay?" Malika blubbered.

"Yup," I said.

We all took a deep breath and motored off.

Our first location was a rough-looking street in the nearly deserted meatpacking district. I had to be coaxed out of my cozy jacket and then separated from my battered sneakers.

I was immediately cold.

John and I posed near an open warehouse door, acting as if we were rushing out. Julian held silver circular light reflectors, and Malika hollered directions. The few passersby stopped to snap pictures of us with their cell phones.

The pavement was freezing my bare feet. We were instructed to hold hands as John tugged me down the street, away from unseen enemies. Julian handed me a tight black pantsuit with a plunging neckline to change into. Everyone stood on the corner while I changed in the backseat. John doffed his sweater and wore an unbuttoned black silk shirt that we felt compelled to tease him about.

John resumed hauling me past various backgrounds while I looked apprehensively behind us. Julian chased us with the reflector, and Malika miraculously navigated the cobblestoned street in her stilettos. The congregation observing us had grown and decided that we were celebrities, even though they had no idea who we were. They were advancing. We crammed back into the Lexus, trying to refold the reflectors, and shot west toward Chelsea Piers.

Malika had scouted a beautiful little pier, with a restaurant at the end and old-fashioned polished wood sailboats anchored around. We commandeered a tiny nautical museum made entirely of wood, Malika and Julian frightening a couple of innocent tourists out so I could change into a long black dress. I shivered outside while John put on a sweater and a knee-length leather coat with a fur collar.

Sexism!

He hollered and beat on his chest a few times, getting into character. Restaurant lunchers craned their necks as we posed in front of a giant ship's wheel and some massive knotted ropes. A group of girls in their early twenties snapped pictures and, much to Malika's annoyance, followed us as we walked to our next location, a nearby pier. The makeup artist examined my face when we arrived. "Cheryl's lips have turned blue," he informed Malika as my teeth chattered.

"Put some lipstick on them, that should work," she said.

John, channeling Tarzan, agreed to clamber up to a wooden beam with only the Hudson River below, while I remained safely beneath him on the dock. Between pictures, he told me of his uncle in Brazil who had recently been kidnapped.

"Did you get him back?" I asked.

"Oh yes, you pay ransom, they let him go. It happens all the time." He shrugged casually.

It was five p.m. when we finished our outdoor location shots. I had lost all feeling in my toes and fingers, and Tarzan and Jane had realized that we had nothing in common. He was very laid-back and relaxed about everything. I am extremely driven and analytical. We had stopped trying to make conversation and lapsed into a peaceful silence, sharing a bag of Milano cookies in the backseat.

"This is what Americans call garbage food. Yes?" John asked.

"No." Julian laughed. "Junk food."

We drove to a subway entrance and descended into its depths. Malika bought a ten-dollar MetroCard and swiped us all through. John and I had to stand barefoot on the gritty subway platform as trains hurtled past, Malika shooting away. We boarded a random train, then Julian and the makeup artist held light reflectors while John and I sprawled against each other on a seat. Our fellow travelers made a point of not bothering us or even staring.

It's a tough city, but you gotta love it.

We reversed subways and managed to find the car in the dark. It had been a marathon shoot. On the way back to Malika's studio, she screeched the car to a halt.

"Look! Look at those lanterns!"

A building's beautiful courtyard was surrounded by paper lanterns, glowing on the trees planted in four-foot-high concrete cylinders.

"Wait here!" Malika told John and me. "We'll check it out!"

The three of them emptied out.

John and I watched them skip across the avenue, holding hands with one another. We grinned and shook our heads.

"They are crazy." He yawned.

"Where do they get the energy?"

"The drugs?" John suggested.

They were back in a flash, banging on the windows and hauling us barefoot out of the backseat. Ignoring the traffic, we formed a caravan and crossed the street. With the help of a cast-iron courtyard chair, John climbed onto the elevated tree container and lifted me up. We were too exhausted and cold to behave ourselves. I jumped up and down in a minuscule black frock, hollering Tarzan yells, while John beat his chest and leaped around wildly.

Malika laughed and snapped pictures. Although I couldn't put that shot in my book, I always kept it; it's the only modeling picture ever taken where I'm smiling.

Back at the studio, we drank green tea, and Malika blushed at everything John said. We changed and jogged downstairs.

Outside, John solemnly shook my hand. "Good luck. Be careful."

I nodded just as seriously. "You too."

Casting us as Tarzan and Jane wasn't much of a stretch. The modeling industry really is a jungle, and you need some luck to make it out alive.

Lottie and I walked purposefully along Thirty-fourth Street, wrapped in our winter woollies, to do some shoe shopping. In Nine West we contemplated choices and commandeered a bench. Lottie took off her pink socks on, which red letters spelled out BOYS LIE.

"Girls lie too," I observed.

"Yeah, but we're better at it."

I grinned proudly.

"There's all this buzz about Elite again." Lottie tried on a gold pump.

There was always talk of Elite Models, usually centering around founder John Casablancas. A notorious modelizer, he lived with Stephanie Seymour when she was fifteen and later excused himself by claiming he thought she was sixteen. His conquests of barely teenage models became too much for even the don't-ask-don't-tell modeling industry, and he was no longer helming Elite. "Yeah," I said to Lottie, "But Elite has bounced back." No small feat after distancing themselves from Casablancas, the man who claimed one top supermodel's infamous breasts were fake and she had slept her way to the top, further stating, "she has nothing to offer from an intellectual point of view . . . she is an empty shell, one big void as a person." Don't hold back John, tell us what you really think.

Lottie wiggled her bare toes before slipping on a stiletto, and I saw the marks.

I knew what they were and groaned, "Aww, Lottie."

She looked up. "What?"

I pointed at her foot. "How long?"

"How long what?" she asked with false innocence.

"How long have you been shooting heroin?"

She avoided my eyes. Injecting between toes is a model's trick so that marks don't show in pictures.

"You've got to stop," I said. What a cliché.

"It's not important." She shrugged.

"Well, your parents would probably freak."

"Yeah, but I've got it under control. It won't kill me."

"Famous last words." I was confused, not sure what to say.

"Shut up, okay?" she snapped. "You're in the industry; here's a question for Cheryl. How do you get through it without drugs?"

"Chocolate helps." I smiled, hoping to bring back her normal pre-drug personality.

"Whatever. I've got to go." She stomped into her shoes and blew out.

My brain was immediately filled with things I should have said—daytime TV things—that might save her. I rushed onto the street in time to see her red head disappear into the crowd.

In an industry phenomenon, shared only by perhaps the CIA, Lottie was seen a few more times and then vanished completely. She became an unmodel, quickly forgotten on the casting circuit and rumored to have left for Paris.

I stood in Rockefeller Center, removing my fuzzy red gloves at a cattle call for Wella Hair. Their headquarters had a projector playing a recent Wella runway show on the slab of white marble between the entrance stairs. About sixty models milled around, lounging on the cool seating arrangements or inspecting the display products on long shelves. I compared books with a blond British male model from Prima, who always seemed on the verge of asking me out but never quite made it. The gang of girls living in Fab's model apartment came over. Sandy, whom I had done Clairol with. Mandy, who was sticking her chest out and boasting about her sugar daddy, couldn't remember even being on the club circuit the night I had seen her. And a quiet, dark-eyed girl who was not deemed important enough to introduce. Allie didn't make it through the summer and had been sent home.

"Hello, Professor," Sandy said.

The nickname had been bestowed on me for declining Sandy's eleven p.m. phone plea to go clubbing with them. I had also been caught reading a book at a casting.

"Cheryl's a dork!" Mandy giggled.

"Are you drunk?" I asked.

"Yes!"

"I like you this way."

Mandy grabbed my book and fled to a corner to examine it.

"How did you get all these shoots?!" she shrieked.

It had not been easy. Malika had lost her mind over John (aka Tarzan) and launched a confusing war against me. She made up fantastic excuses to withhold the disk, while grilling me on whether John and I were madly in love. I thought it was funny, since we never saw each other after the shoot. Veronika figured out what was going on before I did, and it became a favorite discussion of the booking room.

"I'm sick of this stupid woman!" Veronika shouted after a week. "She better cough up the fucking disk."

Veronika had a threat-laced phone conversation with Malika, and I picked up the disk from a reformed and very affectionate photographer.

"Hey, Professor!" Mandy smirked. "Look at this bracelet my sugar daddy got me." She jingled it in front of my nose.

I had seen Mandy accompanied by Wet Noodle at castings. She would make him wait in the lobby holding her things and looking like a wet noodle.

"I'm going to Cipriani's tonight with him," she trilled.

"Oh yeah," I said. "I remember him. How is your bitch these days?"

Sandy burst out laughing, while Mandy struggled to comprehend my question.

The Wella casting worked in two stages. We met with a smiling woman who either said, "Thanks for coming," if they weren't interested, or asked for a comp card and requested that you stay for a few minutes. Forty models were dismissed. The woman grinned at me and said, "Card me."

I handed her a comp card and hung around as instructed.

The Prima gang was among the twenty left standing.

We filed into a huge white marble room, were told to stand in a line, and took part in the most stressful casting I had ever experienced.

Four black-clad Wella execs in their forties stood in front of our row, eyeing us as if we were the Usual Suspects in a police lineup.

"Step forward," said an exec to a male model.

He frowned and stepped forward. The male model was inspected briefly.

"Okay, step back."

They went down the line, asking the models they were interested in to step forward for closer inspection. If they chose a model for their runway show, the lucky subject was placed in the center of the room.

The central colony was growing. Sandy and Mandy had been picked, along with two Prima male models and a Gilla Roos model.

"We only need one blond girl with long hair," announced a solemn line inspector.

Including me, there were three blond, long-haired models.

We looked at one another.

"Step forward," I was told. I did.

"Okay, step back."

The exec stopped in front of the next blond girl. "No, you're not what we're looking for. You can go."

One down, one to go. The poor girl slunk out.

"Step forward," the exec told a long-haired Ford model. She was about my age, with a vulnerable pout. I suspected she was prettier than me.

"Step back."

Were they torturing us?

He stood in front of me. "Step forward. . . . Okay, step back." He walked to the other blonde and repeated his request.

The girl and I glanced at each other nervously. The inspector walked gravely back and forth between us, stopped, and went to confer with the other execs.

I was in knots.

He returned and continued his study of us. Suddenly he halted in front of the other girl, and my heart dropped.

"Not you," he said to her.

The girl's eyes widened with hurt; she'd thought she was being picked.

He turned to me. "You."

Somehow, I didn't feel my usual elation at winning. I dragged my feet to the center and received subdued high fives from the Prima gang.

The girl hurried out, avoiding eye contact.

The casting segment was over; waivers were produced for us to sign. I never liked the blanket waivers that models must sign, allowing the company to do pretty much anything to your hair. But otherwise you simply never book a job.

We were to return at seven the next morning for preshow prep. Leaving Rockefeller Center, I breathed the now icy air and resented winter. I rode the V train downtown to Prima for a comp card restocking.

"It's going to freaking snow," Veronika said.

"I booked Wella."

"Nice."

Fab bounded into the booking room. "Cherilll! I heard you were here. I have a job to discuss with you." He was bundled in a fluffy white sweater. We adjourned to his office. Raquel, the owner, was inspecting some documents, reclining in a comfy chair against the far wall.

She looked up, remembered me, and smiled. "Hi, Cheryl." Fab had probably related long sagas of my naughtiness to her. But I doubt she ever bought it.

Raquel returned to her papers, and Fab leaned across his desk to relay vital information to me. "There is a jewelry showcase tonight at a lovely club/lounge in Manhattan. From ten p.m. to maybe one a.m. I thought you would be perfect as one of the models, because you are so outgoing and friendly."

I restrained a chuckle. A showcase consists of models wearing the designer's jewelry as we mingle with guests and get hit on.

"How much?" I asked.

"Ooee, she will pay you."

"Okay, but how much?"

"I'm not sure, but she will give you cash, and you can pick a piece of jewelry to keep for free."

I grinned. "How much would this piece of jewelry be worth if I sold it?"

"Hee, hee, hee."

"Seriously, though, how much am I going to get paid?"

"I don't know, but she will give you money and it's fun. Like a party."

I looked at him and thought it over. "This designer, she's a friend of yours, right?"

"Ooee, well . . ."

"Fabriziou, I really can't agree to do a job without knowing what I'm getting for it in advance. Also, I have to be at a Wella booking early tomorrow morning."

"But Cherilll . . . ," Fab whined.

I did not feel like doing him a favor, due to obvious past experiences. Fab had this annoying habit of lending his models out cheap to personal pals.

"It will be fun, fun."

"I don't like going to club/lounges. Also, I don't think it's such a good idea to book Prima models out at low prices, because word gets around and people will think those are our regular rates. Then it's difficult to get clients to pay our real rates."

Fab shook his head. "No, no, Cher—"

"She's right."

We both jumped and looked at Raquel.

She continued, "Really, it's not a good idea, Fabriziou. Listen to her."

Don't grin, I cautioned myself.

"Yes, yes, of course." Fab nodded. "You sure you don't want to do the job, Cherilll?"

"Yes, but thanks for thinking of me."

"Okeydokey."

Seven a.m. I sleepwalked into Rockefeller Center and mumbled greetings to my fellow seemingly comatose models. We sat around quietly, staring straight ahead. Chris, a blond male model from Prima, entered the room and announced, "I found coffee." In unison, we rose and followed him like ducklings.

A very cool coffee machine was secreted in an alcove—the kind where you choose a packet of the drink you want, place it in the machine, and the rest is automatic. Chris took charge, placing packet after packet of the strongest coffee in and handing it out to his yawning following. I managed a few sips of the ultraconcentrated brew and almost immediately began to perk up.

Within ten minutes we were unmanageable.

Giggling, we attacked the extensive breakfast buffet that had been laid out. Pete, a green-eyed model with Prima, discovered cameras that were recording live and transmitting to a small screen providing backstage action to include with the footage from the runway show. Pete stood in front of the camera, grinned, and flipped it the finger.

Eventually we were corralled and our hair was worked on. I was told that a nonpermanent red rinse would be applied to only the bottom layer of my hair, so the back would look more strawberry blond in an updo. They said it would wash out within a month, and there was actually no trace of it after a week. I gazed contentedly at the ceiling as a woman in black massaged suds on my head. Mandy boasted about the jewelry showcase she had booked at the last minute and done the night before. I decided not to tell her that she was my replacement after I turned it down.

"I only got two hours of sleep last night!" Mandy squealed, flinging herself onto an unimpressed Pete's lap. There is always competition among models to see who slept the least and yet managed to appear. It's somewhat heroic.

"She paid us three hundred fifty in cash and we got to pick a piece of jewelry." Mandy smirked. The three-fifty was less than half of what we were supposed to receive for four hours' work.

"But guess what! I got soooo drunk on the watermelon martinis that when the cab dropped me off at the model apartment, I handed him some bills. This morning I found out I gave him the whole three hundred fifty dollars!" she said, laughing. Pete rolled his eyes and scooted Mandy off him. Undeterred in her frantic search for self-esteem, Mandy hurled herself at another male model.

"Hey, Professor!" she hollered. "How come you don't like clubbing?"

This was incomprehensible to her.

"Just not my thing," I said.

"Cheryl's a freak, Cheryl's a freak," Mandy, joined by Sandy, singsonged.

They were reverting to kindergarten. How much longer until they called me a doodyhead?

The male models shook their heads. For some reason—perhaps because they are usually older—it's rare to meet a male model who loves clubbing every night like the girls.

"Clubbing's pointless," Pete said, dealing another hand of poker to me and Chris. I had learned to bring a pack of cards to jobs; there's a lot of vegetating involved. I ended up losing a quarter, but it was fun. Lunch was laid out, and we abandoned the cards.

"Have you had trouble getting paid by Prima?" Pete asked, chewing a turkey wrap.

"Of course." It's sadly common for agencies to withhold checks from models—usually for four months after a job is completed, sometimes forever.

"I figured out a way around it." Pete grinned smugly.

"Tell me!"

"Okay, you go to Hilda and say you want the money rushed to you. You have to agree to give Prima an extra five percent, but she'll cut a check in a day. That's really the only way to ever get paid; give them twenty-five percent instead of twenty."

"Wow." I was delighted, munching a Caesar salad.

"Don't tell anyone else, or Prima will stop doing it."

"I won't." I sipped Perrier.

Mandy came over and asked me casually, "Has Fab ever pulled your shirt up and squeezed your boobs?"

My mouth opened and closed a few times. "Uh, no. Why?"

"I was in Fab's office after I signed with Prima. He did that, and I wasn't wearing a bra, so he said, 'Wear a bra, okey?' It was really freaky."

Pete didn't seem the least bit surprised.

"You should tell Raquel," I said.

"Yeah, I did. She said she would talk to Fab, but she hasn't, and now she's, like, 'Just forget about it, Mandy.'"

"Is that why you always wear the, um, push-up bra?" I asked.

"Yeah." Mandy shrugged and wandered off.

Ironically, Fab was a religious churchgoer. He made the models living in his townhouse accompany him to services every Sunday evening and out to dinner afterward. In a way, I had to admire little Fab. Every man in New York was trying to get a date with his models, but Fab went out to dinner every week with three drop-dead-gorgeous girls and made them pay for their meals. Plus the models thought it was mandatory to go.

The man, in my humble opinion, is a genius.

Fab viewed Pete and me as the biggest lost souls at the agency. We questioned things, we made jokes, and worst of all, we managed to get paid for our jobs.

We needed saving!

Fab would routinely chase me around the agency, asking when I would be coming to his church. Pete, a Catholic, managed to stop Fab by calmly informing him that he worshipped Satan.

"What?" Fab had yelped.

"Yes, we sacrifice small animals," Pete said.

"Ooee! Okey." Not sure if Pete was joking, Fab abandoned the cause.

A Wella hairstylist wound sections of my hair into long ropes and secured them in an updo that I wish I could replicate. There would be three different looks, each represented by a girl and a guy model: Secret Agents, Woodland Nymph Fantasy, and Modern Chic.

I, of course, wanted to be a secret agent. Instead, Chris and I were appointed Woodland Nymph Weirdoes, while Pete and Mandy became the new 007s.

We all followed Cathy, an exec, into a large, wood-floored room to be assigned clothes. Mandy and Pete were dressed in slick black; I was assigned layered, gauzy clothes, while flowers were stuck in my hair. The result was amazing. I loved being a Woodland Nymph Thingie.

Cathy unbuttoned Pete's black shirt and rubbed his chest, her close-set eyes glittering. "Arrrren't you hunky!" she squealed.

We all stared at the floor, trying not to giggle.

The show was about to begin. Guests had been let into the room with the runway through a different entrance. I was going to walk the runway alone first, exit, then walk with Chris, and end the show in a feat of organized intricacy, when we would all be onstage simultaneously. We all congregated at the open door to the runway room. A wall prevented the guests from seeing us, but we could see the entire catwalk. Music started.

Sandy, dressed as Modern Chic, walked first. We watched her

from our hiding place as she reached the end of the runway. I put my serious yet ethereal look in place as instructed and walked. I saw the guests for the first time; about two hundred solemn faces stared up at me. I started down the runway; my eyes strayed to all the movement coming from our backlit doorway. Everyone waved, while Chris and Pete made ridiculous faces. The contrast was so outrageous that the instant I turned my back on the audience, I was laughing.

The show went off without a hitch, as it should have, with such consummate professionals as us being the models. Guests swarmed to take pictures of our unique new hairstyles afterward. We were given goody bags with Wella shampoo, conditioner, and a container of bath confetti that I created a huge mess with at home.

Our payment slips were being signed when it was announced that snow was falling outside. Still in full runway apparel, we all rushed out into Rockefeller Center and peered through the glass doors at the fat flakes.

It was my first snowfall in New York.

Respectable businesspeople stared at us clapping our hands in celebration and threatening to bean one another with snowballs. I couldn't resist pointing out that, at this very moment, Al Gore was giving an outdoor speech on global warming.

Mandy, Sandy, and I had a casting for Clairol and agreed to share a cab there. They yelled at me to hurry up as I gathered my stuff.

"C'mon, Cheryl, move it, we've got shit to do!"

"Get over yourselves," I said.

They took offense at this comment—after they had spent the entire day insulting me—and stalked out into the snow. I followed out the doors and kept an eye out for a cab, while trying to catch a snowflake on my tongue.

"I can't believe you said that!" Sandy snapped.

"Neither can I," I said.

"That was so rude. We're not even going to discuss it," Sandy decided.

"Okay." I was in it for splitting the cab fare.

A trio of well-dressed, tanned men in their forties approached to hit on us. Mandy became immediately friendly—could they have connections?—and recommended her favorite club, while I scanned for a taxi.

"We are from Italy," one of them said.

"Oh, cool," Mandy simpered.

"Cab!" I yelled, and charged for one that was letting a couple out. We piled in, and we were off.

"Since you're such a bitch, Cheryl, you have to pay for the cab," Sandy declared.

"No." I gave her my intimidating look. "We're going to split it, like we agreed."

She dropped it.

The tires crunched on the snow, and the windshield wipers squeaked comfortingly as the flakes insulated the taxi. "Is Italy in Europe?" Mandy asked, attaining a new pinnacle of vapidity.

"Yes," I said. "So is France and . . . Japan."

Sandy rolled her eyes at me.

I was enjoying myself. "Also Africa."

Mandy nodded contemplatively, looking out the window.

At the casting, two friendly women from Clairol offered me seven thousand dollars to dye my hair permanently auburn and simultaneously said, "Don't agree to take this job! You'll make *way* more money if you leave your hair natural!" It was the first time a client had pleaded with me not to take a job for my own good. I agreed to pass up the seven thousand, and they seemed relieved.

After the casting, I bid the Prima gang good-bye. They grunted, then Mandy sighed. "I need a drink."

I bounded down deserted Ninth Avenue, leaving deep footprints. I had a date with Tigger, as I do on every year's first snowfall.

Back in Jersey I opened the apartment, patted his head hello, and changed into my old jeans. We banged eagerly down the stairs, and Tigger flew out the front door into the flurry. He frolicked crazily around in the snow as I molded a snowball and hurled it farther down the sidewalk. Tigger gave chase and pounced on it; I tackled him, we rolled around, he ate some snow, and we went back inside, soaking wet.

Some models went home for the holidays. I did not, sensing correctly that fewer models meant less competition for bookings. I crunched through the dirty snow, freezing as usual, and felt sorry for myself as happy families passed, laden down with shopping. Salvation Army Santa Clauses jingled their little bells incessantly, until I had visions of impaling them with a giant candy cane.

At 11:59 on New Year's Eve, I made a resolution: Survive another year.

The renegades in 1C let off what could only have been an atom bomb downstairs and someone screamed.

A couple weeks later, I acted on a tip from a Prima model that a starving artist friend of hers had a breakdown, was fleeing Manhattan, and needed to sublet his tiny midtown apartment. I found that from a number of small jobs I had enough income at my disposal to afford it. I corralled Tigger into his cage and loaded my stuff into a large cab. Through the back window, I watched Jersey vanish. It had been good to us as a staging area, but I was extremely relieved to be getting out.

Tigger and I inspected our new digs with a giddiness that belied how small it was. I was suffused with gratitude when I saw that the artiste has left his fridge, the lone occupant of which was a forlorn pumpernickle bagel, covered with green mold. We settled in, and I purchased an I ♥ NY T-shirt, to be worn only in secret.

It was almost eleven p.m., and I was exploring the origins of an accumulated inch of water under the kitchen sink when my phone rang. Surprisingly, it was Philip's chipper voice informing me that a Fashion Week runway model had fallen ill and a very-last-minute replacement was needed. "Tell me you don't have another important booking tomorrow," Philip pleaded. "I'll be there," I said.

The February air was chill, not yet holding the promise of spring. I eagerly approached the huge white tents of Fashion Week in Bryant Park. The area was crawling with models, our heads wrapped in scarves, feet encased in warm boots, jaywalking across the street. As soon as I was through security and into the complex, using my pass for an afternoon show and my soon-to-be-copyrighted gate-crasher smile, the air turned warm, even tropical. The busy hallways backstage were formed by stark white canvas, resembling the corridors of an insane asylum. Despite the frenetic activity as people rushed to and fro, snapping at tiny cell phones, an air of sanity, even order, overrode the usual backstage chaos. Technicians, stylists, designers' crews, and the fashion press—eager to spot a new trend or make a new star—crowded around. A few confused new models were even being helped by Karolina Kurkova, the Czech supermodel, whom everyone would like to hate but can't, because she's so nice. Champagne was popped in small groups, and fresh-faced, broke newcomers rubbed shoulders with supermodels earning ten million dollars a year. Because it was my first Fashion Week, butterflies were fluttering around my stomach as I navigated by three racks of dazzling red dresses—the Red Dress Collection. A professorial guy, who I am sure was Oscar de la Renta, passed me, and he actually gave me a nod.

IMG, the company that owns Fashion Week as well as IMG Models, puts on only two shows a year: one in September, featuring flirty spring clothes, and one in February, to show the gorgeous heavier fabrics of designers' fall collections. There is a six-month time lag from buyers selecting clothes at Fashion Week until they can be shipped and displayed in local retail stores. When everyone is looking forward to the warm months ahead, models sway down the runway in floor-length fur-lined Muscovite coats, as if preparing for a long winter's hibernation.

Hardly anyone acknowledged my presence, being completely absorbed and focused on the particular function they were responsible for. Two models were gossiping nearby. It's a rule at Fashion Week that everyone must be catty. "Did you *hear* what Karl Lagerfeld said about Kate Moss?"

"What?"

"She's too short and bowlegged!"

Ouch. Not even supermodels are exempt.

An excited woman stood near me, "Oooh, lovely bag, darling."

"Thanks. I got it for five bucks on Canal Street."

"Don't admit it, darling!" She rushed off.

It seemed a lot like other runway shows, except on steroids, with the feeling that one wrong move could make the canvas tent implode. The bane of every runway model's existence was present and accounted for: the Backstage Lurker. These men are wealthy and connected enough to be let back to ogle us hopefully while we're changing. The creepiest ones hang back in the shadowed corners, looking hungry, while pretending to talk on their cell phones. Others are more outgoing and come over to try out their stellar pickup technique. There must be a handbook on this, or a seminar they take, because their identical strategy is analyzable into four distinct steps. A silver-haired man in a charcoal cashmere coat sidled up to me.

"Excuse me for interrupting you . . ."

And he was off.

1. Compliment.

2. Seemingly inadvertent shocking/demoralizing put-down.

3. Reluctant reacceptance of sadly insufficient model.

4. Generous offer to date someone like me, because he is a great appreciator of beauty and will overlook my gross interior flaws.

"Wow, you almost had me there," I said encouragingly, and walked off.

My makeup and hair were done quickly, with military precision. The designer, a highlighted, exuberant, colorfully made-up lady, narrowed her eyes the moment she saw me. She zeroed in, pointing a pink-lacquered nail at my chin. There must be something in my expression alone that allows people to identify me as a likely mischief maker.

"Now, I don't want you trying to celeb-spot in the audience when you walk the runway. You registering this?"

"Yes," I said, thinking, *Celeb spotting—What a great idea!*

She disapproved of my calmness, wanting me to snap to attention.

"No looking around out there going, 'Oooh look, it's Madonna,' okay?"

Madonna is coming? "Okay."

She eyed me distrustfully before moving on.

Another model whispered that a few days earlier the First Lady had sat in the front row and the Duchess of York herself had hit the catwalk, in a gown by Ralph Lauren.

A cool trick is used to hide the backstage area from the audience: A curtain of darkness. The intense floodlights of the runway and the muted light over the crowd rendered the staging area, and the models there, invisible. The show started about twenty minutes late, not unusual. These delays are not due to designers' egos, as many people think, but because of the necessity of changing the hair and makeup on the top models, who may be featured in five other shows that day. With all the buildup about celebrities, when I stomped on the runway, I felt compelled to try to sneak a look at the audience. But the lights were so blinding that it would be easy to misstep, so I fixed my gaze dutifully ahead. Tripping at Fashion Week would have roughly the same result as jumping off the Empire State Building. The runway show took a total of six glorious minutes, and I was done.

When the weather warmed and new April leaves were peeking out, I scoped out the chess players in Bryant Park. Vinnie and Winston Churchill had returned after a long winter's hibernation.

"Cheryl!" Vinnie exclaimed, while Winston went crazy with glee. I occasionally brought him doggie treats.

"Greetings, Vinnie."

"Have you practiced chess over the winter?"

"Nope."

"Excellent."

He went back to winning every game; I couldn't even manage to put his queen in check. But I began to recognize some patterns, which made me very proud.

Life proceeded acceptably until one day, tragedy struck. Veronika vanished. She was "no longer with Prima," and nothing more could be learned. The models speculated that she had become fed up with Fab and defected to saner pastures. Veronika vanished into the industry's black hole and became an unbooker. I watched in horrified disbelief as La-shawnda was appointed head booker. She smirked at me from behind Veronika's old desk, and my castings dropped by 50 percent.

I wasn't her only target. La-shawnda disliked a Czech model, Lana, who bore a remarkable resemblance to me. "Have your castings dropped too?" Lana asked. She was twenty-four, living in Fab's townhouse, and doing well on the runway modeling circuit.

"Yeah," I said, and we decided to get together and mope about it.

Lana had been roped into Fab's churchgoing party and asked me to accompany them. I told her I'd meet her outside the church when it let out, since I have an allergy to sitting on hard benches for long periods of time.

The church was on the Upper West Side, surrounded by pleasant little stores and leafy trees. I arrived when the service ended and well-dressed people spilled onto the sidewalk and milled around, talking. I watched for Lana's blond head above the crowd, since she was six feet tall.

"Cherrrilllll!" Fab fought through people and grasped my hands, his face glowing. "You came! You came to church! Oooee, Cherilll, this will be so good for you!"

I smiled.

"Did you like the service?"

"It was lovely. I think I'll reform myself."

"Ooee, good! How wonderful. Girls, come say hellooo to Cherilll!"

His new crop of models advanced, smiling. Mandy had recently imploded and been sent home. Sandy was dropped, at twenty-five, for being too old.

There's a lot of turnover in modeling.

Lana burst from the church and managed to convince Fab that we couldn't accompany him to dinner. We scurried to a nearby bistro and ate soup and salad. Lana informed me that she hated Fab and wanted to murder him. Then, when the salad arrived, she abruptly shifted subjects. "You know, Cheryl, we're in the same place with our careers, but you're seven years younger than me."

I dodged around this volatile issue until Lana began recounting her experiences as a teenage model in Milan. "Never, ever, ever go there, Cheryl. Or take a bodyguard."

Smitten men had pursued her down the street on their Vespas. One of them had unzipped his pants and pulled his underwear down—to show off, I guess—while zooming after her. Lana fled to New York almost immediately.

I found the story funny from afar, but Lana was traumatized by it.

Prima booked me a swimsuit shoot, and I immediately panicked over whether I was toned enough. Examining myself critically in the mirror, I decided it would have to do. The photographer, Richard, phoned me. "Hi, Cheryl, do you have a pen?"

"Hmm . . . ," I said, sifting through the debris on my coffee table.

"A pencil? A feather? A writing implement of some sort?"

I laughed and took down the shoot information.

His studio was on the twelfth floor of an industrial building in midtown. I rode the unconverted freight elevator and stepped into the dazzling white studio, with huge open windows looking out on New York. Richard, who was wearing a leather vest over a black T-shirt, resembled a burly Hell's Angel. He was perched precariously on an open windowsill, deeply inhaling a cigarette but careful to blow the smoke outside. His wife, a makeup artist, looked like the perfect busty babe to sit on the back of a motorcycle and look cool. I really encourage these marriages of a photographer and a makeup artist. They are so much likelier to show up. A special dating service should be started.

Richard's wife was grumpy, but she was three months pregnant, so all her actions were immediately forgiven. We didn't want to risk making her angry.

Another photographer and co-owner of the studio, Lin, was asking a meek assistant to get ready for checking light readings. Lin passed around a picture of his pretty wife and baby boy. Richard chain-smoked, almost falling out the window, as my makeup was done.

"Keep it natural," said Richard.

"I am keeping it natural!" his wife snapped.

We all shut up.

I changed into a tiny white bikini with boy shorts. For shooting I wore my stilettos, since they help you pose better and make legs appear more toned. Lin rushed over to hold a light reflector near the side of my head, and Richard started snapping away.

"Do you, like, get hit on by older guys a lot?" Lin asked.

I was trying to concentrate on the directions Richard was giving. "Yeah, sometimes."

"So how old is, like, too old?" Lin queried.

"Ah . . ." I pouted for the camera. "Forty, I guess."

Richard lay down on the floor to shoot upward.

"What if a guy is, say, thirty-six? I'm, um, thirty-six."

"I dunno, would your wife mind?" I grinned.

"Don't smile!" Richard yelled.

"Sometimes she doesn't understand me," Lin said, staring at my legs.

"Oh, shut up," Richard groaned. He heaved to his feet, took the light reflector from Lin, and adjusted it on a pole. Lin scuttled off, and Richard lit another cancer stick, which he inhaled in seconds.

"Okay, let's go. Whip your hair around . . . good . . . look directly at the camera, yes."

Richard positioned me directly next to the window for natural light and photographed me from the belly button up. My hair was parted in the middle and covering my chest, so the bikini top was invisible.

"How daring." Richard nodded approvingly and lit up again.

We took a break, sipping 7UP and discussing alternative methods he could use to kick the habit.

"I've tried the gum, the patch, both at the same time. I'm totally addicted, I admit it."

"How about hypnosis?" I suggested for fun.

Richard shook his head, sitting on the window ledge, blowing smoke out.

"Electroshock?"

"Ha-ha."

Lin ate a salad for lunch. "If the smoking doesn't kill you first, you're going to fall out the window."

We smiled; he'd made a good point.

Of all the models I met when I first came to New York, most had quit or been pushed out. I felt like the lone survivor of an unreported war.

In my model uniform of jean miniskirt and black top, I explored along Eleventh Avenue, walking up from Chelsea Piers. The sun shone warm and a wind blew in from the Hudson River. A gigantic all-glass building loomed on the horizon: The Javits Center. I'd never seen it but had certainly heard about the various conventions and luxury car shows it hosted. Curious, I went in.

All the walls and the high ceiling were formed entirely out of triangles of glass. It was big enough to house multiple 747s. I was padding along a red carpet in my flip-flops when I looked up and saw the canvas banner hanging from the ceiling: INTERNATIONAL CANDY CONVENTION.

Be still, my beating heart.

I began to scope the joint. Two escalators led down to endless rows of brightly lit candy stalls. Burly security guys guarded the escalators. It was obviously a convention for candy professionals only; a few well-dressed, middle-aged people went down the escalator with pink passes clipped to their lapels.

Must get pink pass by any means necessary.

I sat on a marble bench near the entrance to think. It was the afternoon, and a large, Greyhound-type bus pulled up outside. Some candy people, pink passes on their lucky selves, went out and boarded the bus.

Ah!

I grabbed a yellow legal pad out of my bag—I carried it around to record my thoughts on life. Positioning myself outside, away from the guards, I waited.

Five minutes passed.

Two innocently smiling women exited and came my way.

"Hello!" I unleashed my very commercial, non-edgy smile.

"Oh, hello." They stopped.

I put my pen to my legal pad and became serious. "Did you ladies enjoy the convention?"

"Well, yes." They nodded, pleased that I had asked.

"Excellent! May I ask if you had any favorite display? Your opinion is very important to us."

They actually blushed. Obviously they weren't from New York. It really wasn't fair.

"We liked everything."

"Ah! Very good. Thank you so much." I scribbled nonsense on my pad.

They seemed disappointed that the interview was over and moved reluctantly toward the bus.

"Oh," I said as an afterthought, "I'm supposed to help collect the lapel clips."

"Of course, dear," one said.

They handed the clips over happily.

I bared my teeth again and walked inside. Picking the tag with the least embarrassing name, I affixed it to my shirt and inserted myself into a small group of conventioneers. We passed the guard and sailed down.

I was intoxicated. So much sugar, so little time. In a maze of stalls I wandered around deliriously, having visions of hurling myself into giant mounds of candy and flapping around. Beautiful, adorable, wonderful people gave me samples. I don't think my unsophisticated taste buds fully appreciated the experience, but I certainly enjoyed myself. A person's happiness is directly proportional to the amount of sugar careening through her bloodstream.

Trust Me

La-shawnda enjoyed relaying castings to me in her snippy, fake British twang. It's a rule in the industry: If you don't have an accent, invent one. She also loved scheduling go-sees too close together, in the hope that I would be forced to sprint acrobatically across Manhattan. I had managed to mature slightly over my year in modeling and picked out only the best castings to attend in a civilized manner. I could harness myself this way only about once a week; the rest of the time, I sprinted.

Speed-walking down 23rd Street past Fifth Avenue, I tried to outdo a woman in a sharp business suit. Outside a modern glass building, a homeless man stretched on his back across the sidewalk, taking up most of it. He seemed to be sleeping peacefully, or possibly, dying. Cell phones glued to ears, an unending mass of New Yorkers stepped over him without breaking stride.

I called Fab on my cell to discuss the dramatic drop in frequency and quality of castings since the vanishing of Veronika. He was inexplicably furious, his accent gone.

"You have been saying bad things about the agency to clients!" he snapped, when I asked where my castings were.

"No, I haven't," I said truthfully. I knew how close-knit the industry is. So much so that when a messenger or anyone else not affiliated with fashion would enter the agency, someone would invariably warn, "There's a civilian here."

"Yes, you have!" Fab practically shrieked. "I have a source!"

"How long have you been withholding jobs without discussing this with me?" I asked.

"A while. You have been saying things!"

I rolled my eyes. "Is this source of yours La-shawnda, by any chance?"

"No. You know, Cherilll, not everyone must like you. You're not running for mayor."

"Neither are you, Fabriziou."

"Yes, well, it's a reliable source."

"No it's not, because it's a lie." I thought quickly about who it could possibly be.

"The agency's reputation is important!"

And Fab was certainly the man to put the agency's best face forward.

"You must respect the agency."

"What's the point of holding me to a contract when you refuse to book me and therefore make no money?"

There was a long silence.

"Not all models are with us only to make money."

I started giggling. The depth of his self-delusion was always entertaining.

"What's funny?"

"Nothing," I said, and then the penny dropped. "Fabriziou, was it Lana who told you this junk?"

"Um . . ." He gulped, giving it away.

"Amazing," I said. I knew that Fab probably didn't really believe Lana, but he was always searching for an excuse to sabotage me. He hastily said that he would generously reinstate my castings. I said okay and hung up.

There is a little-known fact about models: It's best not to be close friends with a model who resembles you too much. Lana and I looked very much alike, and when a client requested a blond editorial model, we were in direct competition with each other. The temptation to get me out of the way—and not have to outdo someone seven years younger—had proved too much for Lana. My quasi-relationship with Prima became even more crippled. I didn't mind much; the drama had become old.

Weeks later, tired out and somewhat disillusioned, I was sent to a casting by another boutique agency with whom I had a deal similar to the one with Classique. Alfaparf, a top Italian hair company, was in New York for a giant runway extravaganza. The call was held in the opulent ballroom of the five-star Jolly Hotel. Executives sat behind a long table, processing the models.

I was plucked out of the line almost immediately by a short blond woman and hustled over to the superstar hairstylist from Milan.

"This," she said, "is Bruni."

Bruni looked me up and down slowly, winked with Italian charm, and ran his hands through my waist-length hair. He winked again and cupped my face in his hands. "Yes," he said.

The woman said, "Congratulations. I'm Candace," and whipped out the compulsory waiver with tiny print for me to sign. Bruni explained with colorful gestures what he wanted to do for the show. "We will put a temporary red tint in your hair, yes? And it will wash out in one day. For the show I will cut a long fringe, bangs, yes?" He demonstrated by holding a small section of my hair near the front and indicated cutting it diagonally at cheekbone level. "Only small fringe, no other hair cut, okay?"

I nodded. "This tint comes out in a day, right?"

Candace sipped Evian. "Yeah, right away."

"Oh, yes." Bruni smiled. "You can show me your runway walk?"

I sashayed a few steps.

"Ah! *Perfetto*!" Bruni kissed his fingertips and grinned.

I signed the waiver and was given the typed job info. Bruni kissed my cheek good-bye, his stubble grating against my chin.

I walked along the dark street outside and made my way home. I seemed to be operating mainly on automatic over the last few months. An unthinking plod from castings, to jobs, to my apartment, without much examination of events. Simply put, I was pooped. I lay on my couch and read a random book from the pile that I picked out by the pound at the Strand.

At nine-thirty the next morning, Saturday, I patted Tigger and headed to the Pier Marco salon on Lexington Avenue. Alfaparf had commandeered it to prep models for the runway show on Sunday night. Two other star hairstylists, besides Bruni, were featured in the show, and I saw them talking to the models they had chosen in the white marbled interior. Bruni saw me enter, wearing jeans and a T-shirt; he rushed toward me, kissed both my cheeks, and hugged me tightly as I stood stiffly.

"Look, look, it's my Cheryl! My models are the sexiest models." He quickly kissed my cheek again while I tried to extricate myself.

A young bleached blonde wearing a black Alfaparf smock approached and, seeing me in Bruni's clutches, said, "It's just because he's Italian. They are sooo affectionate!" She introduced herself as Kyle and led me quickly away to an elegant hair-washing station.

"Are you going to be tinting my hair?" I asked.

"Yes," she chirped.

"It's gonna come out in a day, right?" It never hurts to triple-check.

"Oh yeah, it's only a tinted shampoo, it comes out in the first wash."

Kyle massaged suds on my overworked head, which I thoroughly enjoyed. She led me, dripping, to a black leather seat in front of the long mirror and brought out a bowl with the Alfaparf logo on it, filled with red goopy stuff. Companies brand everything, even shampoo bowls.

"Alfaparf shampoo," Kyle said grandly, using a brush to apply it to my hair as Bruni hovered proprietarily over my shoulder.

"We have to let it sit for fifteen minutes," Kyle declared, and walked off.

I started talking to the model next to me, Julia, a delicately pretty, dark-haired girl based out of DC. Another model sat near us, her hair wrapped in silver foil (likely picking up signals from Pluto), perusing *Vogue*. After twenty minutes Kyle wandered by, and I gently reminded her that it was time to rinse my hair. She washed it off, and I returned to my seat in front of the mirror to contemplate myself. It was slightly redder. Bruni checked me out. "It's not red enough. Use shampoo again."

Bruni leaned down to express some more Italian affection; I leaned deftly away before he could kiss me. He laughed and walked away.

We repeated the routine. On my way back from the hair washing, I noticed the foiled model turning away and wiping a tear from her eye while on her cell phone. I didn't even consider it unusual. Oh, my hardened heart!

Bruni reappeared and winked at me. "It's not red enough," he pouted.

Bruni conferred with his stylists, pulled a chair up next to me, took my hand, and held it. Kyle, Candace, and a chubby blond woman who strongly resembled Candace stood behind me with their hands on my chair. A man in a black suit stood near Bruni and spoke Italian to him and English to me. It was quite the scene.

I slid down slightly in my chair. Bruni looked soulfully into my eyes and intoned, "Now, Cheryl, your hair is too healthy, and it is not, ah, holding the color, yes?"

The suit spoke up. "We want to use a different product on your hair."

I looked at Bruni. "Like what?"

"We want to use permanent color," Bruni declared.

"No!" I yelped. "Most jobs I get are because I'm naturally blond."

Bruni looked pleadingly at me. "It would be so much more easy for me if you let us use permanent color."

Why did people continually think I would be motivated to make things easier for them?

"No. It has to wash out right away."

Julia was listening and nodding to what I said. My lone supporter.

"Are you suuure?" Bruni cooed.

"My whole portfolio is with blond hair. Please don't try to convince me; it has to wash out right away."

The suit looked at Bruni and shrugged. "*Niente da fare, non vuole.*"

I would have thought he was saying, *What a little bitch*, but I knew some Italian from my travels, and, roughly translated, it means, "She won't do it."

"Okay, okay." Bruni sighed. "No permanent color."

I had obviously offended everyone. The giant pressure team around me nodded and muttered okay. Blessedly, they dispersed.

Julia raised her eyebrows. "Wow, that was something."

Bruni, Kyle, Candace, and her look-alike were grouped together in the back of the salon, no doubt lamenting my stubbornness. Julia passed her copy of *Seventeen* to me and began reading the other model's *Vogue*. We had formed a magazine assembly line.

The Candace look-alike appeared behind me and sighed. "Okay, we'll put on the copper tint shampoo. It comes out in a day."

She sighed again to illustrate how much inconvenience I was causing everyone. After the required fifteen minutes of sitting still, my scalp began to burn. It was the third time we had repeated this ritual.

"It's burning my head." I squirmed.

Look-alike came over. "Let's leave it in for another ten minutes."

"Please wash it out, it's burning."

She sighed and washed it out.

I looked in the mirror. The copper tint had done the trick: My hair was a bright orangey-red. I wrinkled my nose, but Bruni loved it. He caught me off guard and kissed my cheek again. It was three p.m., and I was emotionally strung out. Candace came over to inform me that I had to be at the runway venue—Manhattan Center, a division of Madison Square Garden—in forty-five minutes for rehearsals. Everyone admonished me strongly not to wash my hair or even get it wet before tomorrow's show, since all the color would come out. I escaped, breathing the outside air deeply, and had coffee and apple cake at Starbucks. I walked down Thirty-fourth Street and entered the Manhattan Center lobby miraculously on time. The elevator shot me to the Seventh-floor Grand Ballroom. A humongous T-shaped runway was set up, with twelve-foot projection screens hanging on either side. The other models, about ten, were sitting in the drafty backstage area on sofas and being ignored by all the Alfaparf people, who were in total confusion. Some of the girls were semipermanent Alfaparf models and had done similar shows across the country. This was to be the crowning glory before everyone returned to Milan.

After forty minutes of sitting there, Candace announced that we were finally going to rehearse the show. The result was comical. Various Alfaparf people screeched at one another in Italian and expected the models to understand them. Different people would angrily give us completely different directions while the models zigzagged around the stage, not knowing whom to obey. Finally, the models who had been in runway shows before, even a thirteen-year-old from Elite, realized that it was a complete waste of time. The sound technician who was working on the ballroom's second-floor observation crescent grabbed his microphone and boomed in exasperation, "Okay, this isn't working, it's gonna go on forever. Please, will the Alfaparf people stop confusing the models!" We finally managed to leave at eight.

"Don't get any water on your hair!" Candace and Bruni hollered after me.

I slept soundly while Tigger eyed my orange hair, and returned to the Manhattan Center at seven fifteen the next morning, fifteen minutes late.

Most of the models were sleeping on sofas backstage. Only two Alfaparf people were there, and Kyle informed us that everyone would be late, including the breakfast food.

"What time is the runway show?" I asked Kyle.

"At five. It will probably last a couple of hours because of the demonstrations, and we'll need you until eight."

The models' eyes popped open and there was a chorus of, "Then why are we here at seven a.m.?" and, "We can leave soon, take a break, and come back at showtime, right?"

"No," Kyle said. "Sorry, but you guys really have to stay on this floor, in this building, until after the show."

"That's a thirteen-hour day," I said in disbelief.

Kyle responded with the patented Alfaparf shrug. Bruni and the rest of the Alfaparf crew arrived at eight thirty and began chain-smoking in the windowless backstage area. Soon the place was hazy with smoke. A team of makeup artists arrived at nine and covered our faces with heavy stage makeup and applied false eyelashes, after which the models fell back to sleep, their dramatically painted faces propped against cushions. Some models began talking about leaving or calling their agents if they could reach them on the weekend. Candace and her clone were wearing matching black T-shirts that read: DON'T PISS ME OFF. I'M RUNNING OUT OF PLACES TO PUT THE BODIES.

Candace stood intimidatingly over us and barked, "Okay, girls, calm down. Some breakfast will be here soon. Just be happy you were selected to be in such a high-profile runway show. Okay? Don't piss me off."

She gave us a final glare, and all the models stayed inside, slowly contracting lung cancer. Sitting in a carpeted room, Julia and I played snap and poker with my cards for hours. Bruni spotted me and joined us on the carpet for a few hands of poker. By scooting discreetly away, I managed to avoid any of his surges of affection. Faith, the model who had been crying at the salon the day before, was subdued but friendly. She was assigned to a different one of the star stylists.

Faith asked me for my advice on a member of the Manchester United soccer team whom she had met at a club but who then returned to England. "He's so gorgeous. Should I call him?"

"Yes," I said. I'm very bold when advising others.

"He's an ocean away!" Faith said dramatically.

I pondered. "Love bridges everything." I meant it as a joke, but Faith stared at me dewy-eyed.

"That's beautiful, Cheryl. Wow." She tried calling him, but her cell couldn't get any reception. It's the little things that stand in the way of true love. Bruni glided through, flirting and inviting us to his salon in Italy. He picked up the front section of my hair and proudly demonstrated to Julia and Faith the grand, artistically superior fringe he would be creating onstage.

"I will not take any length off the rest of your hair," Bruni declared.

"Will the thickness be the same?"

"Of course!" he boomed. "We only make fringe."

I was intensely bored and tired of talking about hair. At two, everyone rehearsed the show with more success than the previous night's three-ring circus. The ballroom and runway had been decorated beautifully; flowing curtains of golden orange cloth hid the backstage area. Seating for a thousand people was set up, with a wine bar at the far end. We trooped backstage to be assigned our outfits. Bruni's models would all be dressed in red.

"Because my models are the sexiest models!" Bruni informed everyone, slinging an arm around my waist. I wore a flowing red dress with a risqué slit and extremely uncomfortable stilettos that I worried would make me trip. A small, mousy girl was dressed in tights and rehearsing a dance backstage that she would be performing before the show began. A Russian model, who was a trained dancer, caught my eye, and we winced as the girl slaughtered proper technique. If you have really worked at something, it is physically painful to see someone else doing it wrong. While Candace ran a straight iron through my hair, she informed me that the girl was the daughter of someone very high up in the company and had thereby landed the job.

Candace shook her head. "I hope she's not too bad."

The show was about to begin, thirty minutes late, of course. Everyone congregated in the cold and drafty area behind the curtain. A TV screen was set up near some chairs so we could watch a live broadcast of the action; multiple cameras were filming on the stage and transmitting to projection screens. The girl was ready to do her dance and held a large beach-ball-like object that was lit from within.

She was actually quite nice; I felt some concern for her as all the lights shut off and we watched a disembodied lit-up ball travel across the stage on the otherwise black TV screen. An excited whispering was heard from the huge audience. I held my breath as the light technician put a spotlight on the stage and she started dancing. It was funny watching on a TV screen what was happening only a few feet away in front of the curtain.

The girl's routine was choreographed around the lighted ball.

She raised it to the ceiling, knelt to pay homage to it, and generally engaged in some quality bonding. With all the production—music, amazing lighting tricks, and the lighted ball, which was actually pretty cool—she pulled it off. The audience clapped, and we breathed a sigh of relief.

Faith and I stood near each other, since we would be onstage at the same time—me with Bruni and her with an abrasive female star-stylist. Bruni snuck up behind me and grabbed me enthusiastically from behind. I managed to squirm away and reinforced the industry tradition of pretending to laugh it off.

Faith patted my shoulder comfortingly, while Bruni repeated exactly what he would be doing with my hair onstage. Always the paranoid girl, I repeated, "You won't take length or thickness off, right?"

"Right." Bruni nodded, his teeth glowing in the darkness. The announcer onstage began introducing us, and Bruni took my hand to lead me out.

"Trust me," he said, as we stepped into the spotlight.

Faith followed and sat behind me on one of the modern seating blocks being used for the hair-trimming part of the show. The announcer gave a short speech to the rapt audience and then translated profound things Bruni said from Italian to English. Bruni spoke English well, but it never hurts to add some foreign mystery to your superstar stylist. Bruni explained that the motivation for my look was "seductive woman." He combed a shock of hair over my eyes, obscuring the audience and cameraman directly in front of me. He used a few clips to pull the rest of my hair back. Suddenly, with lightning speed, Bruni made a diagonal cut. The audience gasped. I wasn't worried as twelve inches of my hair fell to the stage. This was the fringe. It covered my eyes, and I only caught short glimpses of the cameraman.

Bruni began unfastening the clips and combing my hair. It happened horribly fast: I felt the tug of Bruni's razorlike clippers but couldn't tell what part of my hair he was pulling. There was more painful tugging. The cameraman took his eye from behind the camera, his mouth open, looking worried. I began panicking.

"Stop, stop, stop, stop," I whispered fiercely, the bangs hiding everything.

"It's okay, okay," Bruni whispered. He stopped soon after. I couldn't feel much difference. Bruni spoke to the announcer, who then boomed, "I know that our model was frightened about not having enough hair left, ha-ha. Will you all please let our beautiful model know that she still has long hair."

There was a tense pause from the audience, who then got the idea and clapped. I smiled nervously. Bruni leaned down and said, "Okay, walk on the runway."

As I stood, my hazy vision noticed a pile of fifteen-inch chunks of orange hair. It's not mine, I told myself. I walked the runway. Halfway back, I realized my hair was far too light. My stomach dropped, and I stumbled slightly. When I got backstage I immediately pulled my hair back into a ponytail and realized that Bruni had razored more than three-quarters of the thickness away. Faith exited the stage behind me and said shakily, "Bruni took all your hair off. I saw him cutting it all from behind."

I stood in place, saying nothing. When I thought he had been combing, he had really been cutting.

Faith was angry. "He totally lied to you. I heard him say before the show that he wouldn't change the thickness. I can't believe this. Your hair is gone, they can't do this." Everyone else had seen it on TV and was trying to avoid looking at me. I felt nothing, complete numbness.

Candace rushed over. She immediately pulled me away from Faith. "Don't worry, Cheryl. It will grow back in a couple of years."

"All my hair is gone," I said, trancelike.

"Shhh. I know. I know. Just be calm, you can always get hair extensions."

A bit of anger seeped through. "I didn't need extensions until Bruni lied and cut it all off."

Candace was obviously very worried. She patted my arm. "I know, Cheryl. I know." Pulling me farther backstage, she instructed, "Don't listen to the other models, they will just give you ideas."

"I want to see my hair in a mirror," I said quietly.

"You can't leave the backstage area until you walk the runway again."

"I need to see it now."

"Okay, okay," Candace said, looking panicked. Her clone joined us, immediately saying, "Relax, Cheryl. It will grow back eventually. Take deep breaths."

I was completely detached. Candace grabbed my arm and led my placid self farther backstage to a full-length mirror on a door. It was much worse that I had thought. Three-quarters of my waist-length hair had been chopped off above my shoulders, leaving a thin rat-tail trailing to my waist. Bruni had used razor scissors, so my hair was ragged and uneven, extra short pieces sticking out at odd angles.

"Ohh, nooo." I became completely numb.

Candace paced nervously. She gave a shaky laugh, "Look at it this way. Cheryl. Bruni cut off almost all your ponytail that was dyed orange."

I realized that the top of my head was bright orange while what was left of my ponytail was a lighter orange. Candace grabbed me into an unexpected hug. I faced my head outward and was looking directly into the mirror. A cold draft blew through and chilled my back where my hair had been. Candace began quickly running a straight iron through my hair to make the ragged edges stay down.

"Wow, it *is* thin," Candace marveled as she brushed what was left.

"Come on, Cheryl." Candace led me back to where the other models were. "You just have to walk the runway some more. Okay?"

I had gone officially into shock and didn't speak again until I left the building. Candace maneuvered me into a chair near the TV monitor. The show was progressing as if nothing had occurred. Faith came over immediately and sat beside me, patting my back. A blond model who was one of the more permanent Alfaparf models started trying to make me feel less alone.

"One time before a show, Bruni teased my hair so much that when he tried brushing it out afterward, it just fell out. See?" Her hair was very thin, and she had a bald spot on the side of her head. I closed my eyes and willed it away.

Bruni lurked guiltily in a corner and avoided eye contact. I wanted to cry but couldn't; I felt that I should at least react in some way, but there was just nothing left. I knew that my career—made by endless days pounding the pavement and fighting impossible people—was finished. It took more than a year to build something that was destroyed in three minutes. The other models knew it too and remained silent, their eyes downcast.

I shivered in my thin evening gown. Feeling someone approach my chair, I looked around in time to see Bruni place his expertly tailored jacket over my shoulders. He brushed the ragged strands of my hair aside and placed his fingers briefly on the back of my neck. There must have been a spark left somewhere in me, because I shrugged his jacket off my shoulders, letting it fall, and walked toward the curtained runway.

"Good, good." Candace appeared at my side, Julia and another model in tow, and pushed me out onto the catwalk. It occurred to me as the lights hit that this might well be the last time I walked a runway. The cameraman's head popped out from behind his machine and watched me, concerned. There was no joy in being onstage this time. I didn't like the music, the cameras, my image on the huge dual projection screens, or the audience's faces staring hungrily up at me. I hated the lights.

The show ended, and the models stood onstage in a V while Bruni and the two other hairstylists were applauded by the audience. It had been quite a show.

We all trooped zombielike backstage and changed. Faith put a piece of paper in my hand with her e-mail address and phone number.

"Call me, Cheryl. You have to do something about this."

A woman called Lindsay filled out our payment slips, billing the production company. I walked onto the darkened sidewalk at about seven thirty and went straight to a phone booth. My dad picked up, and I managed to blurt out what happened before I started crying. My mother came on the line before I ran out of quarters.

"I'm coming, all right? It's going to be okay," she spoke soothingly.

I sniffed, and the phone cut me off.

Walking quickly up Eighth Avenue, I sensed someone following me and turned around to see three short blond-haired women in their late thirties. "Wow, you must be really upset about your hair," one said. "We were near the front."

"He cut more than half off!" said another.

"Yeah." I kept walking, hoping they would leave me alone.

"You must really be trained as a runway model, right? We thought you were the best."

"Thanks."

"So . . . ," their leader pressed, "your career's over now, right?"

I was suddenly furious, looking at their pleased faces.

"Go to hell," I said.

Their mouths fell open, and they gawked as I walked off. How did I manage to attract these people?

At my apartment, I should have recharged my phone and called my parents again, but I didn't want to talk to anyone. Instead I stood in the steaming shower and furiously shampooed my hair, knowing that it probably wouldn't make any difference. None of the orange color came out at all. I lathered up three times, with no change except that strands were falling out. They had used permanent color. I wrapped a towel around myself and stared in the mirror above the sink. If anything, it was a brighter shade of orange. Ragged pieces hung around my chin, the razored ends sticking out in all directions.

For the first time in a long while, I burst out sobbing and slid down the wall to sit on the tiles. Time passed; Tigger meowed and clawed on the other side of the door. I leaned forward and let him in. He climbed onto my lap and rested his head on the towel. I kept on crying about everything in general. Stiff and cold, I fell onto my bed and blessedly passed out.

The sun was starting to glare through my closed eyelids as someone knocked on my door. Wrapped in my towel, I peeked suspiciously out the peephole. My mother stood there; she had driven all night. I opened my door. She took in my face and hair without flinching, came inside, shut the door, and hugged me. I started crying again, a reflex action that I was beginning to find extremely annoying in myself. I was tucked back into bed, patted and fussed over in a satisfactory manner. My mom stood outside my room, calling my father to report the extent of the damage. My mother whispered that I was "shattered." I realized that I really was; she is the last person prone to exaggerate. *What a sucky life*, I thought, staring at the ceiling.

My mother was furious. I smiled to think what would happen if dear Bruni ever passed her on the street. She tried to feed me soup, which I was too upset to eat, then began making phone calls. A few hours later she announced, "We are going to see a lawyer."

"They're expensive," I said automatically.

"This one is very good and will take it on contingency if it's a strong case."

I stared at the ceiling some more. "'Kay."

Obediently I led my mother to ritzy Madison Avenue and up to the lawyer's spacious office. I was impressed with her phone techniques—we were meeting with one of the partners. He sat us down and asked me to give a detailed account of what had happened. The last thing I wanted to do was relive the whole miserable experience, but the welcome numbness returned and I impressed all with a point-by-point description.

The lawyer and my mother seemed outraged. He agreed to take the case on contingency, although the waiver I had been made to sign troubled him.

"If it's a blanket waiver, they can get away with pretty much anything." He reviewed pictures in my book showing my hair pre-disaster and shook his head. "We'll try anyway." He asked me to write an in-depth account of what happened from the casting to when I staggered out of the Manhattan Center freshly shorn.

I slept some more and then immersed myself in the writing. "She's still in shock, but functioning." I eavesdropped on my mother's reports to Dad and was relieved to hear that I was operational. I wasn't so sure anymore.

Over the next week, sitting solemnly behind my legal pad, I carefully recorded events. My mom slept on the foldout couch, which I'd tested and deemed comfy. When the week passed, my mother observed that I was not suicidal or prone to heft an Uzi and seek Bruni out in Milan. She had taken charge of my schedule and actions—something I hadn't allowed since the coup d'état of my family that I staged at the age of three. Mom informed me that I would be allowed to stay in Manhattan as long as was necessary to deal with my lawyer. Then, whether I liked it or not, young lady, I would be collected by my father and transported to North Carolina for rehabilitation. I nodded agreeably from behind my legal pad. Mom had to drive back home but left unbreakable instructions to phone morning, noon, and night.

I walked around New York. The streets felt tilted, sounds oddly muffled. I typed my grand summary and e-mailed it to my lawyer. When we met a week later, a printed copy of my summary was on his desk. He stared at me, wide-eyed. "I read this." He tapped the stacked paper. "It's so vivid. I felt like I was *there*."

"Uh, thanks," I said, my usual bundle of personality.

Later, I called Faith and she met with my lawyer to supplement and second what happened, although she insisted her name not be relayed to Alfaparf or the company that owned it, Beauty & Business, fearing she would be blacklisted. Her hair, she discovered, had been fried as well and was turning an ominous red/orange color while feeling like straw. She lost jobs because of it and had to chemically dye her hair brown so it would be presentable, damaging it further.

The consequences of Bruni's rampage on me were even worse. My agencies instantly distanced themselves from the-train-wreck-formerly-known-as-Cheryl. I was sent on a casting, before the extent of the damage became widely known, to Lancaster London. At their offices, I tried on blue-and-white checkered capris and a blue top. The executives were looking nervously at one another, and before I left, one confided, "Cheryl, we really love your face and you fit the clothes perfectly. I felt I should be honest with you: Your hair clashes with everything. I'm really sorry. Did someone do this to you at a hair show?"

I became officially unbookable. In reaction, I conducted a tour of all Manhattan's best hair salons and was given the same verdict. It was permanent color. If I bleached my hair back to blond, the damage would be severe. I moped in Starbucks and was hit on by an Orthodox Jewish man who operated on Wall Street and offered to pay my lawyer fees. It surprised me to be hit on, because after the industry's reaction to me I felt I looked hideous.

"Have you heard the story of Samson?" he asked, the ringlets of his hair on either side of his head bobbing.

I wondered if he used a curling iron. "Yeah."

"Butchering someone's hair is symbolic of robbing their strength and spirit. That's why this man did it to you."

"He's a sick puppy," I answered.

My father arrived a few days later to take me home. He hugged me and reached up to do his usual ruffling of my hair but thought better of it. We loaded my bags into the trunk and Tigger into the backseat. We sat for a while in the front seat outside my apartment building.

"Listen, pal," he began earnestly, as I eyed him warily from under a shock of Day-Glo orange hair. "One of these days you'll be able to look back on all this and weep uncontrollably."

I burst out laughing, for the first time in months.

"We have signs of life!" he declared, pretending to take my pulse and delivering a hand chop above my knee to check reflexes. A bag of Doritos appeared, and we zoomed through the Lincoln Tunnel and into Jersey.

"Where did you live here?" my dad asked.

"You really don't want to know."

Sadly I watched Manhattan vanish while our "Margaritaville" CD played.

Don't know the reason
Stayed here all season
Nothin' to show but this brand-new tattoo,
How it got here, I haven't a clue.

Many hours later, we neared home base.

"There's a little hill coming up—you'll love this," my dad said. We have been catapulting the car off hills for ages. He started to floor the accelerator.

"Ah, Dad, is this safe?"

"Sure."

A warning bell sounded in my head. Although he's an excellent driver, in situations involving cars and speed, my dad reverts to a teen-age-boy level of caution. His blue eyes were open wide, anticipatory grin fixed in place, leaning forward in his seat. The problem with my dad and me is that we are far too alike, almost carbon copies of each other's slightly crazy personalities. His enthusiasm began to catch.

"So how much air do you usually get?" I asked, with a grin beginning on my face.

"Two to three feet." His eyes glittered dangerously.

"Cool. Can you see if cars are coming the other way?"

"No."

"This is gonna be fun!" I squealed, holding Tigger tightly on my lap.

We took the hill at fifty, shot into the air, and slammed down so hard that we bounced up and hit our heads on the roof.

"Yessssss!" we both yelled. A little way down the road my dad cleared his throat. "Don't tell your mother."

My mother was waiting with chocolate chip cookies when we stomped through the door. Dad tried to grab most of them before I kicked his shin; it was time to re-establish who was boss. He retreated to another room while I ate cookies, only to reappear holding a severed arm. He waved it. "I found Fred!"

Fred's realistic plastic arm wore a white dress-shirt sleeve, a cufflink, and a pinkie ring. A line of blood dribbled down his hand. My dad had purchased Fred when I was three, and we'd hang it out our rent-a-car's trunk while driving into a new neighborhood, shaking up the locals.

The good ol' days.

It occurred to me that if I had survived my childhood, I could survive pretty much anything. Dad tossed Fred to me, and I grinned.

It was good to be home.

New York Model

The rehabilitation of Cheryl was progressing smoothly, according to my parents' late-night discussions, which I eavesdropped on. Then I received a call from my lawyer, informing me that after some correspondence with Beauty & Business, where they tried to distance themselves from Bruni, they had unearthed the waiver. It covered them for anything short of tossing me out of the window. He advised me to drop it and go on to better things.

Easier said than done.

It was chilly and gray outside. For a few hours I wavered on the edge of getting depressed again, while my parents watched me worriedly. It had been months since the AlfaBarf Incident—as my dad christened it—and for the first time, while staring out the window, I became angry. Would I, Cheryl Diamond, descend into despair, hiding my orange head from the world?

No!

I would rise like a phoenix from the ashes. A blond phoenix!

I whirled around, feeling more like myself, and declared dramatically, "This won't stop me!"

My parents, relieved that I was communicating, smiled and bobbed their heads.

I went into training, jogging bravely for an entire sixty seconds before developing a massive side cramp. I had lost weight and was pale, with neon orange hair and blond roots. I ran on, tilting to one side while nursing my charley horse and hoping no one was watching me.

Delighted that my normal take-no-prisoners personality had returned, my mother confiscated the Doritos and enforced a healthy diet. I bounded off in my very uncool jogging outfit every day and was soon competitively outrunning other well-behaved joggers. Cue the *Rocky* movie sound track.

My mom, the only person I have let cut my hair since AlfaBarf, snipped off half a foot of the ridiculous rat-tail. A ray of light, in the unlikely form of a woman at a hair salon, informed me that there might be hope. "How healthy was your hair before it was fried?" she asked.

"Very healthy."

"If it was really in perfect condition, you might be able to get some of the orange out by doing deep conditioning. It would loosen the color."

A detailed description of a hair follicle followed. I researched the subject as if calculating for the first time that $E = mc^2$. We mounted a family-wide campaign to eradicate all the orange in the universe.

Each evening was spent with my conditioner-soaked hair in a

shower cap and then covered with a towel turban. When the sun was out, a glass of fresh-squeezed lemon juice was dumped on my hair, and I sat on the balcony in the direct sunlight.

To our amazement, more than six months after AlfaBarf, some blond highlights began peeking though. Gradually, strangers stopped cornering me wherever I went and asking what had happened to my follicles.

I missed New York: the smog, the people, the kamikaze bike messengers. I even missed the lights.

"Tell me honestly, are you a masochist?" my dad asked when, eight months after the incident, he drove me back to Manhattan.

I smiled. "Nope, just stubborn."

Tigger was chilling in the backseat; he knew the drill.

I adjusted the CD player to Crowded House, a really underappreciated Aussie group. "Hey!" my dad yelped, staring at my hand. "You stopped biting your nails!"

"It was a crutch," I pronounced grimly.

Tigger and I secured a small apartment in Manhattan, not far from where my former abode had been. The sun shone, the air was warm, and New Yorkers marched forward, dressed in black, ignoring me. It was wonderful.

I drank coconut champagne on my way to a casting. Sitting on a comfortable chair at Max Mara, I looked up when Brianna, a nice model I had known in the bad old days, entered. She immediately sat down, staring at me as if she was seeing a ghost.

"I thought you were gone!"

"I was, but I'm back."

This was a foreign concept; unmodels don't return to the scene of their humiliation. She leaned forward, inspecting my hair. The blond was growing in quickly, still uneven and light orange in my ponytail, but overall, an amazing recovery-in-progress.

"Wow!" she said.

I felt brave.

"So," Brianna said, "are you, like, traumatized?"

"No." I grinned. "But I'm, like, getting there."

She clapped her hands in delight and handed me her portfolio, opened to a tear from *Seventeen* magazine.

"Will you look at that?" Brianna jabbed her finger at the page with her carefree, smiling picture on it. Underneath her face, red letters spelled "Do You Have Hepatitis B?"

I laughed.

"Don't laugh." She smacked my shoulder. "My parents are gonna see this!"

She didn't have to worry; when it comes to models, New York is a no-parental-extradition state.

"I didn't know they were gonna use my picture for this article!"

"You look good." I snickered.

"Shut up!"

The hazard of modeling is that after you're paid for your picture, it can be affixed to any tagline.

"So, do you?" I said.

"What?"

"Do you have hepatitis B?"

She set her book aside and started to strangle me.

I reinserted myself into the flow of the industry, avoiding Prima like the plague. One day, walking down 25th Street, I spotted La-shawnda heading the other way. I ducked into a doorway before she saw me. It was surreal; I had never really seen her out from behind her desk in the booking room. She was a bit shorter than I thought and belonged back in the agency, making sure I would never get booked.

I was "discovered" by a well-known photographer while eating a bagel in Au Bon Pain. His wife, Lila, a makeup/hairstylist, stared unnervingly at me until they finally came over to discuss shooting.

A few weeks later, over lattes at Starbucks, we discussed the theme and mood for the shoot. I routinely go along with whatever photographers say, since they've already made up their minds on how to shoot me within sixty seconds of our first meeting. Besides, they really know better. The photographer, Eugene, was a calm Greek man; his pretty wife was from the Caribbean, with a musical voice and absolutely unshakeable opinions.

"Eugeeeeene," she sang, "I want to do a really wild updo with her hair."

I found myself nodding to her cadence as if she were a rock band. A location shoot was scheduled: elegant clothes against the backdrop of Manhattan's gritty streets. We agreed to shoot it the following Sunday and I left them nibbling a giant cookie.

Avoiding one of New York's torrential rainstorms, I ducked into a café near Bryant Park, where a pretty girl with a button nose and her aunt struck up a conversation with me. As the storm raged, I debated world issues with them. They were delightfully intelligent but unusually intent on world peace. I gently explained that world peace was not possible with rampantly enterprising people like me on the planet.

"We like to think that it is possible," Tala, the girl, said, glowing with hope.

"I like to think a lot of things, but that doesn't mean they happen." I grinned.

Tala was very tolerant of my bluntness. "It may be possible. All people are basically good."

I stared at her. "You haven't been in the city long, huh?"

We met up in Bryant Park a few days later. She wanted to introduce me to some friends who were "smart and knowledgeable" like *moi*. We walked to a place almost directly next to the Grace Building and entered what resembled a charming little tea shop. I was introduced to a group of young people with serene expressions and modest clothes. They showed me a pamphlet with the somewhat menacing picture of a man glowering forth. "The Reverend!" they said.

"Oh!" I smiled. "You're Moonies, right?"

Tala blinked. "Well, we do follow Reverend Moon."

"Moonies!" I was happy. This would be interesting.

They began the programming process in earnest. I was taken through a door in the back of the tea shop and into the main part of the building. Upstairs, in a screening room, the lights were turned off and I was shown a fifteen-minute puff piece on the courageous and infallible Reverend Moon. He fought communism! The voice-over boomed. He strove for peace! He was indicted for tax evasion! This was glossed over quickly to make it seem like he did time for wanting peace. I was immensely amused. Being in the modeling industry, I knew what a good public relations push looks like.

We retired back to the tea shop, where an assortment of free muffins was laid out. I quickly grabbed a chocolate one, and we filled cups with green tea.

"Omigod, she's a model!" Two women were starring at me.

"A high-fashion model!" one whispered. They seemed afraid that a normal-pitched voice would make me vanish.

I sat with Tala and a friendly, freckled girl. It was impossible to dislike the Moonies, since they were so genuinely well-intentioned. A cheerfully smiling man appeared. "This," Tala said, glowing, "is Reverend Jules."

"Hello," he said in a Jamaican accent.

Tala declared, "Reverend Jules has agreed to give us a lecture!"

I almost recoiled. I hate lectures of all kinds. But the reverend was off in a booming, hypnotic voice. Between making points on world peace and avoiding temptation, he openly tried to look up my skirt.

"If people *spread* the wealth out, we can have harmony."

"Isn't that communism? Aren't you against that?" I asked.

"Not really. It's about nonviolence." He tried to keep a straight face.

"Did you know that Reverend Moon's son is in the arms manufacturing business?" I smiled sweetly. My dad had informed me of it when I called him surreptitiously to say that I had infiltrated the Moonies.

"Well, that aside, we believe we must spread peace."

"Yes!" I declared, grinning. "Let's go borrow some guns from Reverend Moon's kid and smack some peace into the world!"

Standing tall, Reverend Jules spread his arms wide in the tea shop and actually began singing, *"Somewhere over the rainbow, WAY UP HIGH . . ."*

I stared at him, openmouthed, along with everyone else. He had a fantastic voice and no self-consciousness. *"THERE'S A LAAAAND THAT I HEARD OF, ONCE IN A LULLLLLABY . . .* join in, join in," he sang. When words I knew rolled around, I sprang up from my seat and hollered, *"SOMEWHERE OVER THE RAINBOW, WAAAAY UP HIGH . . ."*

Soon after, I marched out onto the sidewalk, trailing five Moonies of both sexes. I had decided to take them to a hidden place in Manhattan that makes the best burgers and was a closely guarded secret.

We entered the Burger Joint off 56th Street, down a cloaked corridor in Le Parker Meridien Hotel. Tiny, dimly lit, with famous people's autographs written on the exposed brick walls and iconic movie posters, it was packed and loud as usual. We shouted orders for burgers and fries over the din, and they insisted on splitting the check. Dusk was setting outside as we walked back downtown to the Moonie compound.

"Ohh!" Tala squealed when she spotted the artwork on Sixth Avenue spelling out LOVE, the huge red letters stacked on top of each other.

LO
VE

"That's what we're all about!" Tala squealed. She snapped pictures with all of us standing in front of it. One of the guys tried climbing the giant *E* with the goal of sitting inside the *O*. He got stranded in the middle rung of the *E* and had to be helped down.

Although I was enthusiastically recruited to become a Moonie, I'm too much of a street kid to ever believe in peace and harmony, or even want it. I bade them farewell.

On Sunday, I was ten minutes early for the shoot with Eugene, eager to update my portfolio. Eugene and Lila were just arriving and complimented me on my punctuality as we rode the elevator up to his brother's apartment in the Village. Since Eugene's studio was in Brooklyn, we commandeered the place for the day as a base of operations. They had brought an assortment of elegant black clothes, which I supplemented with a black swimsuit we would use for one look.

My makeup was done in an hour, and I was scolded for not using enough moisturizer. Lila was probably right—you can never be too dewy. If makeup artists ever did ad campaigns, the tagline would read: "Got moisture?"

The black bikini was shot indoors so we wouldn't attract a crowd. I wore black stilettos with my hair slicked into a high ponytail and tightly braided.

Being in front of the camera, flashes blinding me, felt amazingly good. I was officially back.

The wild updo was unleashed. Employing massive amounts of spray, Lila piled my hair atop my head like a very cool croissant. I changed into a tiny black dress, à la Audrey Hepburn. With Eugene leading the way, laden down under his equipment, we headed out. Our base was on Christopher Street, conveniently near the Hudson River and its scenic background. No one even gave my hair or outfit a strange glance. It was, after all, the Village.

A beautiful fountain shot water toward the blue sky near the walkway along the Hudson. I balanced on the two-foot-wide concrete border surrounding the fountain in my stiletto boots. As Eugene knelt down to shoot upward, the sun got in my eyes and I raised my hand to shield them.

"Yes! Hold that, very good."

The best pictures always happen by accident.

I sat on the fountain while, musically spouting opinions, Lila expertly undid my updo and transformed it into a slick bun. I gazed across the Hudson at Jersey's rambling skyline and pondered the last few years of my crazy life.

It had been worth it, I decided.

Comp cards: $350
Prints of pictures: $100
Portfolio: $40
The Experience: Priceless

"Eugeeene, she's ready!"

I changed into black leather pants and an off-the-shoulder black top in a visitor center nearby. Eugene positioned me looking on an expanse of green grass. New Yorkers relaxing during their lunch break politely scooted over to give us shooting space.

"Okay, good," Eugene said after fifteen minutes. "I want some of you with the water in the background."

I turned and set off for the shimmering river.

"Hey," Eugene called, and I looked over my shoulder. Snap. "That," Eugene said, grinning, "was a picture."

We returned to base to raid his brother's kitchen. We tried not to look guilty when the lady of the apartment, the brother's beautiful, dark-eyed girlfriend, dropped in to say hi. We stopped chewing briefly to acknowledge her presence.

Loading ourselves into Eugene's black Cadillac, we sped to our next location in the meatpacking district, just above the Village. It really was originally used for packing meat, but lately the gritty vibe attracted trendy restaurants and clubs. There was still enough grit to attract us. Eugene drove fast, racing against losing light as the sun began to set. We pulled up outside a recently abandoned warehouse, graffiti coloring the walls. I hopped out onto the cobblestoned street wearing a floor-length puffy black skirt and a tiny, cutoff, belly-baring sweater. The smell hit us.

"Uggghhhh," Lila screamed.

"Well, something definitely died," Eugene observed calmly.

We shot against the incomprehensible graffiti, with me employing my edgy look. Sleepily, we called it a wrap and collected our stuff from the apartment. They were nice enough to chauffeur me all the way uptown to my secret burger place, since I was starving. We agreed to meet later in the week and go over the pictures to compile a disk of the best shots.

A few nights later, my model friend Brianna decided to conduct an experiment to rate our importance.

"It's this exclusive lounge called Bungalow 8. If you can get in, you're automatically fabulous," she informed me as we neared the entrance on West Twenty-seventh Street.

"That simplifies things," I agreed.

There was a long, eager line that we immediately decided to attempt to cut. Brianna whispered that the bouncers—supposedly named Disco and Armin—were notoriously tough. In our model uniforms, we approached politely and smiled. We were surprised when they let us in; with all the hype, we expected to be required to perform a tap dance or yodel.

"We are officially fab-u-lous," Brianna declared as we entered, people screaming objections behind us. The inside was relatively small, with potted palm trees reaching high and soft lighting. Comfortable chairs were grouped around the VIP tables, which cost about six hundred dollars just to be able to sit there with a bottle of vodka. Having accomplished our objective of infiltrating the joint, our adrenaline vanished, and we contemplated going out for french fries.

"Let's at least make the effort of going to the bar," Brianna said, smiling. As we set off bravely, something smashed full force into my chest. I caught my breath and looked down. One of the Olsen twins was rubbing her nose after the impact. She was tiny, barely more than five feet, and very slim. I proudly identified her as Mary-Kate, since her hair was dark.

"Sorry," she said unhappily.

"It's okay," I assured her, and continued to the bar.

"Did you hurt her?" Brianna asked.

"Possibly." I frowned.

"She's way too skinny."

Soon after, the news of her eating disorder broke. It was known much earlier in the industry, as everything seems to be. Brianna moved away to ask a girl what her very hip silver-blue drink was called.

"Cheryl!?"

I turned around and came nose-to-nose with Giovanni's menacing bulk. My feet wanted to bolt for the door. My brain—which alternates between complete stupidity and shattering brilliance—decided to be smart.

"Hey, man," I said with an insolent little smirk, while secretly wondering if this was the end.

"Well, you haven't changed." He chuckled.

Despite his best efforts to the contrary.

I glanced at a nearby VIP table with an empty seat Gio had just vacated. A mean-looking guy in a five-thousand-dollar suit was watching us. The other seats were occupied by a type of girl that seemed to populate Gio's life in an unending stream. Identical bleached blondes with breast implants and brain outplants, who all insist their real names are Candy, Honey, or Amber.

Following my gaze, Gio said, "They're actually quite nice."

"The conversation must be fascinating." I was feeling mischievous now that my life didn't seem in danger and looked directly into Gio's bottomless eyes.

"I heard about what happened," Gio said, assessing my hair.

I looked away and sighed.

"I didn't think you'd be back," he said.

"You didn't think I'd last six months, either."

He liked that, and we smiled at each other. Brianna was sipping a drink and keeping her distance in the interest of self-preservation.

"How are you?" Gio asked.

"Great." And for the first time, I actually meant it.

"Well, you look fantastic. That was a bad break."

"I seem to have had a lot of those."

"But Cheryl, you don't need luck!"

"Ah, how true." I actually kind of liked Gio. Navigating Manhattan, smoothing his way by handing out crisp fifty-dollar bills from his endless supply to any nuisance in his path. I tilted my head at Brianna, indicating that we should go while the going was good. Surprisingly, Gio offered his hand, and after some consideration, I shook it.

"I've got to revise my earlier opinion," he said. "I think you'll go the distance."

I smiled from ear to ear. "Finally we can agree on something."

After a casting the next day, I walked through Manhattan, the only place where in one day you can encounter an obese man in a kilt, a guy jogging down Park Avenue in a Speedo, a woman beating a man with an umbrella, and a strange, slightly orange-haired model having the time of her life.

In sun-dappled Bryant Park, Winston Churchill spotted me and went nuts; it had been a while. Vinnie's partner was unceremoniously booted, and I took his place.

"Cheryl!"

I smiled, lining up the pieces.

"This is great," Vinnie said, and Winston yipped in agreement.

We began playing. Between moves, I gazed at the big lawn where New Yorkers lounged. Fashion Week, once again, was imminent. The giant white tents would spring up and the glamorous illusion would unfold.

"How's modeling?" Vinnie asked.

"Pretty good."

"Well, you've definitely paid your dues."

"I've overpaid!"

"Perhaps you could see about getting a refund."

"Ooooh, good one, Vinnie."

"Is modeling what you really want to do?"

"I'm thinking of diversifying."

He gave me a quizzical look. "What are you up to?"

I grinned, moving my bishop forward.

"On guard."

Acknowledgments

Special thanks to: my great literary agent, Adam Chromy; my super-lawyer, Liz; editor extraordinaire, Anica Rissi; and the enthusiastic team at Simon Pulse.